FIGHTING FOR FREEDOM

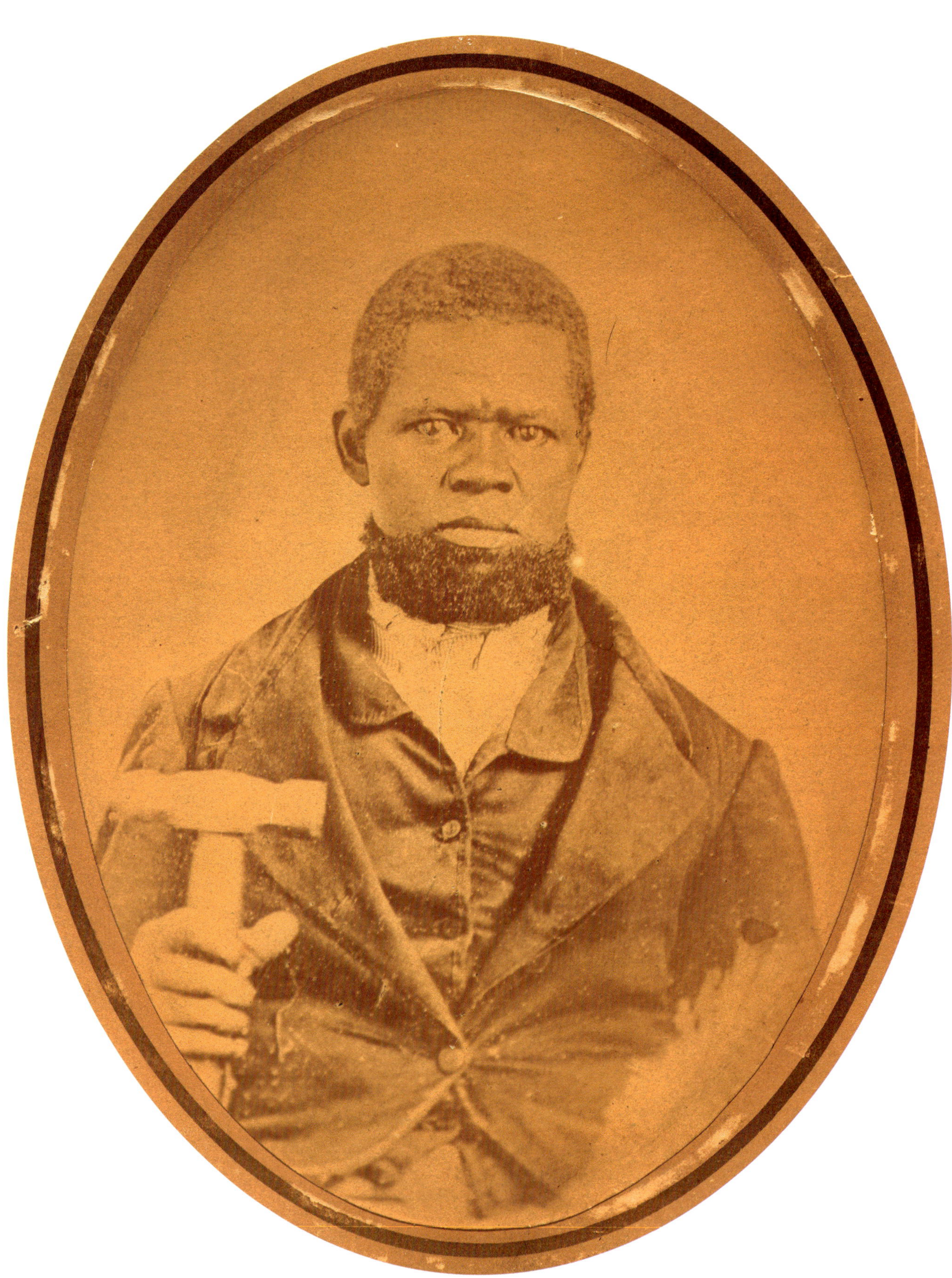

FIGHTING FOR FREEDOM

Black Craftspeople and the Pursuit of Independence

EDITED BY TORREN L. GATSON,
TIFFANY N. MOMON, AND
WILLIAM A. STROLLO

THE UNIVERSITY OF NORTH CAROLINA PRESS
Chapel Hill

Designed and set by Jamison Cockerham
in Arno, Scala, and Sentinel

Cover art: *Craftsperson with a Hammer,* by an unidentified photographer, ca. 1863, Pennsylvania. Courtesy of private collection.

Manufactured in Canada

LIBRARY OF CONGRESS CATALOGING-IN-PUBLICATION DATA
Names: Gatson, Torren L., editor. | Momon, Tiffany N., editor. | Strollo, William A., editor. | DAR Museum (Washington, DC), organizer, host institution.
Title: Fighting for freedom : Black craftspeople and the pursuit of independence / edited by Torren L. Gatson, Tiffany N. Momon, and William A. Strollo.
Other titles: Fighting for freedom (DAR Museum [Washington, DC])
Description: Chapel Hill : The University of North Carolina Press, [2025] | Includes bibliographical references and index.
Identifiers: LCCN 2024050310 | ISBN 9781469686257 (cloth) | ISBN 9781469683164 (epub) | ISBN 9781469686264 (pdf)
Subjects: LCSH: African American decorative arts—Exhibitions. | African American artisans—Social conditions—Exhibitions. | Art and freedom—Exhibitions. | BISAC: ART / American / African American & Black | SOCIAL SCIENCE / Ethnic Studies / American / African American & Black Studies
Classification: LCC NK839.3.A35 F54 2025 | DDC 745.089/63073—dc23/eng/20241214
LC record available at https://lccn.loc.gov/2024050310

For product safety concerns under the European Union's General Product Safety Regulation (EU GPSR), please contact gpsr@mare-nostrum.co.uk or write to the University of North Carolina Press and Mare Nostrum Group B.V., Mauritskade 21D, 1091 GC Amsterdam, The Netherlands.

TO THE THOUSANDS OF BLACK CRAFTSPEOPLE,

known and unknown,

who never imagined their skilled artistry

would be the subject of esteem and praise

and to

FAYE, NELLIE, EMORY, KACY, KINGSTON, AND KARSYN

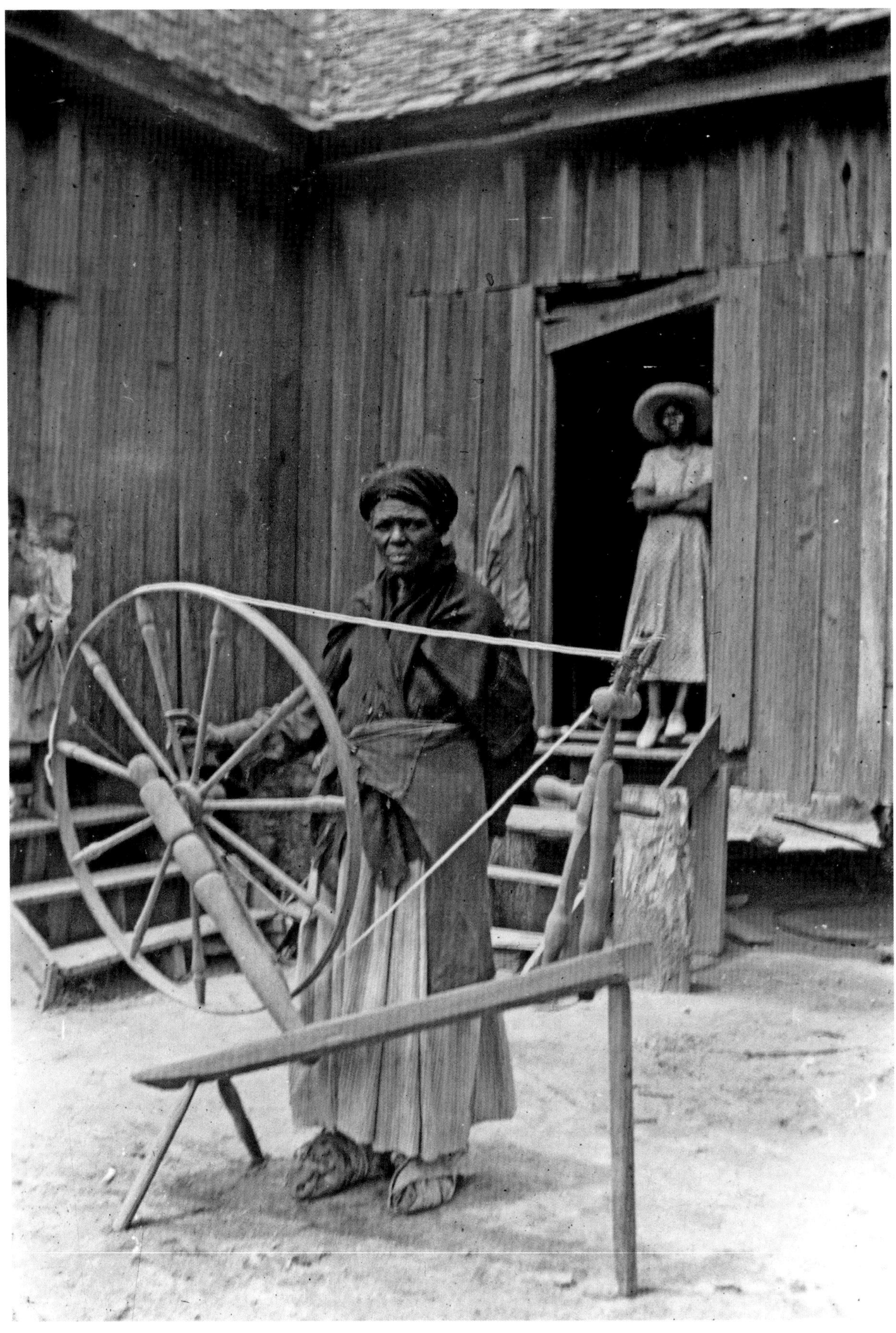

Contents

FIGURE 0.1. *Lucindy Lawrence Jurdon, Age 79*, between 1936 and 1938, Alabama. Photograph courtesy of Library of Congress, https://www.loc.gov/item/mesnp010242/.

Foreword

As our nation approaches the 250th anniversary of the signing of the Declaration of Independence, the National Society Daughters of the American Revolution (DAR) is committed to highlighting the creations, contributions, and legacies of Black craftspeople with a comprehensive and cohesive narrative. Our hope is that this volume stimulates dialogue around the myriad interpretive pathways Black crafters used to frame ideals and principles of freedom.

Founded in 1890, the DAR is a nonprofit, nonpolitical volunteer women's service organization dedicated to promoting patriotism, preserving American history, and securing America's future through youth education. In 2020, the DAR launched an important ongoing effort called the E Pluribus Unum Educational Initiative to increase awareness of often unrepresented Revolutionary War Patriots, including those who were African American. Given the DAR's purpose to perpetuate the legacy of all men and women who achieved independence, DAR has a decided role to play in researching and promoting how diversified participants assisted in the creation of our nation. The *Fighting for Freedom: Black Craftspeople and the Pursuit of Independence* exhibition is one such opportunity to tell the stories of these individuals, who have all too often been left out of the pages of history.

This exhibition is a critical initiative for the DAR Museum as we continue showing the inclusivity of American history. As highlighted through this exhibition of Black decorative arts, the DAR Museum collections are not only aesthetically beautiful but also reflect our mission to collect, preserve, and interpret objects in ways that inspire conversations about the diverse American experience. We are committed to intentional approaches to the safeguarding of Black craftspeople's treasured history through our collection practices and this exhibition, *Fighting for Freedom: Black Craftspeople and the Pursuit of Independence.*

Pamela Edwards Rouse Wright, President General
Susan Lee Metzger, Curator General

Preface

CARROLL VAN WEST

Making African American hands central to the story of early American craftsmanship has been long in the making. At the turn between the nineteenth and twentieth centuries, W. E. B. Du Bois bitingly observed that "the problem of the twentieth century is the problem of the color-line," and generations of white scholars in material culture, museums, and the decorative arts proved him right. Their books, articles, papers, and exhibits about early American craftsmanship paid little to no attention to African American crafters, except for those creative hands such as the stone carver William Edmondson in Nashville whose work Depression-era writers could conveniently label as primitive.[1] No one much in the scholarly field of material culture studies, the decorative arts, or museum studies as it took on a professional sheen in the 1960s made much of a fuss when folklorist Henry Glassie proclaimed that "much of the Negro's folk culture is European in origin," because his summary reflected the European- (and white-) centered research and assumptions of the 1960s.[2] Or when anthropologist James Deetz produced his popular and influential *In Small Things Forgotten: The Archaeology of Early American Life*, subtitled as and said little about African American culture or even presence, relegating it to a brief overview of a forgotten New England rural neighborhood known in the 1970s as Parting Ways—a name he preferred to that given by the Black residents who once lived there, New Guinea.[3]

Objects from African American hands received little attention in the American Bicentennial of 1976, even though all sorts of serious scholarship and multiple exhibits on early America took place at many if not all major American institutions. In the nation's capital alone, the National Gallery of Art's exhibition *The Eye of Thomas Jefferson* presented the cosmopolitan Jefferson; the Smithsonian had the *We the People* and *"The Dye Is Now Cast"* exhibits, while it also hosted the promising yet incomplete *A Nation of Nations* exhibit, whose exhibition catalog promised to explore "The People Who Came to America as Seen through Objects, Prints, and Photographs at the Smithsonian Institution," but since the institution at that time held so few artifacts related to people of color in its collection, the depiction of African Americans was sparse.[4]

The content of these "national" exhibits stood in glaring contrast to what happened at four African American museums, the DuSable Museum of African

American History in Chicago; Detroit's International Afro-American Museum; the Smithsonian's Anacostia Neighborhood Museum; and the newly established African American Museum of Philadelphia. As ably chronicled by Andrea A. Burns, these museums, along with museums at Historically Black Colleges and Universities, pushed back against the Bicentennial mainstream.[5] However, the weight of authority and scholarship from the mainstream institutions drowned the collective African American voices in the fervor and hype that consumed the Bicentennial period in 1970s America.

Fifty years later, at the time of America's 250th commemoration, what was normal and acceptable in 1976 is no longer considered acceptable, or even the least bit correct. Many people and events helped to turn the tide in scholarship, but perhaps the most important event was "A National Conference on Black Museums: Interpreting the Humanities," organized in 1980 by Dr. Bettye Collier-Thomas, director of the Mary McLeod Bethune Memorial Museum, funded by the National Endowment for the Humanities, National Council of Negro Women, and the African American Museums Association, which had formed just two years earlier and was headquartered in Boston. Held at the DuSable Museum in Chicago, this huge gathering of Black museum professionals embodied the organizing principles of the African American Museums Association:

> Who, if not we, will make sure that the impact of our contributions from the very beginning of this nation, is perpetually preserved for the benefit of our own generations to come and for the enlightenment of the larger community? Who, if not we, will ensure that the work, the heroes, the heroines, the extraordinary lives of our people who built communities and industries in every region of this nation and continue to do so is documented with material object and written record? Who, if not we, will celebrate the cultural creativity of the Black men and women by providing the space for continually telling the stories and singing the songs and making new ones in the land?[6]

These questions and many others come flooding into your head upon viewing the objects and text of the *Fighting for Freedom: Black Craftspeople and the Pursuit of Independence* exhibit. This exhibition is a powerful statement of purpose and scholarship from the present generation of historians, curators, public historians, and historic preservationists who seek to find the objects and places crafted by Black hands and share those traditions and accomplishments to both scholarly and public audiences. It is an exhibit for our times, for Torren Gatson, Tiffany Momon, William Strollo, and their collaborators center the Black experience at the heart of America's revolutionary eras, be they the War for Independence or the post–Civil War Reconstruction era. A balanced mix of established and new voices explore the challenging idea of African American craft as a catalyst for freedom seeking and how Black hands through art and craft have shaped the American experience.

The essays range provides thematic overviews as well as highlighting key individuals. Tiffany N. Momon begins with an insightful overview of how the decorative arts create a powerful lens through which long struggles for Black liberation, expression, and community can be better understood. Lauren Applebaum, Susan J. Rawles, Jennifer Van Horn, R. Ruthie Dibble, and Philippe L. B. Halbert lean into the stories and impact of individual crafters and artists. Applebaum revisits the career of sculptor Edmonia Lewis and identifies her challenging language of identity, persistence, and empowerment. Rawles considers David Drake's words on his magnificent pottery from South Carolina's Edgefield District, emphasizing how his "literacy became a medium of freedom." Taking on the career of Robert Duncanson, Van Horn sheds needed light on the tradition of Black house painters and the many ways they expressed themselves as they transformed from crafters to acknowledged artists in nineteenth-century America. Dibble dives deep into the records of the American Colonization Society to assess the work of Black crafters such as Augustus Washington and Robert Griffin who left the land of their oppression to the promise of freedom in Liberia. Halbert adds to the broader contexts of the exhibit through his exploration of silversmith François Mentor as a freed man of color practicing his craft in Canada.

Other essayists weave broader themes into the narrative. Connecting craft to community building is a key theme is Lydia Blackmore's essay on cabinetmakers of color in early nineteenth-century New Orleans. Alexandra Alevizatos Kirtley untangles the webs of relationships, commerce, craft, and enslavement that characterized the famed cabinetmaking shops of Philadelphia. In his introductory essay, contemporary chairmaker Robell Awake reinforces the exhibition's dialogue between past and present by admitting, as it always has been, that "history informs both how I design and construct my chairs as well as the stories I want to tell through them."

The scholarship is illuminating, but the objects shine the brightest. There are handmade bricks, with the fingerprints from their Black makers forever part of the object itself, from Wilton Plantation in Virginia, a colonoware bowl from Mount Vernon, a post–Civil War ladderback chair from Tennessee, a fanning basket from South Carolina, a powder horn from Connecticut, and a coverlet from Kentucky. Then comes the story of a Charleston-made coffeepot, which suggests convincingly that it was sold along with its enslaved maker, Abraham, at an estate sale in 1768.

The exhibition and catalog bring the names of crafters to the forefront, some well known, some not: Lewis Buckner, Gershom Prince, John Gough, Thomas Commeraw, David Drake, Ellen Morton, Margaret Morton, Dutreuil Barjon, Thomas Day, Augustus Washington, Thomas Gross, Robert Duncanson, Tobias Scott, Lucius Jordan, Peter Bentzon, Abraham Spencer, Moses Williams, Isham Hudson, Cesar Chelor, John Hemmings, Altimore McKeethen, and Taylor McKeethen. For most, until recently, their art and their lives have been marginalized. Say their names. Then there are the makers where, at best, a first name is known, such as Abraham or James or Lucy. The exhibit dignifies the work of those who were refused the dignity of their own name or even a full name, by reminding us that crafters grasped that dignity for themselves through their art and skill. Say their names, too. Say them louder.

Notes

1. W. E. B. Du Bois, *The Souls of Black Folk* (1902; Greenwich, CT: Fawcett, 1961), 41; Robert Farris Thompson et al., *The Art of William Edmondson* (Jackson: University Press of Mississippi, 1999), 15–60.

2. Henry Glassie, *Pattern in the Material Folk Culture of the Eastern United States* (Philadelphia: University of Pennsylvania Press, 1968), 116.

3. James Deetz, *In Small Things Forgotten: The Archaeology of Early American Life* (New York: Anchor Press, 1977), 138–39.

4. William H. Adams, ed., *The Eye of Thomas Jefferson* (Washington, DC: National Gallery of Art, 1976). A companion volume of essays, also edited by Adams, touched in depth Jefferson and his relation with the arts but had nary a word to say of his relations with John Hemmings, who became a skilled carpenter and whose work is now featured in the DeWitt Wallace Decorative Arts Museum at Colonial Williamsburg. William H. Adams, ed., *Jefferson and the Arts: an Extended View* (Washington, DC: National Gallery of Art, 1976); *We the People* (Washington, DC: Smithsonian Institution); Lillian B. Miller et al., *"The Dye Is Now Cast": The Road to American Independence, 1774–1776* (Washington, DC: National Portrait Gallery, 1976); Peter C. Marzio, ed., *A Nation of Nations: The People Who Came to America as Seen through Objects and Documents Exhibited at the Smithsonian* (Washington, DC: Harper and Row, 1976), front cover.

5. Andrea A. Burns, *From Storefront to Monument: Tracing the Public History of the Black Museum Movement* (Amherst: University of Massachusetts Press, 2013).

6. "Keepers of the Story," *Ebony*, February 1981, 84–90.

Acknowledgments

In the years leading up to the installation of this exhibition and publication of this catalog, we have received generous support, guidance, wisdom, and encouragement from countless colleagues, donors, friends, family, and strangers. We would like to express our deepest gratitude to all of those individuals who have helped make this work possible. We express our gratitude to the National Society Daughters of the American Revolution, the University of North Carolina Greensboro, the University of the South, the Middle Tennessee State University Center for Historic Preservation, and Dr. Carroll Van West for their support and encouragement on this project over the years. The curators would like to thank Pamela Wright, President General; Susan Metzger, Curator General; and the Wright administration for their unwavering support for this exhibition.

We would like to thank the following individuals and institutions for lending to the exhibition: American Folk Art Museum, Tennessee State Museum, Battle of Franklin Trust, Historic New Orleans Collection, Museum of the Shenandoah Valley, George Washington Foundation, Mount Vernon Ladies' Association, Charleston Museum, Museum of Early Southern Decorative Arts, Luzerne County Historical Society, Colonial Williamsburg Foundation, Museum of Fine Arts Houston and Bayou Bend, Menokin Foundation, Thomas Jefferson's Monticello Foundation, Kentucky Historical Society, the University of the South, Philadelphia Museum of Art, Historic Charleston Foundation, Robell Awake, Dana Shoaf, and private lenders.

We would also like to thank the following institutions and individuals who helped bring this exhibition to their museums: Sara Arnold, director of curatorial affairs at the Gibbes Museum of Art; Lydia Blackmore, curator of decorative arts at the Historic New Orleans Collection; Annabeth Dooley; Executive Director Ashley Howell, Chief Curator Richard White, and Senior Curator of Fine Art Candice Candeto at the Tennessee State Museum; Dana Hand Evans; and Curator of Collections Nick Powers at the Museum of the Shenandoah Valley.

Finally, we express our gratitude for the generous financial support of the following individuals, whose donations made this publication possible: Jeffrey S. Evans & Associates Auctions, Andrew and Lauren Brunk, John and Stephanie Case (Case Auctions, Inc.), and Leland Little Auctions.

FIGHTING FOR FREEDOM

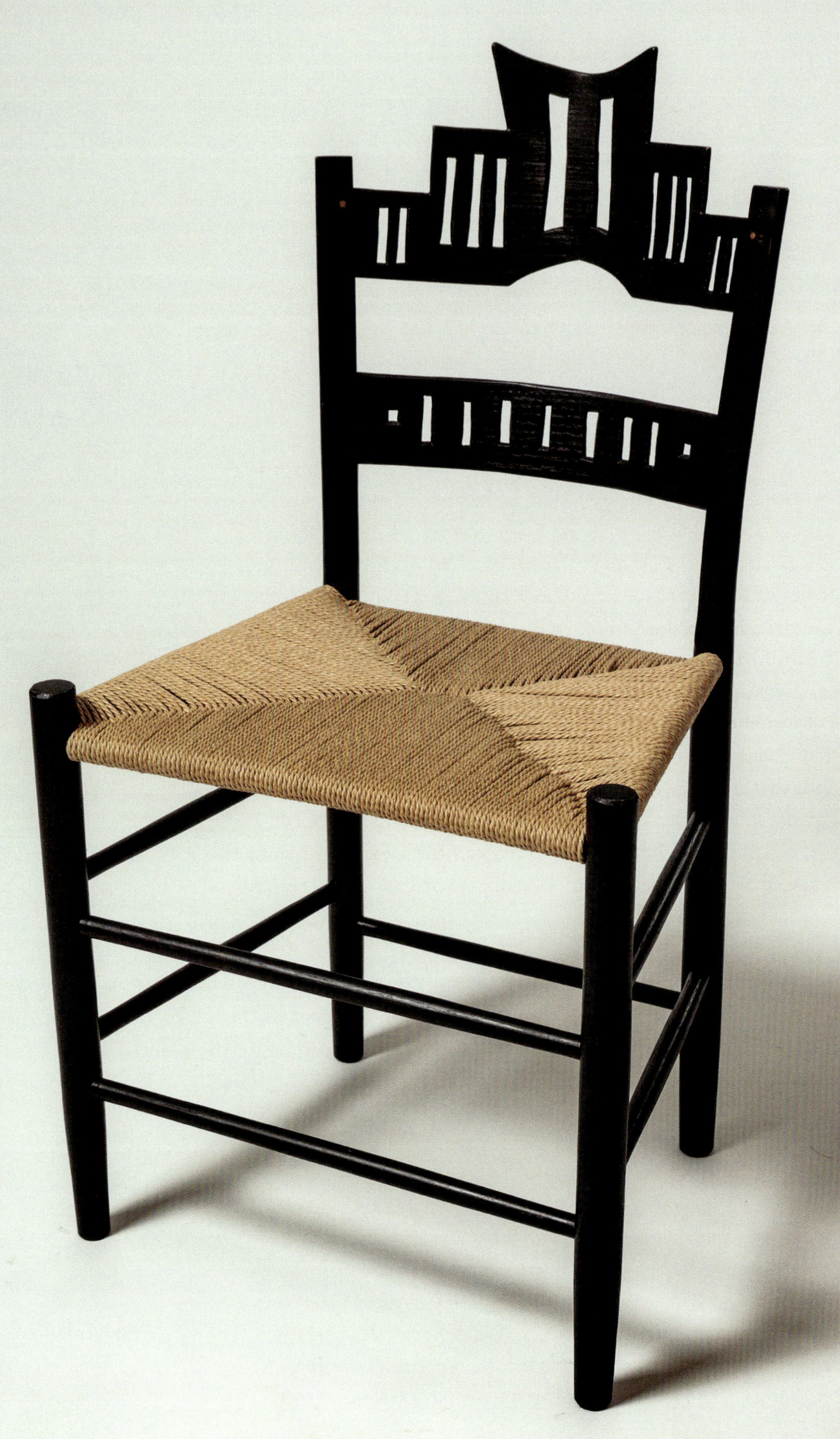

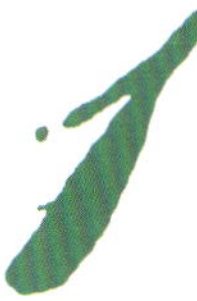

Artist's Statement

ROBELL AWAKE

When I started making furniture a decade ago, it was unclear to me if furniture making was something Black people do or ever did. Woodworking magazines were filled with people who didn't look like me, who were often making furniture that didn't speak to me. The whiteness of the field and the myths about who has historically made furniture felt just as real of a barrier as the financial cost of getting started. Research has become an integral part of my practice as I reclaim traditions and stories of Black craftspeople whose enormous contributions to decorative arts have largely been erased.

I make furniture informed and inspired by decorative arts research to explore and reference the diversity of craft traditions from across the Black diaspora. Like chairmakers throughout history and across cultures, I practice green woodworking—a preindustrial method of making furniture that employs newly felled regional hardwoods that are split, processed, and shaped using hand tools and assembled using traditional methods of joinery. In my current body of work, I use this technique to explore two chairmaking traditions that reflect my identity as an Ethiopian American—ladderback chairs pioneered by enslaved American chairmakers and Jimma chairs from Ethiopia. By merging and reinterpreting these two forms, my work offers a new furniture aesthetic rooted in Black design traditions that are often overlooked, appropriated, or altogether obscured by dominant Eurocentric myths and narratives.

With a practice heavily informed by research, I make chairs that are as much archival as they are a form of self-expression. Each design on the back slats is unique and rooted in improvisation—a time-honored modality that shows up in Black art and craft traditions across the globe. While my carved chair backs start with a sketch, these carvings evolve as I work and respond to the material, balancing an intuitive approach to the design while remaining rooted in Black histories and artistic traditions. Yet, as with hip-hop or the quilts of Gee's Bend, Alabama, improvisation happens within clear structures and from a deep understanding of an artist's medium. Like creators working in those traditions, I allow myself to respond intuitively to my materials and create intentional yet spontaneous designs on each chair slat that reference a story or an inspiration from the Black diaspora. My chairs are made by hand using traditional green

(*opposite*) FIGURE 1.1. *Chair*, by Robell Awake, Atlanta, Georgia, 2023. Wood. Image courtesy of Dustin Chambers.

woodworking techniques and local hardwoods. I split each log myself, steam bend the posts and back slats in a homemade steam box, and shape the wood using a drawknife and a spokeshave. I shape the intricate carvings on the back slats using a fretsaw and a carving knife.

History informs how I both design and construct my chairs as well as the stories I want to tell through them. My material-based practice of traditional green woodworking and improvisational carving are central to my approach and connect me to Black chairmakers and artists across time and disciplines who have engaged in similar modes of craft and artistic expression.

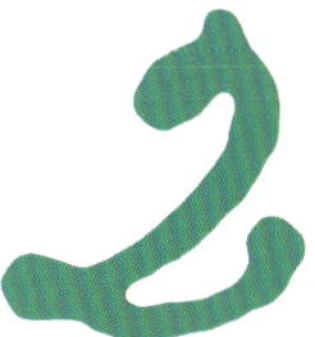

Black Decorative Arts Exhibitions, Then and Now

TIFFANY N. MOMON

The Black presence in the decorative arts is best understood through the people, objects, and places often located in the margins of major museum collections. The stories of the Black artisans behind the objects are often misunderstood in favor of a decorative arts story that neatly discusses objects and makers without interrogating the conditions in which they lived and were created. Over time, researchers and museum curators sought to tell the stories of Black artisans how they needed to be told, not shying away from the uncomfortable past, but embracing it and addressing the oppression under which Black artisans lived and created. Because of the work of these researchers and curators, Black Americans could visit museums and see objects that documented the presence, skill, and artistry of people they were connected to. The power in these exhibitions is that they brought people together to recognize and celebrate the Black artisan, which many major museums had sought to ignore. This essay takes as its subject but a few of the groundbreaking exhibitions that made possible the Black decorative arts exhibitions of today.

In 1976, Regenia Perry curated the exhibition *Selections of Nineteenth-Century Afro-American Art* at the Metropolitan Museum of Art and boldly declared, "One of the most remarkable facts about Afro-American art is that it exists at all. No people in the history of America have survived under such adverse conditions as the slaves . . . exposed to the vicissitudes of slavery for over two hundred years."[1] Perry's declaration highlighted what African Americans already knew and what likely sounded foreign to others—that a group of people so oppressed, consistently despised, and relegated to the margins of society created art in spite of their status as enslaved men and women. Not only that, but their art persevered in the face of anti-Blackness, persistent ignorance surrounding their contributions, and the lack of recognition for many of them and their works. Additionally, Perry noted, "The earliest Afro-American artifacts belong to the category of the decorative arts and are slave-made handicrafts—pottery, ironwork, baskets, woodcarving, textiles and quilts."[2] Despite this knowledge, portions of the decorative arts field were reluctant acknowledgers of their work, preferring to recognize only those they saw as the most exceptional African American artisans, such as Thomas Day and David Drake, and preferring to ignore the others who reminded them too much of the brutality of slavery.

Objects featured in the exhibition included Harriet Powers's Bible quilt; a nineteenth-century walking stick by Henry Gudgel exhibited with a nineteenth-century bronze tube from the Benin peoples of present-day Nigeria, well known for their Benin bronzes; face vessels from Edgefield, South Carolina; woven baskets; oil portraits by Joshua Johnston; marble sculptures by Edmonia Lewis; and more. Overall, through loans from private collectors and institutions such as the Museum of Early Southern Decorative Arts and the Museum of Fine Arts, Boston, Perry's exhibition included a variety of media and artisans, effectively presenting African American decorative arts to audiences at The Met. Although the exhibition did not travel and was on display for a short time, it was groundbreaking, comprising ninety-two pieces of African and African American art. The exhibition broke barriers that made other exhibitions solely featuring African American decorative arts and art possible. *Selections of Nineteenth-Century Afro-American Art* put forth before the masses the art of enslaved labor.

Several objects featured in The Met exhibition were included in the Los Angeles County Museum of Art exhibition *Two Centuries of Black American Art*, also presented in 1976. Curated by artist David C. Driskell, this exhibition spanned the years 1750–1950. Much like the New York exhibition, *Two Centuries of Black American Art* broke new ground. It featured over 200 works by sixty-three artists and included paintings, sculptures, drawings, graphics, crafts, and, of course, decorative arts. As the first comprehensive survey of African American art, the exhibition sought to acknowledge the work of Black artists whose contributions to American art had largely been neglected and ignored. To share this important message, the exhibition toured multiple venues, including the High Museum of Art, the Dallas Museum of Fine Arts, and the Brooklyn Museum.

Driskell's exhibition checklist reads like a who's who of African American artists, artisans, and craftspeople and includes Thomas Day, David Drake, Robert Duncanson, Edmonia Lewis, Clementine Hunter, Aaron Douglas, William Edmondson, Joshua Johnston, and Horace Pippin. These artisans and others shared the spotlight with several creators listed simply as "Unknown." The Los Angeles exhibition highlighted the need to recognize the art of African American craftspeople whose names we do not know. Driskell understood the importance and significance of including in the exhibition works of art by African American artisans even if we could not identify the makers. He recognized the complexity of the African American experience in our country, and he knew that he needed to include everyone, not just those artisans that we could name, a lesson that many in the current decorative arts field still struggle with.

In the exhibition catalog, Rexford Stead, deputy director of the Los Angeles County Museum of Art, wrote, "The artists represented were not selected because of their African ancestry alone, however direct or mixed, but to consider how this has obscured their contributions to American art history." He continued, "And so it is not mere skin color that gives this survey a unity although it is true that many of the artists represented underwent uniquely personal torments because of a majority society's prejudices."[3] Stead's observations were correct, and he rightfully questioned how much art had been lost over time due to bias and anti-Black racism. Stead's comments paired well with Driskell's goals for the exhibition, as he echoed scholar Alain Locke, calling on Black Americans to center art in their lives and to use art as a liberating force.[4]

Stead's remarks were optimistic and showed his hope for what could come out of this exhibition, but critics had doubts. In his review of the exhibition, art critic Hilton Kramer wrote, "This is a difficult show to review, and this difficulty ought to be acknowledged at the outset. At least for a critic whose primary interest lies in assessing artistic merit and who remains unpersuaded that he is performing a useful service if he allows extra artistic standards to obscure the difference between superior artistic achievement and its absence, this exhibition presents problems that ought to be more openly discussed than they usually are nowadays." The show, Kramer continued, was "more interesting as a social history than for its esthetics." He also stated that "there is simply too much here that does not belong in a serious museum exhibition." He concluded by noting that the exhibit, by and large, "was a social documentary about the black American artist rather than an anthology of achievements."[5] Kramer's critique was without a doubt misguided, but the damage was done. Newspapers across the country carried the article, and its language sought to discredit and minimize the work of Black artisans during the country's bicentennial celebrations. Kramer also made the mistake of attempting and encouraging the public to divorce social history from how we understand the work of Black artisans, completely erasing, as Rexford Stead so aptly put it, "the uniquely personal torments . . . and impossible odds" that Black artisans faced.[6] For Black creators, the work they completed was often deeply spiritual and representative of their lives and experiences. To disconnect that from the object is inherently disrespectful.

In 1978, folklorist John Michael Vlach's exhibition *The Afro-American Tradition in the Decorative Arts* debuted at the Cleveland Museum of Art. The exhibition included basketry, musical instruments, wood carving, quilting, pottery, boat building, blacksmithing, architecture, and more. It is estimated that more than a quarter million people saw this exhibition as it traveled the country for two years. The exhibition was not without its critics, and arguments about whether this was an exhibit on decorative arts or one about craftwork persisted.

Vlach described this exhibition as "an attempt to trace and substantiate African influences in the traditional arts and crafts of Black Americans."[7] He also noted that through this exhibition and its subsequent publications, he hoped to "provide inspiration for more investigation, for rechecking materials and findings, for further discovery, and that he hoped it would ultimately help develop a richer and more complete understanding of African American culture."[8] Vlach's exhibition confirmed what preceding exhibitions and Black people already knew and had preached for decades: that the complexity and creativity of African American culture certainly carried over into the decorative arts.

Each of these exhibitions fell roughly near the nation's Bicentennial—the 200th anniversary of the Declaration of Independence—a nationwide celebration that paid tribute to historical events leading up to the creation of the United States. However, when Regenia Perry's *Selections of Nineteenth-Century Afro-American Art* opened at The Met, it was on display only from June 19 through August 1, 1976, for roughly five to six weeks. That five-to-six-week period just so happened to include the Fourth of July, the precise date of the Bicentennial. Yet the museum did not see the value of a show like this, did not see the true value of co-curator Perry, and certainly did not fully understand the use of the exhibition as an opportunity to show African Americans how objects made by their ancestors fit not only into the celebrations of 1976 but also into one of the nation's largest art museums. In the present moment, the decorative arts field, museums, and the nation must reckon with past mistakes while also making tangible change that leads to the creation of inclusive exhibitions that do not minimize the roles and contributions of Black artisans. At a time when Black history is being attacked across the nation and described as divisive, we have an opportunity to show that this history is anything but. In fact, this history brings us together to acknowledge and celebrate the many, many hands that made American art what it is today.

As we approach the nation's upcoming semiquincentennial, the 250th anniversary of the signing of the Declaration of Independence, nearly fifty years removed from the exhibitions discussed here, *Fighting for Freedom: Black Craftspeople and the Pursuit of Independence* picks up the torch and presents an opportunity to discuss the Black presence in the decorative arts through the lens of Black liberation and the continual fight for freedom that has plagued Black Americans for hundreds of years. Through the objects and stories presented in the exhibition, we see that Black artisans were not just creating under the coercion of slavery but were also using their skills to free themselves and others and uplift their community. While *Fighting for Freedom* includes works from many artisans featured in earlier exhibitions, it also embraces lesser-known artists and unites some of the greatest decorative arts objects under the same banner for the first time. The story of the Black presence in the decorative arts is an American story, with many of the artisans featured bearing arms in support of a country that did not support them but believing in its ideals of freedom and liberty anyway. These Black artisans held this country accountable in their demands and actions and recognized that no one is free until we all are free.

Notes

1. Regenia Perry, *Selections of Nineteenth-Century Afro-American Art* (New York: Metropolitan Museum of Art, 1976), 3.

2. Perry, *Selections of Nineteenth-Century Afro-American Art*, 3.

3. Rexford Stead, "Introduction," in David C. Driskell, *Two Centuries of Black American Art* (New York: Alfred A. Knopf, 1976), 9.

4. Driskell, *Two Centuries of Black American Art*, 59.

5. Hilton Kramer, "Black Art or Merely Social History?," *New York Times*, June 26, 1977.

6. Stead, "Introduction," 9.

7. John Michael Vlach, *The Afro-American Tradition in the Decorative Arts* (Athens: University of Georgia Press, 1990), 199.

8. Vlach, *Afro-American Tradition*, 20.

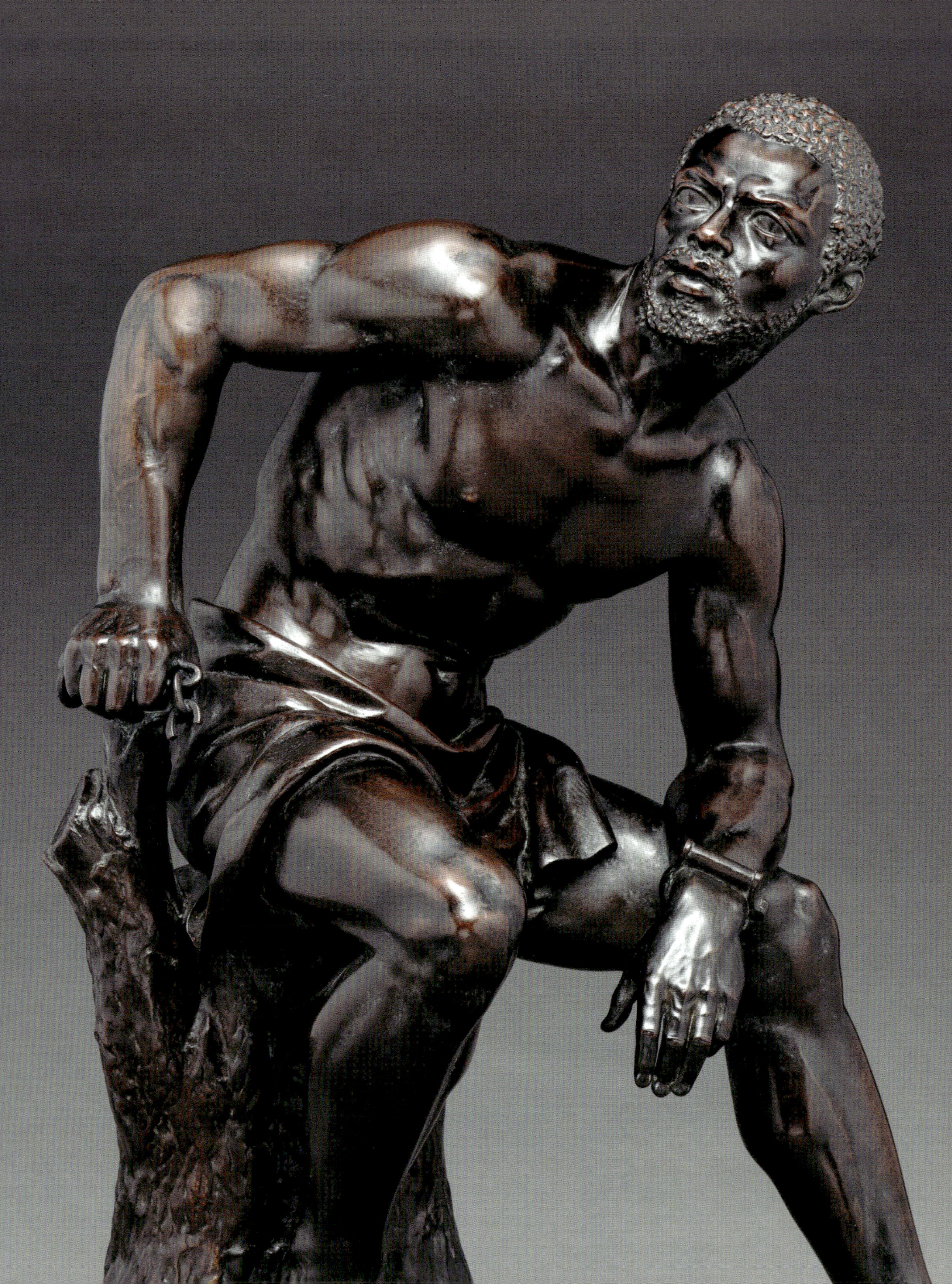

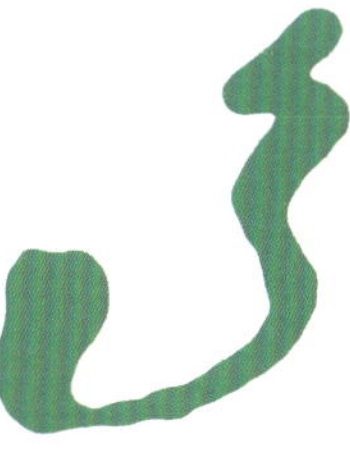

Carving a Vision of Freedom

Edmonia Lewis and Black Representation during the Fight for Emancipation

LAUREN APPLEBAUM

In October 1864, the Colored Ladies' Sanitary Commission held a fair in Boston's Mercantile Hall "for the benefit of the sick and wounded colored soldiers."[1] With the onset of the Civil War, women's wartime relief organizations were founded across the North to offer supplemental aid to the Union Army. When the federal government authorized the enlistment of United States Colored Troops in the spring of 1863—during the months following the signing of the Emancipation Proclamation—it withheld from Black soldiers sufficient medical care, supplies, and pay equal to that of their white counterparts. African American women mobilized out of necessity. The Colored Ladies' Sanitary Commission was a Massachusetts-based offshoot of the Contraband Relief Association (renamed in 1864 to the Ladies' Freedmen and Soldier's Relief Association). Founded in Washington, DC, by the formerly enslaved seamstress and antislavery activist Elizabeth Keckley, this organization, and others it gave rise to, sought to supply basic necessities to formerly enslaved African Americans and to provide for Black regiments what was unfairly denied to them by the American government.[2] Funds were raised through donations and the sale of handmade goods. Writing of the Colored Ladies' Sanitary Fair, a reporter for the African American daily newspaper the *New Orleans Tribune* noted, "The tables are . . . amply supplied with the fancy articles and nic-nacs that always constitute the *matériel* of such fairs."[3] Displayed alongside tables of regionally handcrafted goods, and among the main attractions for some of the correspondents reporting on the event was "[a] small statue representing Sergt. Carney of the 54th regiment, in a kneeling attitude holding up the colors lest they touch the ground . . . the work of Miss Edmonia Lewis of this city."[4]

Sergeant William H. Carney was a celebrated Black officer of the Fifty-Fourth Massachusetts Infantry, one of the first African American regiments to serve in the Civil War. Led by the revered (and widely commemorated) white officer

Colonel Robert Gould Shaw, the regiment carried out an attack on the Confederate Fort Wagner in South Carolina in July 1863. Although Shaw and many others perished in the battle, Carney, severely injured, heroically saved the regiment's flags from the fallen color bearer.[5] This now unlocated sculpture was unusual in its centering of a powerful Black narrative in the nation's fight for freedom. Portrayed by Edmonia Lewis, an artist of African American and Mississauga (Ojibwe) descent, and debuted at a fair organized by Black women for the benefit of colored troops, this work is one of the turning points in the nineteenth-century visual discourse of antislavery.

Lewis had arrived in Boston the previous year to begin her artistic career. After training briefly with the renowned sculptor Edward Brackett, she took up a space in the Studio Building on Tremont Street, the city's epicenter of artistic production.[6] During this time she began carving a number of plaster portrait medallions and sculptures of some of the most famous figures associated with the abolition movement, for which Boston was a major hub. Among the people she portrayed were Abraham Lincoln, the antislavery activist John Brown, the lifelong stalwart abolitionist and civil rights champion Wendell Phillips, the statesman Charles Sumner, the antislavery writer Maria Weston Chapman, the social reformer and founder of the widely read antislavery newspaper *The Liberator*, William Lloyd Garrison, and the celebrated officer and "martyr for freedom" of the Fifty-Fourth Massachusetts Infantry, Robert Gould Shaw.[7] Copies of such works, all portraying white advocates of Black freedom, were advertised in newspapers such as *The Liberator* and sold to those invested in the abolitionist cause, enabling Lewis to finance her travels to Rome in 1865, where, against all odds, she would go on to become the first Black and Native American woman to achieve international recognition and acclaim as a marble sculptor.

FIGURE 3.1. *Antislavery Medallion*. Metropolitan Museum of Art. Gift of Frederick Rathbone, 1908.

Stemming from these Civil War years in Boston, during which time Lewis was deeply entrenched in abolitionist political circles, the artist began crafting a visual language of Black liberation, resilience, and empowerment. Scholars have written extensively on the social and political dynamics of this early body of work.[8] Most recently, Caitlin Beach has explored these antislavery medallions and statuettes at length, focusing on the subjects Lewis portrayed and the venues in which they circulated, especially their engagement with Black women–led activism and relief efforts at events such as the Colored Ladies' Sanitary Fair, where "the praxis of making was central to a project of relief for African American soldiers, their families, and the formerly enslaved."[9] As Beach argues, these factors "reveal how the realm of sculptural practice constituted a form of political action in its own right."[10] Drawing on the work of Beach and other recent scholarship, I focus here on two of Lewis's works that demonstrate her investment in reinventing Black representation during the fight for emancipation and beyond.

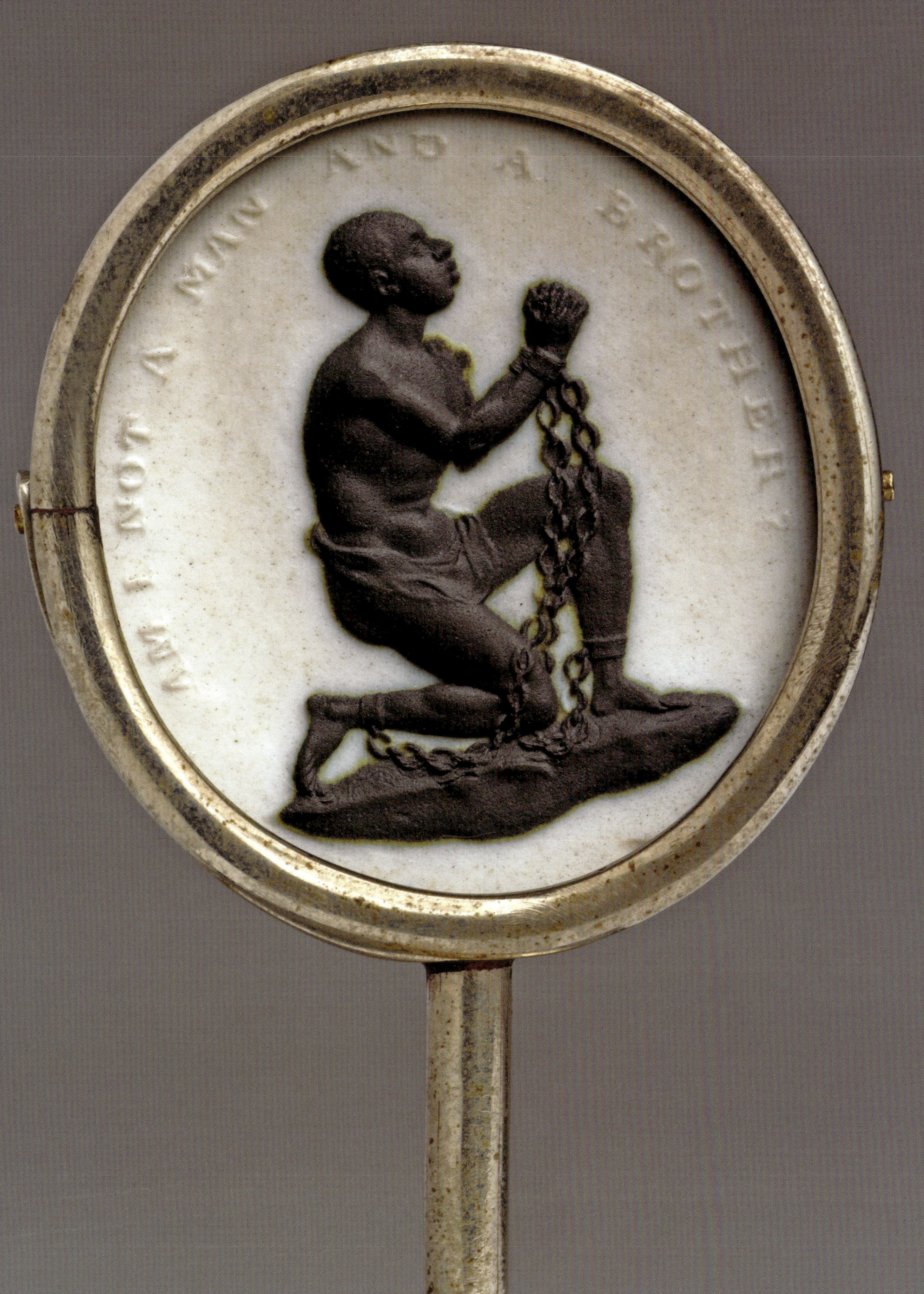
AM I NOT A MAN AND A BROTHER?

Sergeant William H. Carney and the Black Antislavery Figure

If Lewis's participation in the efforts of the Colored Ladies' Sanitary Fair was its own kind of activism, her statuette of Carney was radical within the context of visual representation as well. During the era of transatlantic slavery, representations of Black figures across American and European visual and material culture were most often shaped by the context of bondage, submission, or parody.[11] Even images created to promote abolition portrayed Black figures sublimated in bondage. Among the most well known of such images was the British potter Josiah Wedgwood's antislavery cameo medallion created in 1787, which portrayed the enslaved body of an anonymous man shackled on his knees, hands pleading, inscribed with the words, "Am I not a man and a brother?" (fig. 3.1). Meant to elicit sympathy, this widely circulated motif was used to promote abolition movements across the Atlantic World, even as it perpetuated and reproduced the representation of bondage.[12] As Beach notes, the Lewis scholar Marilyn Richardson has crucially identified Lewis's portrayal of Carney as an anomaly in American sculpture as it uniquely captured "the singular experience of a specific, named, and in turn nationally recognized individual African American soldier . . . fighting for . . . freedom."[13] Born enslaved in Norfolk, Virginia, in 1840 and later self-emancipated, Carney would become the first Black man ever to receive the Congressional Medal of Honor, awarded in 1900 for his actions at Fort Wagner.

Though it is now lost, we know from the brief description of it in the period press, cited above, that Lewis portrayed Carney carrying out the actions that made him a patriotic symbol for freedom, kneeling in his efforts to protect the flag from falling to the ground. Indeed, these actions were recounted widely in the weeks after they took place. For example, an article from August 1863 in *The Liberator* narrates the bloody battle, highlighting Carney's bravery amid the scene. As the flag bearer fell, Carney "caught the colors, carried them forward, and was the first man to plant the Stars and Stripes upon Fort Wagner. As he saw the men falling back, himself severely wounded in the breast, he brought the colors off, creeping on his knees . . . holding up the emblem of freedom."[14] Lewis would have certainly read such accounts, as she would have likely seen a widely circulated Currier and Ives illustration from 1863 visualizing these words before modeling her statuette (fig. 3.2).

The Currier and Ives illustration dramatizes the moment the regiment's white colonel, Shaw, is fatally wounded. Leading the charge over the fort's wall, he grabs his chest as his legs give way, his drawn sword about to fall from overhead. As *The Liberator* accounts, "Col. Shaw, was one of the first to scale the walls. He stood erect to urge forward his men, and while shouting for the men to press on, he was shot dead, and fell into the fort."[15] Storming from behind is Carney clutching the flag with both hands in an unwavering forward motion, the inverse of Shaw. The two figures together form the composition's key narrative—the martyred white colonel falling backward, and the unwavering Black officer rushing forward, determined to protect the nation's colors through the battle's end.

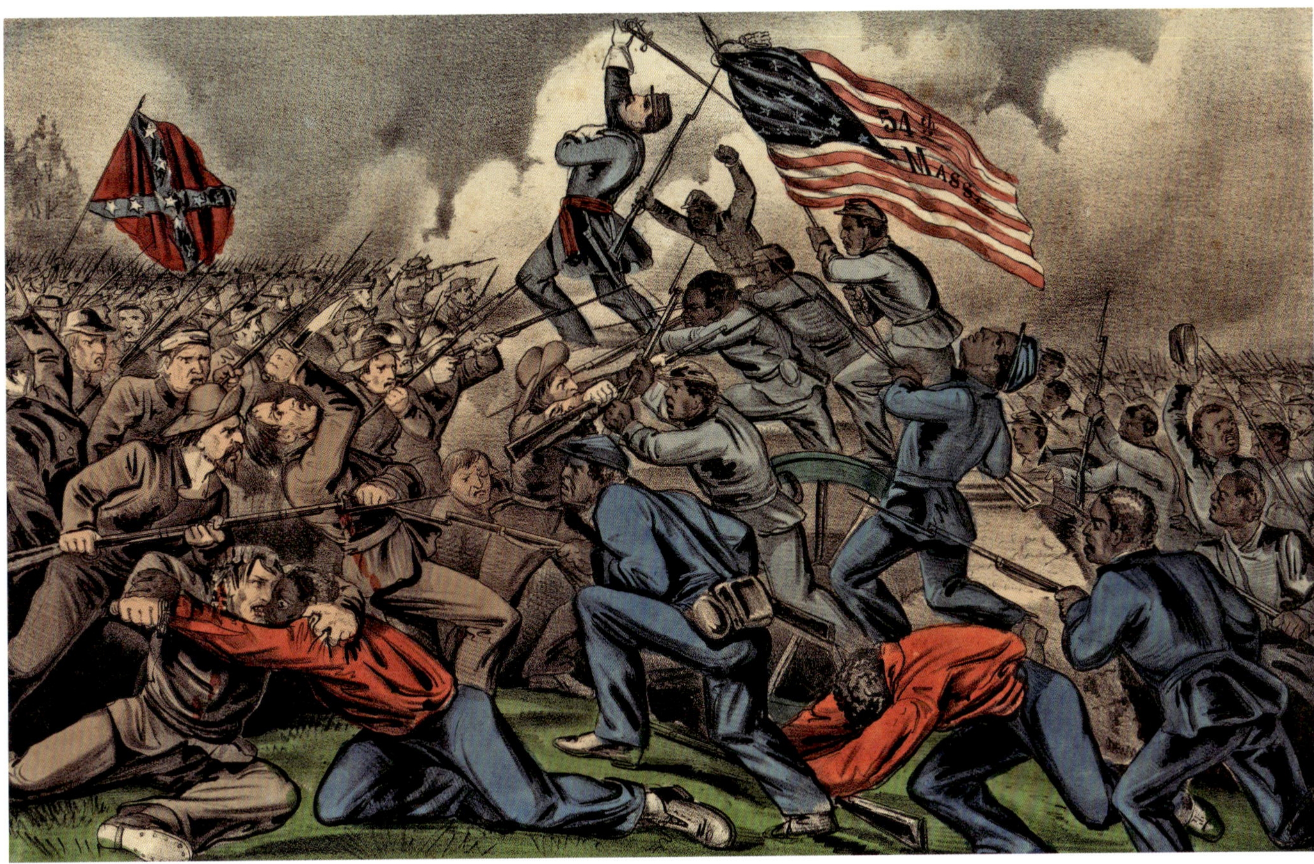

FIGURE 3.2. *The Gallant Charge of the Fifty-Fourth Massachusetts (Colored) Regiment*, by Currier and Ives Lithography Company, 1863. Hand-colored lithograph on paper. National Portrait Gallery, Smithsonian Institution.

Whereas the progressive antislavery *Liberator* gives primary focus to Carney's triumphant gesture, Shaw is the theatrical focal point in the more mainstream Currier and Ives illustration. Beach and Richardson have both interpreted the public's processing of these events, noting how white audiences consistently chose to celebrate the figure of Shaw rather than any individual member of the Black regiment. As Richardson has observed, "The possibilities of memorialization and historical immortality of the black men of the Fifty-fourth were intrinsically bound up with the martyrdom of Shaw."[16] This construction of public memory would continue decades into the future, with the white sculptor Augustus Saint-Gaudens's well-known memorial to Robert Gould Shaw and the Fifty-Fourth Regiment, dedicated on Boston Common in 1897. The sculptor consulted numerous photographs of the white commander for his likeness on horseback in the center foreground of the memorial. Though dozens of photographs of uniformed Black soldiers who served in the Fifty-Fourth Massachusetts were available to consult, Saint-Gaudens sculpted the infantrymen from models he hired in New York.[17] Rather than portraying specific soldiers' faces, the sculptor instead modeled the troops, on foot in the background in lower relief, as "a generally undifferentiated presence."[18]

Lewis was surely conscious of these racial dynamics in both visual and journalistic accounts and in public commemorations of the Fifty-Fourth Massachusetts, as seen in her decision to model a plaster bust of the white Colonel Shaw, which was met with such great success among her patrons and Shaw's family that reproductions were made both in the form of plaster casts as well as more affordable cartes de visite. Despite suppositions during the period, noted by Beach, that Lewis's choice of subject was made out of gratitude to Shaw, several scholars have made the important point that Lewis displayed a keen understanding of her market's desires and chose her subjects with her own enterprise in mind.[19] Indeed, it was the sale of these reproductions that financed her travels to Italy, suggesting that Lewis's choice of subject was, at least in part, strategic. As the artist later recalled, "I was practically driven to Rome in order to obtain the opportunities for art culture, and to find a social atmosphere where I was not constantly reminded of my color. The land of liberty had not room for a colored sculptor."[20]

Envisioning Self-Emancipation in *Forever Free*

Among the first major projects she completed shortly after settling in Rome, Lewis began modeling *Forever Free*—a celebration of emancipation in the United States—in 1865. The marble sculpture took form as the Thirteenth Amendment to the US Constitution was ratified, unquestionably outlawing slavery throughout the country. Originally titled *The Morning of Liberty*, it portrays a young Black man and his female companion at the dawn of emancipation.[21] The young woman rests on bended knee, holding her hands in prayerful thanks. With her other foot planted on the ground unchained, she is positioned to rise up alongside the man standing next to her. He has one hand placed protectively around her and the other held triumphantly overhead, shedding the broken manacles of bondage. Though the female figure's pose echoes that of the subjugated figure in Wedgwood's antislavery medallion, the scholar Kirsten Pai Buick has made the point that Lewis was, rather, presenting a unified post-emancipation image of the African American family, demonstrating the ideals of stability and respectability that were promoted by the societal norms and expectations of her day.[22]

FIGURE 3.3. *The Freedman*, by John Quincy Adams Ward, 1863, cast 1891. Bronze. Metropolitan Museum of Art. Gift of Charles Anthony Lamb and Barea Lamb Seeley, in memory of their grandfather Charles Rollinson Lamb, 1979.

Indeed, *Forever Free* is distinct from other contemporary abolition and emancipation works. With the international ubiquity of Wedgwood's medallion and its success in advancing the abolitionist cause, artists on both sides of the Atlantic began emulating this archetype for the unclothed, chained, and servile Black figure in their works meant to honor emancipation.[23] One notable American example is John Quincy Adams Ward's sculpture *The Freedman*, displayed at the National Academy of Design in New York in 1863 (fig. 3.3). The seminude figure sits on a tree stump, one arm still chained, the other free and poised to hoist himself into a standing position. The liminality of the figure, positioned in between bondage and freedom, speaks to its creation as the Emancipation Proclamation was signed but not ratified until more than two years later. In this way, Ward's *Freedman*, as the art historian Kirk Savage states, "remains somewhere between the two sculptural poles of abjection and triumph."[24] Another well-known example is a public memorial designed by Thomas Ball and unveiled in Lincoln

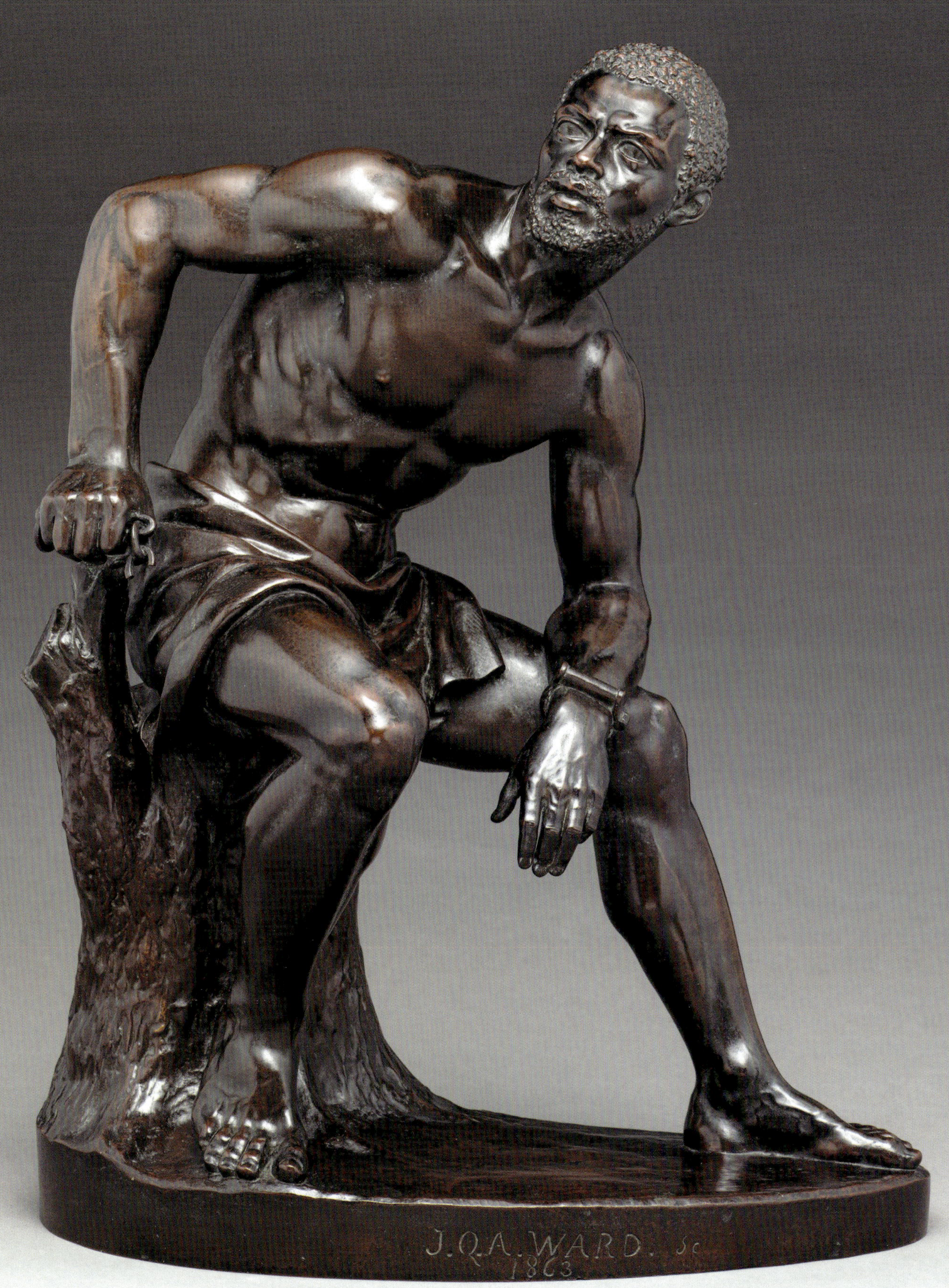
J.Q.A.WARD. Sc
1863

Park, in Washington, DC, in 1876, eleven years after the passage of the Thirteenth Amendment. Known as the Freedman's Memorial, it portrays Abraham Lincoln clutching the Emancipation Proclamation in one hand, the other outstretched over an unclothed enslaved man kneeling at Lincoln's feet, as if metaphysically breaking his shackles.

Unlike these other works, *Forever Free* rejects this oppressive formula of Black representation. Lewis portrays the free Black man standing up. Correcting contemporary narratives that cast the heroic white figure of Lincoln as the savior who freed the enslaved, Lewis offers empowering images of Black individuals waging their own liberation. As the scholar Adrienne Childs has said, "The man holds up broken chains in a gesture of strength and empowerment, implying that *he* broke them."[25] Unveiled in Boston in 1869, *Forever Free* was presented to prominent abolitionist the Reverend Leonard Grimes. Indeed, it was Grimes and his congregation who raised the funds to help found the Colored Ladies' Sanitary Commission and his wife, Octavia, who was the organization's leader.[26] Throughout her career, and especially in her representations of Sergeant Carney and *Forever Free*, Lewis was driven by the Black political circles in which she was deeply entrenched during the years leading up to the American abolition of slavery. While actively participating in organizations leading relief efforts for African Americans, Lewis also invented a mode of representation that subverted contemporary artistic norms by uplifting Black individuals as agents of their own emancipation.

Notes

1. The event was advertised in Boston newspapers, including the *Boston Morning Journal*, October 18, 1864, and was reviewed in African American publications, notably G. J. H., "From Boston," *New Orleans Tribune*, November 1, 1864, 1; and G. W. P., "Affairs about Boston," *Weekly Anglo-African* (New York), November 5, 1864, 2–3. See Caitlin Beach's discussion of this historical context of Black women's-led relief work surrounding the Colored Ladies' Sanitary Fair in her book *Sculpture at the Ends of Slavery* (Oakland: University of California Press, 2022), 131–40.

2. In her memoir, Elizabeth Keckley describes her founding of the Contraband Relief Association as well as her trip to Boston to visit abolitionists and philanthropists, including Wendell Phillips and Rev. Leonard Grimes. During her visit, Grimes and his congregation raised the money to establish this Boston branch of Keckley's organization, led by his wife, Octavia Grimes. See Elizabeth Keckley, *Behind the Scenes; or, Thirty Years a Slave and Four Years in the White House* (New York: G. W. Carleton, 1868), 113–15. See also Beach, *Sculpture at the Ends of Slavery*, 132–33.

3. G. J. H., "From Boston," 1.

4. G. J. H., "From Boston," 1; G. W. P., "Affairs about Boston," 2–3. The other works praised in both of these articles were Lewis's "life-like medallion of Wendell Phillips" and "a life-size three quarter length portrait of the lamented Colonel Shaw, the hero-martyr of the assault on Fort Wagner," painted by Edward Mitchell Bannister. For more on the appearance of the now-lost Carney statuette and its context alongside goods at the fair, see Beach, *Sculpture at the Ends of Slavery*, 128–29, 134–36.

5. For more on the Fifty-Fourth Massachusetts, see Sara Greenough and Nancy K. Anderson, *Tell It with Pride: The 54th Massachusetts Regiment and Augustus Saint-Gaudens' Shaw Memorial* (Washington, DC: National Gallery of Art, 2013); and Martin H. Blatt, Thomas J. Brown, and Donald Yavocone, eds., *Hope and Glory: Essays on the Legacy of the 54th Massachusetts* (Amherst: University of Massachusetts Press, 2001). See also Beach, *Sculpture at the Ends of Slavery*, 125–27.

6. Other artists working in this building included Edward Mitchell Bannister, John LaFarge, William Rimmer, and her teacher, Edward Augustus Brackett. See Beach, *Sculpture at the Ends of Slavery*, 121–22.

7. Lewis inscribed these words into the marble version of her portrait bust of Shaw (1867, commissioned by Shaw's family), who was widely described this way after his death in the Second Battle of Fort Wagner in Charleston, SC.

8. See, for example, Marilyn Richardson, "Taken from Life: Edward M. Bannister, Edmonia Lewis, and the Memorialization of

the Fifty-Fourth Massachusetts Regiment," in *Hope and Glory: Essays on the Legacy of the Fifty-Fourth Massachusetts Regiment*, ed. Martin H. Blatt, Thomas J. Brown, and Donald Yacovone (Amherst: University of Massachusetts Press, 2001), 94–115; Kirsten Pai Buick, *Child of the Fire: Mary Edmonia Lewis and the Problem of Art History's Black and Indian Subject* (Durham, NC: Duke University Press, 2010); Charmain A. Nelson, *The Color of Stone: Sculpting the Black Female Subject in Nineteenth-Century America* (Minneapolis: University of Minnesota Press, 2007); and Melissa Debakis, *A Sisterhood of Sculptors: American Artists in Nineteenth-Century Rome* (University Park: Pennsylvania State University Press, 2014).

9. Beach, *Sculpture at the Ends of Slavery*, 116, 131. As Beach also notes, Lewis has been more widely associated with the white abolitionist circles, patrons, and artists in her orbit.

10. Beach, *Sculpture at the Ends of Slavery*, 115–16.

11. There is a vast body of scholarship that explores portrayals of Black figures in Euro-American representation. For a succinct summary of this history, see Adrienne L. Childs, "The Vanquished Unchained: Abolition and Emancipation in Sculpture of the Atlantic World," in *Fictions of Emancipation: Carpeaux's "Why Born Enslaved!" Reconsidered*, ed. Elyse Nelson and Wendy S. Walters (New Haven, CT: Yale University Press, 2022), 22–26. By the mid-nineteenth century, photography would become the primary medium through which Black individuals would assert and reclaim control over their self-representation.

12. For more on this paradox, see Nelson and Walters, *Fictions of Emancipation*, esp. Childs, "Vanquished Unchained," 26–28. In an American context, see Kirk Savage, *Standing Soldiers, Kneeling Slaves: Race, War, and Monument in Nineteenth-Century America* (Princeton, NJ: Princeton University Press, 1997). See also Beach, *Sculpture at the Ends of Slavery*, 22–24.

13. Richardson, "Taken from Life," 114; Beach, *Sculpture at the Ends of Slavery*, 136. See also Nelson, *Color of Stone*, 171.

14. "The Mass 54th at Fort Wagner," *The Liberator* (Boston), August 28, 1863, 2.

15. "Mass 54th at Fort Wagner," 2.

16. Ricardson, "Taken from Life," 107. See also Beach, *Sculpture at the Ends of Slavery*, 126.

17. Captain Luis F. Emillio of the Fifty-Fourth Massachusetts published a history of the regiment in 1891 that included such photographs of infantrymen captioned with their names and ranks. See Luis F. Emillio, *History of the Fifty-Fourth Regiment of Massachusetts Volunteer Infantry, 1863–1865* (Boston: Boston Book, 1891). For more on these dynamics at play in Saint-Gaudens's construction of this memorial, see Richardson, "Taken from Life," 108–9.

18. Richardson, "Taken from Life," 108–9.

19. For more on the context and reception of Lewis's bust of Shaw, as well as scholarly critiques and reevaluations of Lewis's strategic aims, see Beach, *Sculpture at the Ends of Slavery*, 126; Buick, *Child of the Fire*, 13–14; and Richardson, "Taken from Life," 104.

20. Edmonia Lewis, quoted in "Seeking Equality Abroad: Why Miss Edmonia Lewis, the Colored Sculptor, Returns to Rome—Her Early Life and Struggles," *New York Times*, December 29, 1878.

21. Marilyn Richardson proposes that this title was inspired by a famous speech that Frederick Douglass gave on December 28, 1862, to a crowd of Rochester, New York's Black community who anxiously awaited Lincoln's long-anticipated signing of the Emancipation Proclamation on January 1, 1863. As Douglass said, "This is scarcely a day for prose. It is a day for poetry and song, a new song. These cloudless skies, this balmy air, this brilliant sunshine, (making December as pleasant as May,) are in harmony with the glorious morning of liberty about to dawn upon us. . . . It surpasses our most enthusiastic hopes that we live at such a time and are likely to witness the downfall, at least the legal downfall of slavery in America. It is a moment for joy, thanksgiving and Praise." See Douglass, "The Day of Jubilee Comes: An Address Delivered in Rochester, New York, on December 28, 1862," printed in *Douglass' Monthly*, January 1863, available at The Frederick Douglass Papers digital edition, https://frederickdouglasspapersproject.com/s/digitaledition/item/9164. See Marilyn Richardson, "Edmonia Lewis and the Boston of Italy," online proceedings of The City and the Book V: International Conference on Americans in Florence's "English" Cemetery, October 10, 2008, www.florin.ms/CBVa.html#richardson.

22. Buick, *Child of the Fire*, 55–59.

23. Childs, "Vanquished Unchained," 30; also see Savage, *Standing Soldiers, Kneeling Slaves*, 23. Beach explores this dynamic in transatlantic sculptural production throughout *Sculpture at the Ends of Slavery*.

24. Savage, *Standing Soldiers, Kneeling Slaves*, 55.

25. Childs, "Vanquished Unchained," 32.

26. See Beach, *Sculpture at the Ends of Slavery*, 142; and Keckley, *Behind the Scenes*, 113–15.

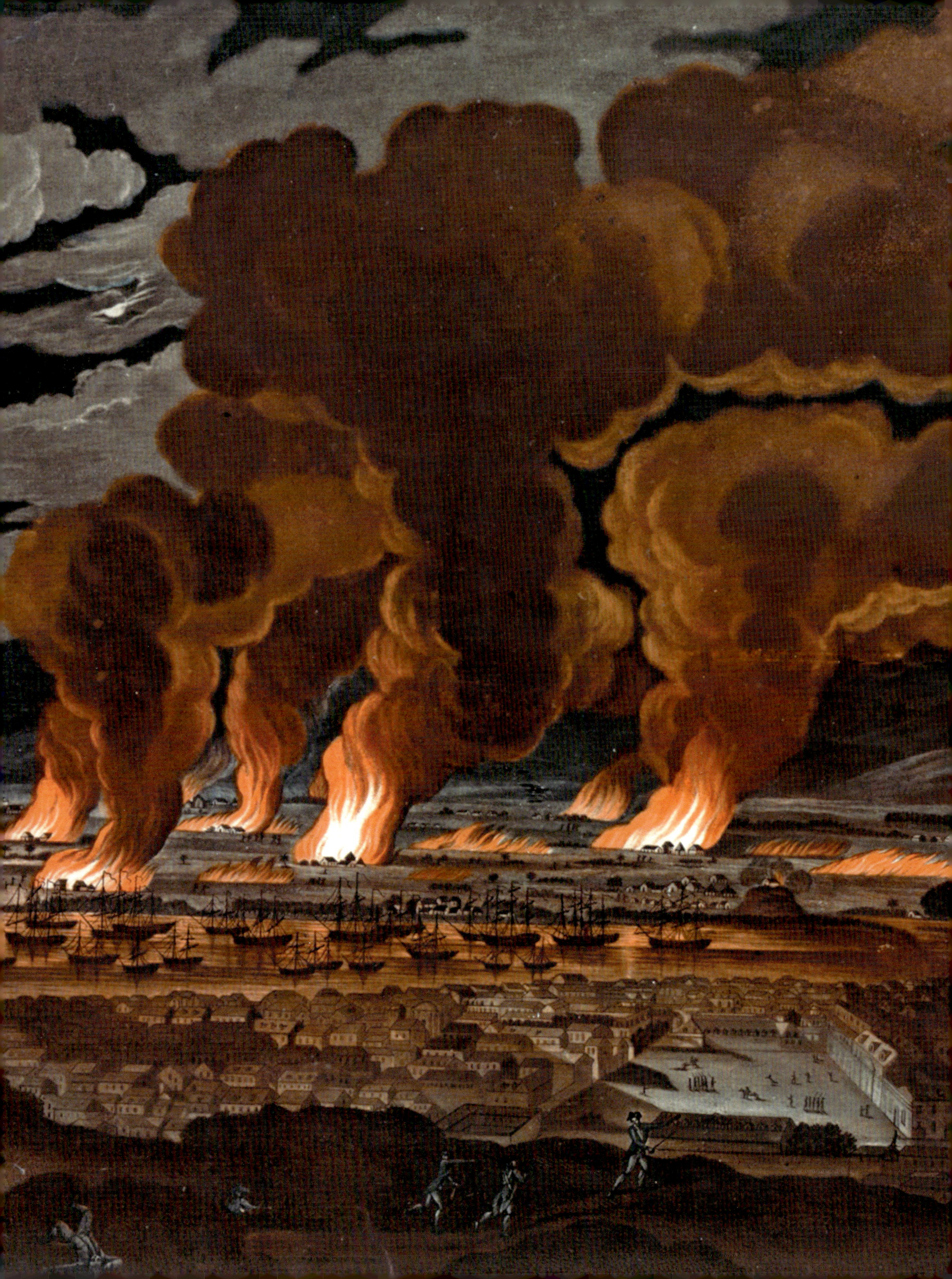

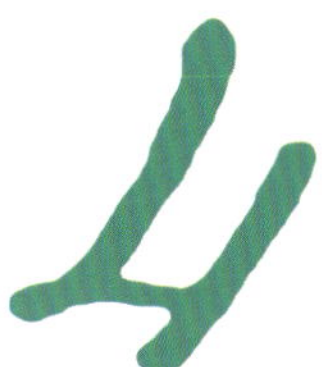

Crafting Community

Cabinetmakers of Color from Saint-Domingue in New Orleans

LYDIA BLACKMORE

The revolution that most changed the fate of people of color in New Orleans was not from 1775 to 1783 but from 1791 to 1804 in what is now known as Haiti. Thousands of free people of color fled the French colony and started new lives in territorial New Orleans. Among the refugees were skilled cabinetmakers who took on the training of a generation of young men. In this essay I track the fates of two men, master craftsman Jean Rousseau and his first apprentice, Dutreuil Barjon, as they created a new community of craftspeople in New Orleans.

Refugees of Revolution

The Haitian Revolution was a series of revolutions and rebellions with changing loyalties among the free white, free Black, and enslaved residents of Saint-Domingue; the colonial empires of France, Great Britain, and Spain; and the changing political leadership of the French Republic. Before the revolution, Saint-Domingue was the most profitable colony in the world, providing sugar and coffee to the French empire. The population of nearly 500,000 was unevenly divided, with about 30,000 free whites, 25,000 free people of color, and 445,000 enslaved people.[1]

At the same time, Louisiana was a colonial outpost at the edge of North America and the Gulf of Mexico. Founded by the French in 1718 but operated by the Spanish since 1763, New Orleans was not part of the American Revolution against the British. Like Saint-Domingue, Louisiana had an economy based on enslaved labor and global trade connections. Its population was much smaller than Saint-Domingue but was similarly divided into three tiers: free whites, free people of color, and enslaved people of African and Indigenous descent.

On August 22, 1791, enslaved workers in Saint-Domingue sparked a rebellion, burning plantations and killing more than 1,000 people (fig. 4.1). Over the next thirteen years, repeated and violent destruction of plantations and urban areas by enslaved people fighting for freedom and by various European empires trying

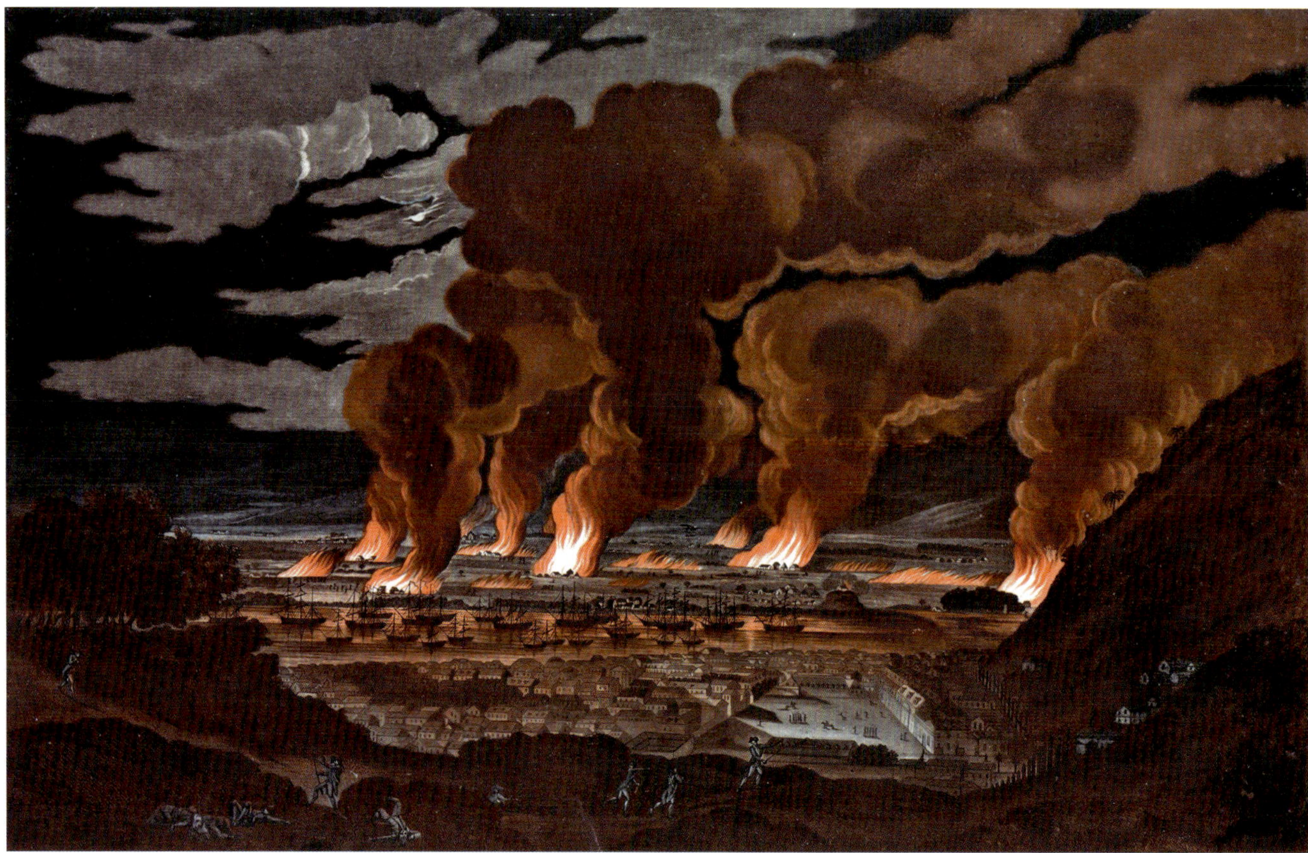

FIGURE 4.1. *Vue des 40 Jours d'Incendie des Habitations de la Plaine du Cap Français*, by Jean Baptiste Chapuy, engraver; after J. L. Boquet, artist, 1795. Colored copperplate engraving. Historic New Orleans Collection. Gift of Dr. and Mrs. Fritz Daguillard, 2017.0003.139.

to seize economic control caused waves of white and free Black colonists to flee the island. Free people of color were caught in the middle, not considered equals by white colonists, and not considered brothers in the fight for liberty by the formerly enslaved militants. French forces evacuated Saint-Domingue in November 1803, and the self-liberated Black army completed a scorched-earth campaign to destroy any remaining plantations and kill all whites and those loyal to them. This led to an exodus of remaining white colonists and colonial free people of color. On January 1, 1804, the renamed country of Haiti declared its independence as the first Black republic in the Western Hemisphere.[2]

Some of the Saint-Domingue refugees went straight to New Orleans, but most were scattered to ports around the Caribbean, Gulf of Mexico, and Eastern Seaboard. A large number, especially free people of color, ended up in Cuba. In 1809, after Napoleon invaded Spain, the Spanish governor of Cuba expelled all French-speaking people from the island, spurring a final wave of Saint-Domingue refugees to take to the seas seeking a new home.[3]

More than 10,000 Saint-Domingue refugees arrived in New Orleans following the expulsion from Cuba. They doubled the population of New Orleans, which in 1805 numbered only 8,000. Over 3,000 free people of color arrived, tripling that population in the city. Of this group, a majority were women and children. The gender disparity was for multiple reasons: more women were emancipated in colonial Saint-Domingue, more free men fought and died during the revolution, and Louisiana actively barred entry to men of color from Saint-Domingue in hopes of limiting their revolutionary influence on the local enslaved population.[4]

The New Orleans these families settled in was in a period of transition. Purchased by the United States in 1803, New Orleans was part of the Orleans Territory until Louisiana became a state in 1812. A cosmopolitan port city, its prominent language was still French, but Spanish and English were heard in equal measure. Within a few years of their arrival, the Saint-Domingue refugees and the new Louisiana Americans proved their loyalty to the republic by defending the city from the British at the Battle of New Orleans.[5]

As refugee families settled in the city, free people of color entered the trade class, especially as market vendors, builders, and craftspeople. Many sought to set their sons up for success by sponsoring their indenture to a master craftsman.[6] Of the 1,152 apprenticeship indentures recorded by the office of the mayor between 1809 and 1843, about half were for free boys of color.[7] Of those, 93 indentures for free men of color were to learn the cabinetmaking trade, nearly half of whom were part of the refugee diaspora. Seven boys were born in Saint-Domingue during and following the Haitian Revolution. Twenty-one were born in Cuba between 1804 and 1809. It is likely that the boys recorded as having been born in Curaçao, Jamaica, and Charleston, South Carolina, were also refugees.[8]

The apprentices of color worked with twenty-four master craftsmen, half of whom were free men of color. At least six of the masters were from Saint-Domingue. The two master craftsmen with the most apprentices were Jean Rousseau (twenty-nine apprentices) and Dutreuil Barjon (eleven apprentices), both free men of color born in Saint-Domingue.[9]

Jean Rousseau

Jean Rousseau was born in Saint-Marc, Saint-Domingue, before 1791.[10] He probably received training as a cabinetmaker as a teenager during the revolution and likely arrived in New Orleans before 1806, when the governor of the Orleans Territory banned entry of adult Black men with origins in Saint-Domingue. By 1813, Rousseau had a store with mahogany furniture and cabinetmaking tools worth $3,000. In that year, he took on three apprentices and married Jeanne Marie Mallet, a free woman of color.[11]

Over the next fifteen years, Rousseau took on two dozen more apprentices. Half of the young men were born in Saint-Domingue or Cuba, the rest in New Orleans. All were free people of color, except for two, Lolo and Mars, who were put into apprenticeship by their enslavers. Extending this complicated web of free, indentured, and enslaved, the Rousseau household included at least four enslaved boys who may also have been learning the cabinetmaking trade.[12]

Although Rousseau's cabinetmaking shop must have been busy, there are no pieces of furniture attributed to him. There is plentiful documentary evidence of his trade, in the apprenticeship indentures, advertisements, and the estate

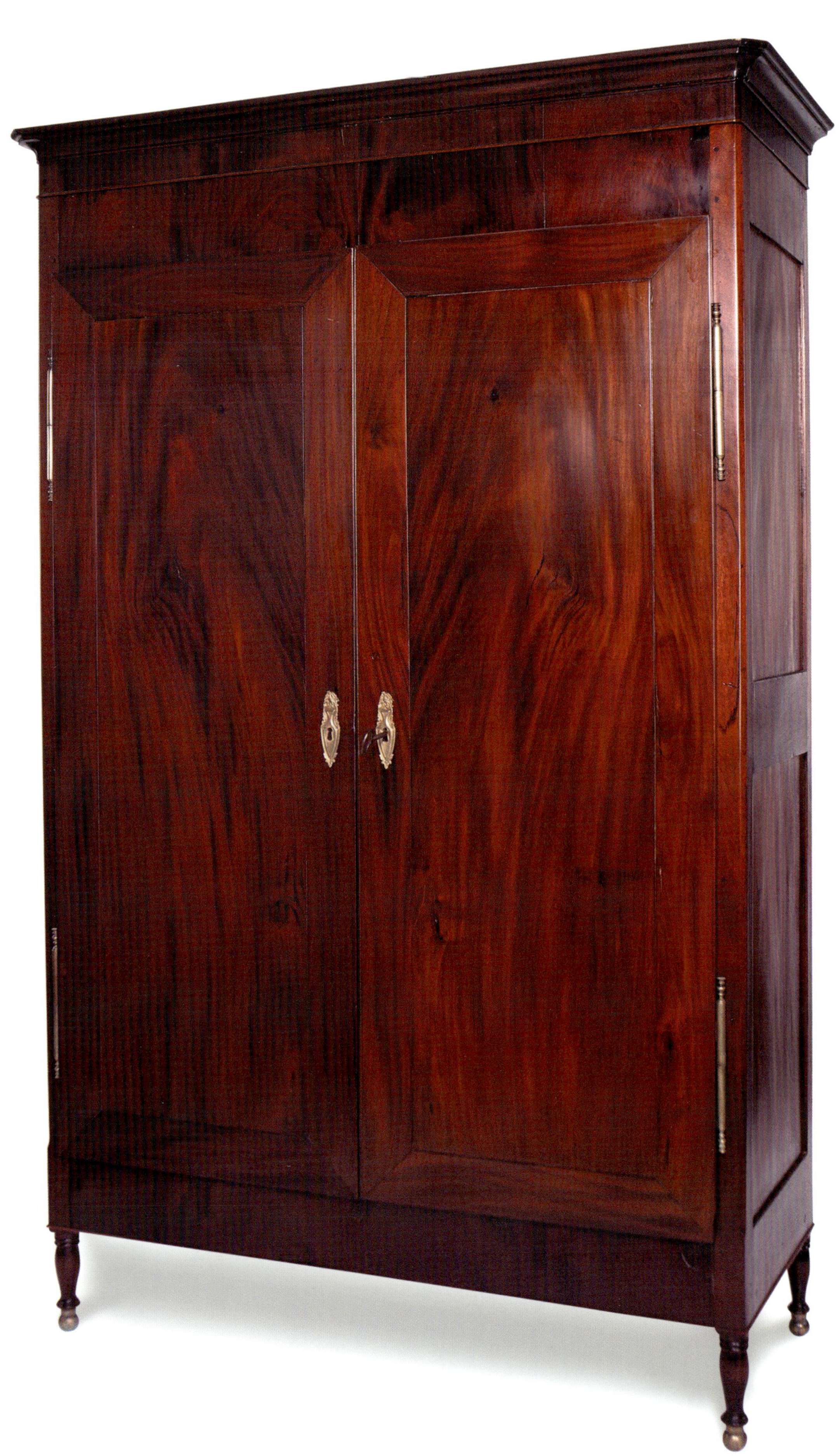

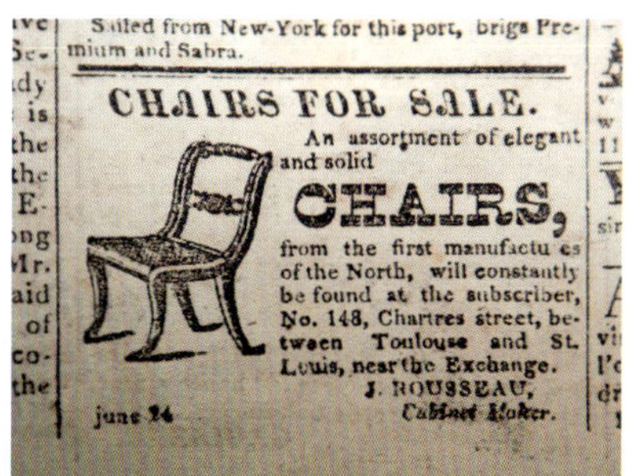

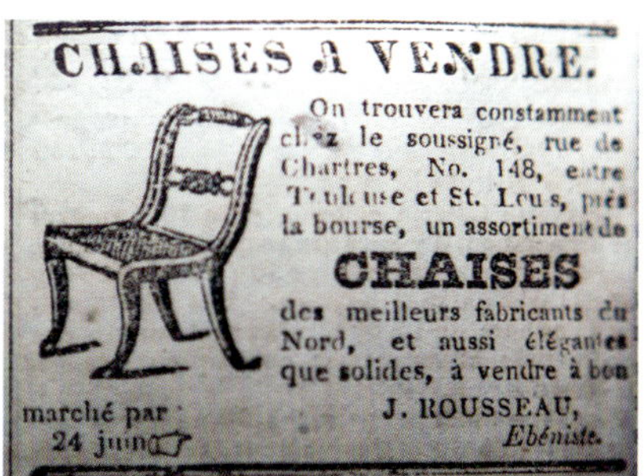

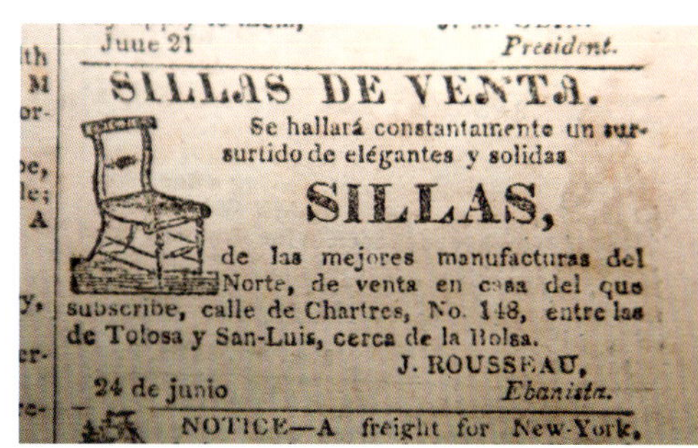

(*opposite*) FIGURE 4.2. *Flush-Panel Armoire*, Louisiana, between 1815 and 1830. Mahogany, tulip poplar, cypress, brass. Collection of Wayne and Cheryl Stromeyer.

(*above*) FIGURE 4.3. "Chairs, Chaises, Sillas," *L'Abeille* (New Orleans), June 25, 1830. From Jack Holden, H. Parrott Bacot, and Cybèle T. Gontar, with Brian J. Costello and Francis J. Puig, *Furnishing Louisiana: Creole and Acadian Furniture, 1735–1835*, ed. Jessica Dorman and Sarah R. Doerries (New Orleans: Historic New Orleans Collection, 2010), 111.

papers filed after his wife's death in 1827. At that time, the Rousseau family lived in a three-room cottage on Bourbon Street with a work yard in the back. The small house was heavily furnished in mahogany, including columned beds, couches, armoires, and tables. The yard held several thousand board feet of wood. Rousseau's atelier and workshop on Chartres Street held armoires, sofas, bookcases, tables, and beds valued at $5,000.[13] There are many unattributed pieces of New Orleans–made mahogany furniture from the period, but none have tell-tale signatures or documented provenance to say that they were produced in Rousseau's shop.

Mahogany was native to Saint-Domingue, and the few pieces of furniture with documented ties to the French colony use the species. Although the use of mahogany was not unique to Saint-Domingue, one construction detail has been attributed to the island: the use of flush panels in armoire doors, showing off fine mahogany grains across a smooth facade (fig. 4.2). Flush-panel construction became prominent in New Orleans after the influx of Saint-Domingue refugees. As a prolific cabinetmaker in the city at the time of this change in armoire construction, Jean Rousseau may have originated the flush-panel trend and passed the style to his numerous apprentices.[14]

In 1827, Rousseau advertised furniture recently imported from New York for sale in his store, following a general trend in furniture retail in New Orleans.[15] Representing the multicultural nature of his business, he advertised "Chairs," "Chaises," and "Sillas," in English, French, and Spanish in the local papers (fig. 4.3).[16] The cabinetmaker bought and sold six properties in the French Quarter as investments and for use by his business and family. Rousseau left New Orleans about 1838 and was living in Kingston, Jamaica, when he died a decade later.[17]

Pierre Charles Dutreuil Barjon

Pierre Charles Dutreuil Barjon was born in Jérémie, Saint-Domingue, about 1799 to Marie Therese "Fillette" Latapie Cambray.[18] Before he turned five, his mother fled with him from his birthplace. They went first to Cuba, where Cambray gave birth to a second son in 1806.[19] The family likely came to New Orleans in the wave of refugees that arrived in 1809. On April 27, 1813, when Dutreuil was about fourteen, his mother sponsored him in apprenticeship with Jean Rousseau to learn the trade of a "menuisier ou ebeniste."[20] He was Rousseau's first apprentice.

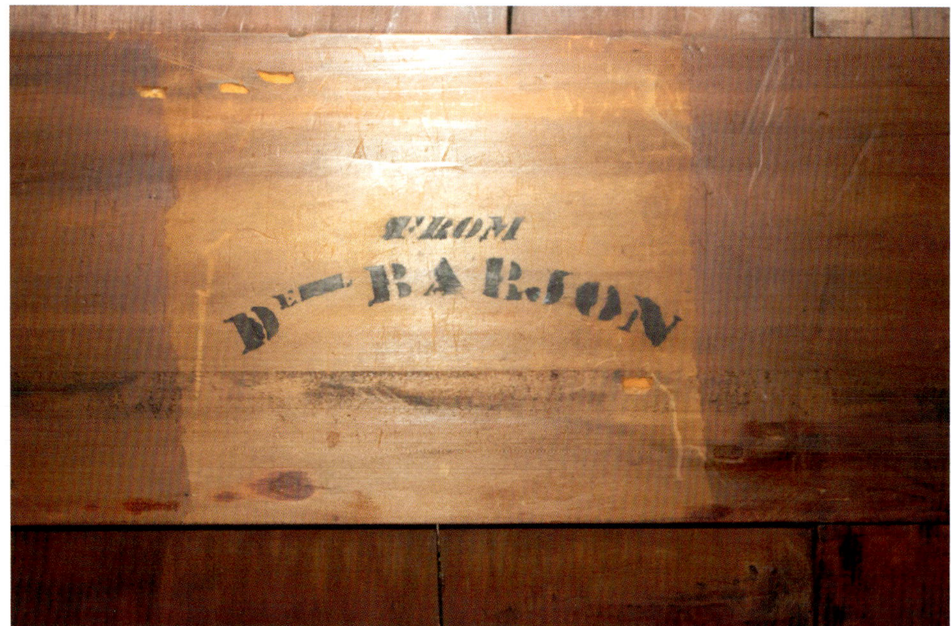

FIGURE 4.4. *Armoire*, detail. Historic New Orleans Collection. Gift of Mr. and Mrs. Robert J. Patrick, 2008.0088.

During the 1820s, Barjon took on eleven apprentices of his own. The two oldest were born in Saint-Domingue and Cuba; the rest were born after the final wave of refugees arrived in New Orleans. Like Rousseau, Barjon was expanding his immediate family while taking on young men to train. In 1823, he married Eulalie Lanna, the natural daughter of Celeste, a free woman of color, and Jean Lanna, a white real estate investor. They had four children in six years. Barjon set up his home and business at a property owned by his father-in-law on Royal Street. The business included a store, a workshop, and a sawmill to cut boards and veneers suitable for cabinetmaking.[21]

When Eulalie Lanna died in 1836, the Barjon store contained dozens of beds, armoires, sideboards, couches, and other furniture made of mahogany and fine cherry. He also had 30,000 board feet of mahogany in various widths stored on the property.[22] Barjon declared bankruptcy in 1843 and was forced to buy half of his belongings from his children to maintain their inheritance from their mother. The sale included three enslaved men, Thomas, Tom, and Mingo, who may have worked with the sawmill. Barjon owed wages to six employees of the cabinetmaking shop. As a result of the bankruptcy, Barjon's twenty-year-old son, Dutreuil Jr., took over the management of the business. Little is known about the end of Barjon Sr.'s life. He may have moved to France, where there was less discrimination against people of color.[23]

Unlike Rousseau, pieces of furniture signed by Dutreuil Barjon do exist. They reflect the inventories of his property, including beds with columns, daybeds, and armoires. They were purchased by white and Black creole customers.[24] His work shows his access to prime wood and various tools of the sawmill. Instead of using the colonial Caribbean flush-panel construction, his armoires reflect the sleek curves of Biedermeier style, as seen in a monumental armoire bearing Barjon's stamp (fig. 4.4 and fig. 33 in Exhibition Catalog of Objects).

Rousseau and Barjon were just two of the cabinetmakers of color with roots in Saint-Domingue who created a community of craftsmen in New Orleans. Despite the documentary evidence of their trade, only Barjon signed his work. No signatures or receipts exist from Barjon's master, Jean Rousseau, his compatriots who apprenticed with Rousseau, or his own apprentices. There are many beds, armoires, and case pieces that have been passed down the branches of creole New Orleans families who would have purchased mahogany furniture in the French Quarter in the early nineteenth century. When looking at those unattributed pieces of furniture, we must assume that many were made with Black hands that had felt the waves of revolution.

Notes

I wish to thank my colleagues at the Historic New Orleans Collection, especially Libby Neidenbach and Sarah Duggan. Special acknowledgment goes to HNOC interns Joseph Will, Ashanty Felipe, Saidah Rothleuther, Skye Spencer, and Ella Mayfield for their work adding Louisiana craftspeople to the Black Craftspeople Digital Archive.

1. Nathalie Dessens, *From Saint-Domingue to New Orleans: Migration and Influences* (Gainesville: University Press of Florida, 2007), 7–15.

2. Dessens, *From Saint-Domingue to New Orleans*, 7–15.

3. Dessens, *From Saint-Domingue to New Orleans*, 7–15.

4. Elizabeth Clark Neidenbach, "Refugee Revolution," *64 Parishes*, https://64parishes.org/refugee-revolution.

5. Carolyn Cosse Bell, *Creole New Orleans in the Revolutionary Atlantic, 1775–1877* (Baton Rouge: Louisiana State University Press, 2023).

6. "A Graphical Overview of New Orleans Indentures, 1809–1843," New Orleans Public Library, accessed January 14, 2024, http://nutrias.org/~nopl/inv/indentures/graphs.htm

7. Indentures including apprentices or master craftspeople of color have been digitized by Louisiana State University as part of the Free People of Color in Louisiana: Revealing an Unknown Past digital archive: www.lib.lsu.edu/sites/all/files/sc/fpoc/index.html. Apprentices in the cabinetmaking trade have been documented in the Black Craftspeople Digital Archive by interns at the Historic New Orleans Collection.

8. New Orleans (LA) Office of the Mayor, Indentures, 1809–43, Louisiana Division/City Archives, New Orleans Public Library, Louisiana Digital Library.

9. New Orleans (LA) Office of the Mayor, Indentures, 1809–43.

10. Sacramental records, Archdiocese of New Orleans, SLC M3, 47.

11. John and Jean Rousseau Collection, 1814–38, Louisiana State Museum Historical Center, New Orleans, available online at Louisiana Digital Library, https://louisianadigitallibrary.org/islandora/object/fpoc-p16313coll51%3A50655.

12. "Louisiana, U.S., Wills and Probate Records, 1756-1984," s.v. "Jeanne Marie Mallet," Ancestry.com.

13. John and Jean Rousseau Collection.

14. Jack D. Holden, "West Indian Armoires and Their Derivatives: Louisiana Creole-Style Flush-Panel Armoires," in *Furnishing Louisiana:* Creole and Acadian Furniture, 1735–1835, ed. Jessica Dorman and Sarah R. Doerries (New Orleans: Historic New Orleans Collection, 2010), 128–30.

15. *L'Abeille* (New Orleans), December 11, 1827, cited in Dorman and Doerries, *Furnishing Louisiana*, 111.

16. *L'Abeille* (New Orleans), June 25, 1830, cited in Dorman and Doerries, *Furnishing Louisiana*, 111.

17. "1227–1229 Bourbon St.," Vieux Carré Digital Survey, Historic New Orleans Collection, www.hnoc.org/vcs/property_info.php?lot=22987-01D.

18. "Indenture of Pierre Dutreuil with Jean Rousseau Sponsored by Marie Cambry, Volume 1, Number 110, 1813 April 27," New Orleans (LA) Office of the Mayor, Indentures, 1809–1843, Louisiana Division/City Archives, New Orleans Public Library, available online at Louisiana Digital Library, https://louisianadigitallibrary.org/islandora/object/fpoc-p16313coll51%3A60662.

19. "Indenture for Severin Latapy with Jean Rousseau sponsored by Marie Cambrie, Volume 3, Number 95, 1819 January 25," New Orleans (LA) Office of the Mayor, Indentures, 1809–43, Louisiana Division/City Archives, New Orleans Public Library, available online at Louisiana Digital Library, https://louisianadigitallibrary.org/islandora/object/fpoc-p16313coll51:37866.

20. "Indenture of Pierre Dutreuil."

21. "Louisiana, U.S., Wills and Probate Records, 1756-1984," s.v. "Eulalie Lanna," Ancestry.com.

22. "Eulalie Lanna."

23. Stephen Harrison, "Furniture Trade in New Orleans, 1840–1880: The Largest Assortment Constantly on Hand" (MA thesis, University of Delaware, 1997).

24. Creole is defined as having been born in Louisiana with at least one parent of French or Spanish ancestry.

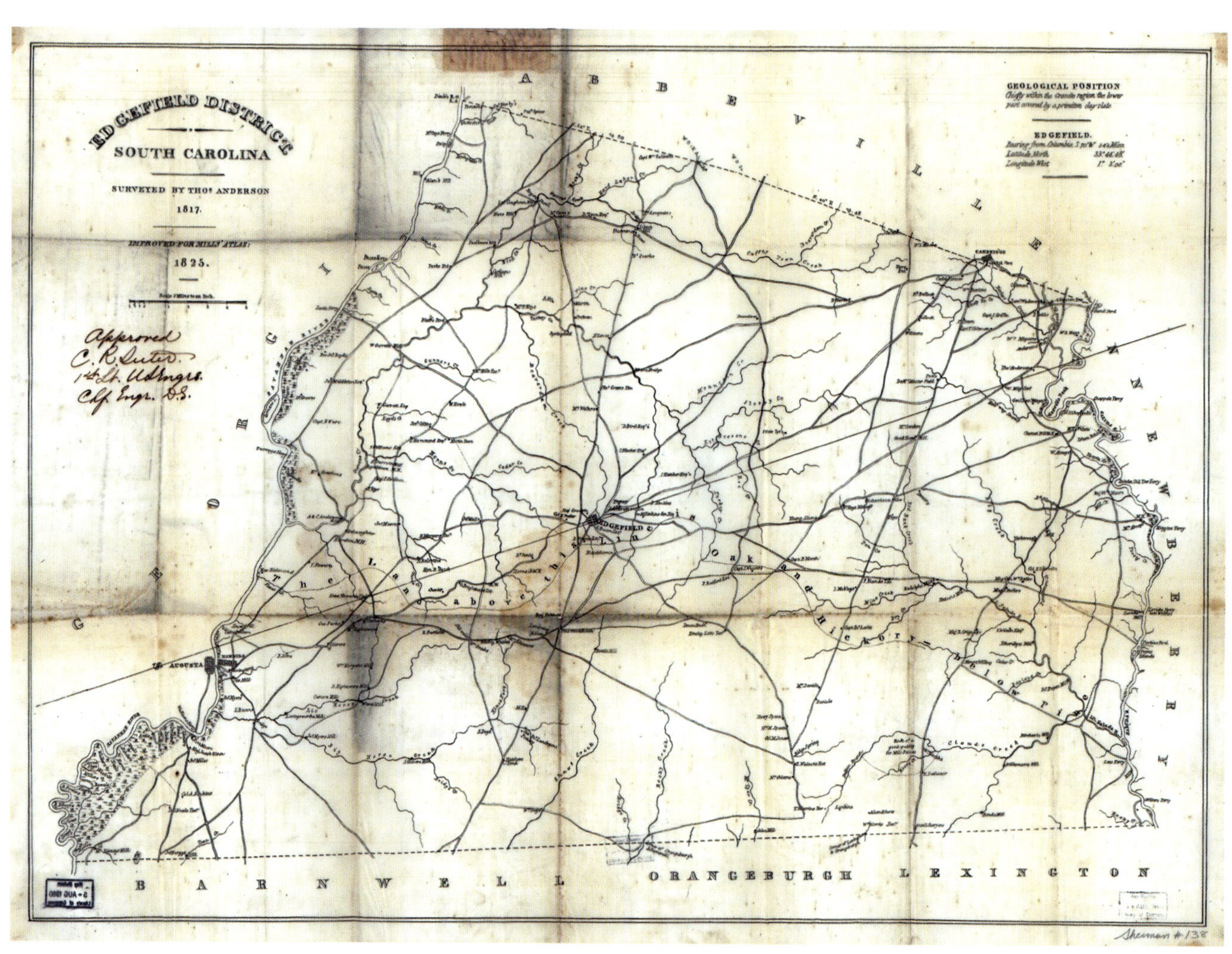

FIGURE 5.1. *Map of Edgefield District, South Carolina* [1825]. Library of Congress.

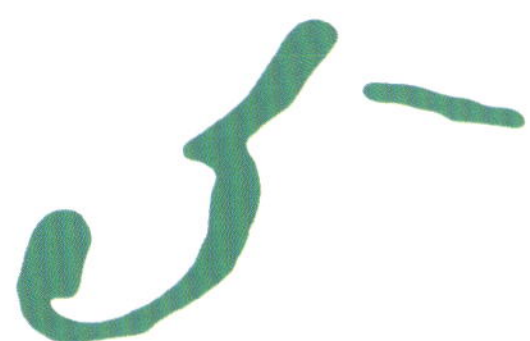

Literacy as Freedom

Dave the Potter and the Act of Inscribing

SUSAN J. RAWLES

The life and work of Dave the Potter (ca. 1800–1870s) has attracted the attention of scholars and collectors for more than a century, signaling the importance of enslaved artisans to the American craft tradition while cementing Dave's fame in the history of South Carolina's stoneware industry.[1] Among the most skilled potters of the nineteenth century, Dave spent his lifetime in the Edgefield District (fig. 5.1), a western region of the state bordering the Savannah River, where the perfect convergence of water, wood, and white kaolin clay facilitated the development of more than a dozen potteries.[2] Conducted within the plantation economy, these manufactories were unique in America for their scale of operation, providing functional domestic wares—jugs, jars, churns, and so on—on a year-round basis in numbers sufficient to store staples for the region's free and enslaved populations.[3] Within this community, Dave crafted jars prized for their size, symmetry, and glaze.[4] Even more valued are their extraordinary inscriptions: the names, dates, and poetic couplets he incised onto the surface of selected works. These inscriptions are remarkable for several reasons. Not only do they document Dave's ability to read and write, but they suggest Dave's resilience to South Carolina's "Negro acts," which outlawed literacy among its enslaved populations.[5]

Like its Anglo-Caribbean neighbors, South Carolina developed as a "black-majority colony," and in 1691, the growing number of free Blacks, coupled with the labor demands of an evolving rice trade, prompted the colony's adoption of slave codes based on Jamaica's Slave Act of 1684.[6] As the concept and language of "race" was consolidated, the status of "all [enslaved] negroes, mulatoes, mustizoes, or Indians" was changed from a condition of debt bondage—akin to indentured white servitude—to a form of chattel property that could be used as currency in the transfer and payment of debts.[7] This increasingly racialized codification of masters, slaves, and indentured servants progressively limited opportunities for literacy among people of color in the Anglo-Atlantic world. In 1740, white supremacy was codified in South Carolina in *An Act for the Better Ordering and*

Governing Negroes and Other Slaves in This Province. Code XLV of the act proclaimed: "And *whereas,* the having of slaves taught to write, or suffering them to be employed in writing, may be attended with great inconveniences; *Be it therefore enacted* by the authority aforesaid, That all and every person and persons whatsoever, who shall hereinafter teach or cause any slave or slaves to be taught, to write, or shall use or employ any slave as a scribe in any manner of writing whatsoever, hereafter taught to write, every such person and persons, shall, for every such offense, forfeit the sum of one hundred pounds current money."[8] The subsequent act of 1800 reinforced the 1740 codes while further authorizing "twenty lashes on every slave found in an assembly convened for the purpose of 'mental instruction.'"[9] In 1834, additional legislation extended the offense to reading.[10]

The antiliteracy campaigns of the antebellum period were prompted by mounting fears of slave rebellion in the decades preceding the Civil War.[11] Yet evidence suggests that the escalating restrictions were treated with varying levels of enforcement.[12] Even during the most tumultuous periods, evangelical Christians defended "Bible literacy" as essential to individual salvation, and many Edgefield Baptists endorsed this position.[13] Moreover, writing was treated as a separate discipline even among the free white population.[14] Though most whites were "literate" by 1850, the very term was redefined in the modern period, from a measure of one's facility with classical languages to the basics of reading and writing. This was owing, in part, to the influence of slavery, the ideals of democracy, and the evolving nineteenth-century association among literacy, freedom, and progress. By the late nineteenth century, Beth Schweiger writes, "Reading became a category of political economy, a mark of productivity and potential, the most reliable measure of progress."[15] In tandem with these developments, the written word became intellectually fragmented, divided into categories of print and script that were ascribed distinct functions and values. Together, these conditions—the influence of evangelical Christianity, the inconsistent enforcement of anti-literacy measures, and the reinterpretation of script as a medium of self-presentation—created opportunities for gifted enslaved craftspeople to impose their presence on the public sphere.

Enter Dave the Potter. Dave first appeared in the public record in 1818 when, as collateral on a loan, he was recorded as "a boy about 17 years" and "country born" in the United States.[16] His last known mention was in the *Edgefield Advertiser* on October 30, 1873.[17] Between these years, Drake inscribed at least forty-two stoneware objects.[18] His first known inscription, "Concatination" (to be linked together), appeared on a two-handled jar dated June 12, 1834. It was followed a month later by his first known couplet: "Put every bit all between / surely this jar will hold 14."[19] But a brick attributed to Dave and inscribed "April 18" suggests that he began learning to write sometime during the 1820s, a period of escalating political and racial tensions in South Carolina.[20] This emerging literacy culminated in what is believed to be his first signed and dated poem piece, now in the collection of the Virginia Museum of Fine Arts (figs. 5.2–5.4). Dated "January 29th 1840," the jug was produced at Lewis Miles's pottery on Horse

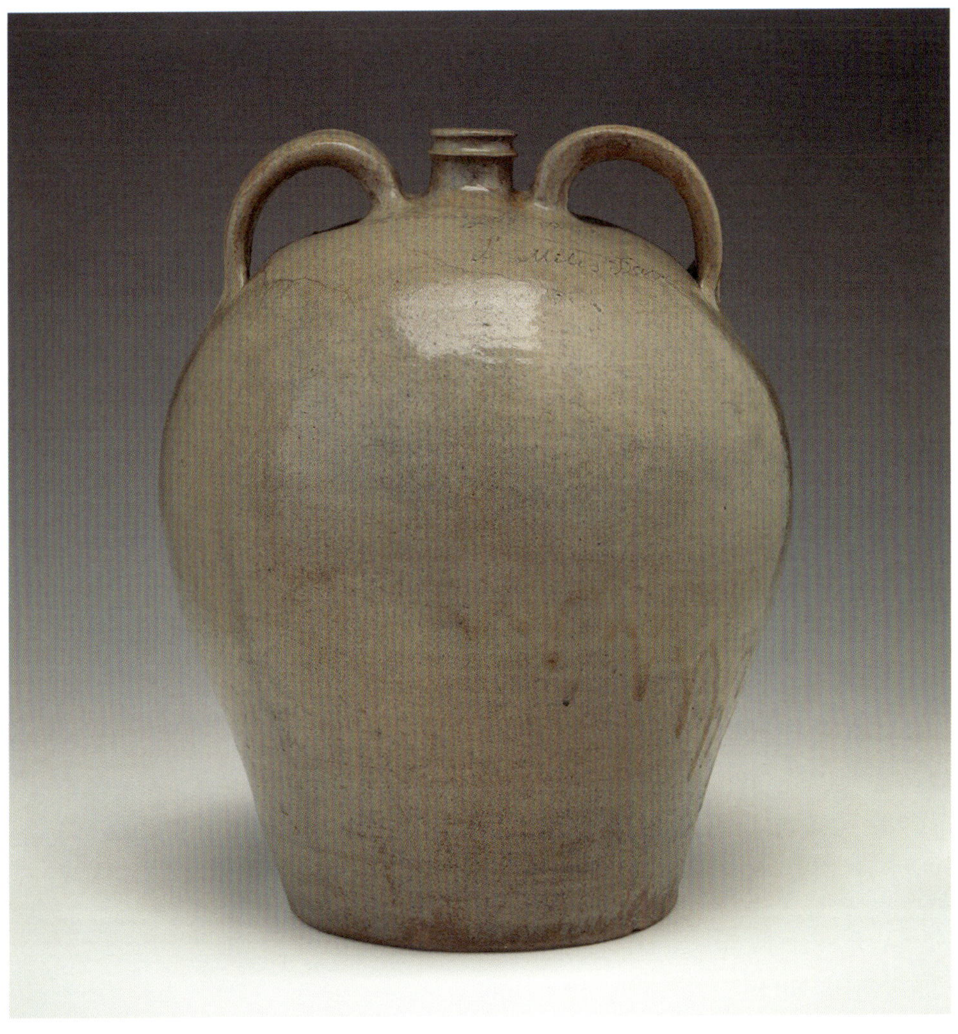

FIGURE 5.2. *Two-Handled Jug*. Stoneware with alkaline glaze. Virginia Museum of Fine Arts, Richmond. Floyd D. and Anne C. Gottwald Fund and partial gift of Dr. and Mrs. John E. Hoar, 2017.150. Photo © Travis Fullerton.

Creek, just south of Edgefield Village, and bears the name "L Miles" as well as a horseshoe-like imprint possibly made with a typesetter's "U."[21] In a nod to the plantation's tannery operation, it is inscribed with the couplet, "Ladies & Gentleman's Shoes / Sell all you can: & nothing you'll loose! x." Most remarkably, Dave impressed his own name on the jug. Though there is a long history of marking words in clay, this rare assertion of personhood merits consideration.[22]

Scholars have speculated about the meaning of Dave's signature: Is it the mark of an artist or a rebel? As Michael Chaney has noted, pairing "Dave" with "L Miles" complicates the attribution of authorship. On one hand, the pairing might be read as complicity on Miles's part, not just in the fabrication of the object but in the rebellion of the inscription. On the other hand, it highlights Dave's condition as chattel property—"Dave belongs to Mr. Miles," as it were.[23] This latter required a substitute means by which to present Dave's extralegal personhood. For Chaney, it transpires through the commodity itself; the "concatenate" *linking together* of discordant parts, the self (signature) and its object (jug), represents "the transubstantiation of author into [a] work" that synchronizes two parts—the artistic talents of the potter and

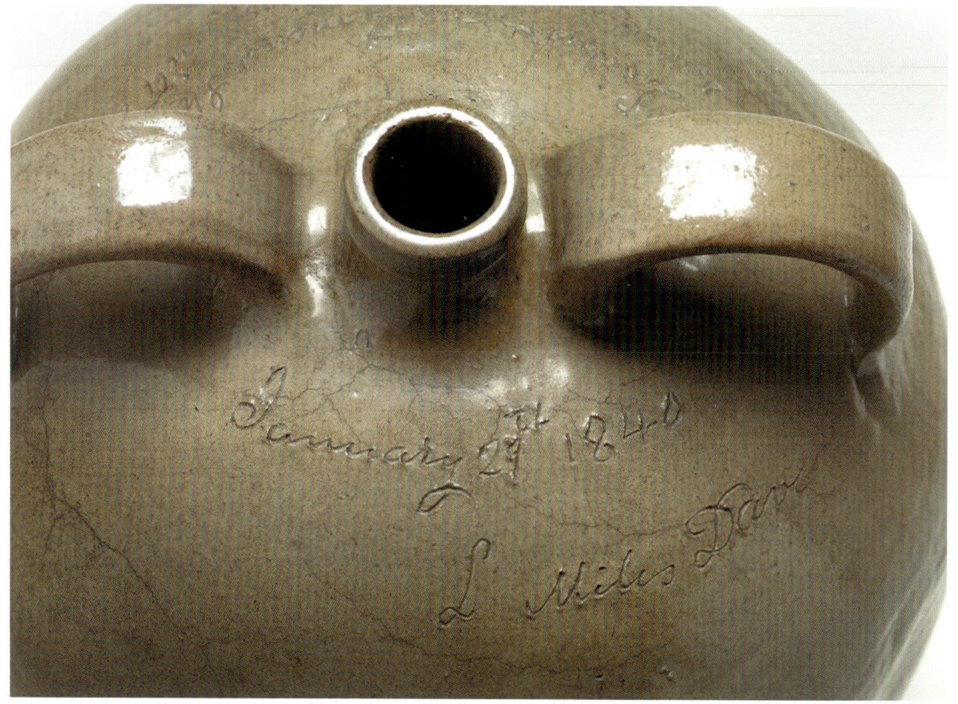

FIGURE 5.3. *Two-Handled Jug, with "Horseshoe,"* detail. Stoneware with alkaline glaze. Virginia Museum of Fine Arts, Richmond. Floyd D. and Anne C. Gottwald Fund and partial gift of Dr. and Mrs. John E. Hoar, 2017.150. Photo © Travis Fullerton.

the body of the enslaved man—whose values are determined by the marketplace.[24] But the union of the jug's body (form) and mind (text) also invites an alternative interpretation, one in which Dave is metaphorically restored to a divine wholeness beyond the reach of slavery. Dave grew up in a community of people committed to the Baptist faith; the Drake and Landrum families were not just followers but founders of Baptist churches and preachers of its word.[25] Baptists believe that salvation requires an individual's direct relationship with God—one mediated by neither priest nor slaveholder. Moreover, the history of African American verse suggests that poetry served as a vehicle for spiritual salvation, particularly during the two eras of religious revivalism known as the First and Second Great Awakenings.[26] For enslaved potters such as Dave, the combined influence of the Second Great Awakening and the abolitionist movement may have encouraged the weaving of spiritualism with liberty, his "rebirth" in the jug invoking a religious freedom that imparts the promise of a higher, New Testament self—a unity of mind, body, and spirit that begins with baptism and ends with resurrection.[27] As Tamara Thornton might put it, the jug becomes "one of the places where the self happened."[28]

Dave the Potter was among an estimated 2,500 literate, enslaved South Carolinians.[29] Through self-determination and the assistance—or negligence—of others, enslaved people memorized and copied random alphabetic characters, went to nighttime classes held in hidden school "pits," bribed delinquent strangers for assistance with Noah Webster's ubiquitous *Elementary Spelling Book*—the "blue-back speller"—and learned from educated children as playmates and caretakers.[30] Yet Dave's handwriting was not the print of the typesetter or the "speller"; Dave's handwriting was fluid cursive, a more

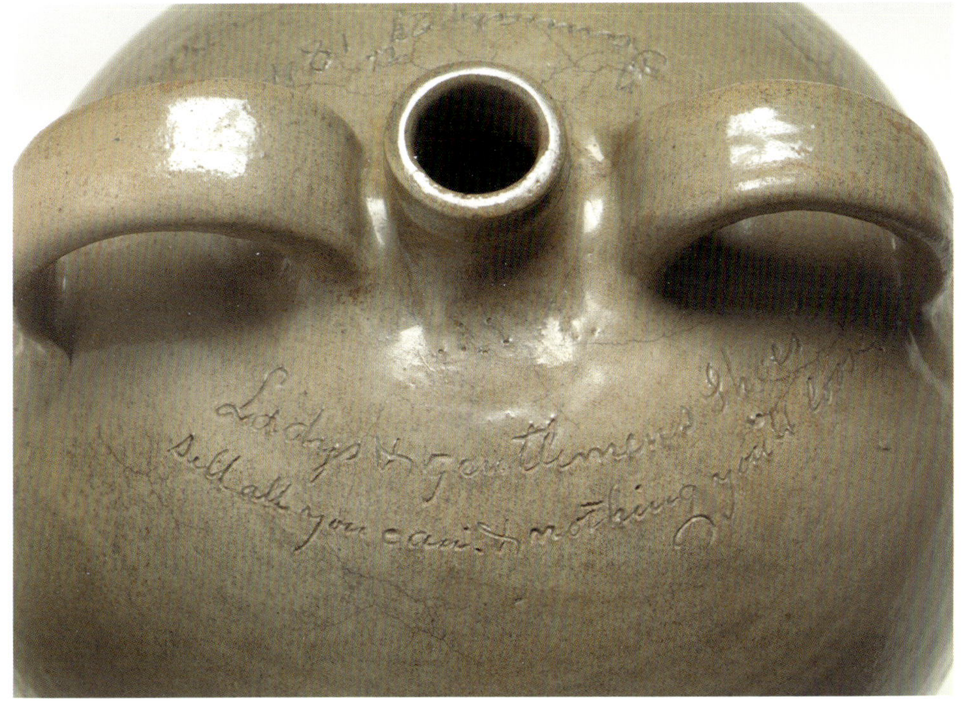

FIGURE 5.4. *Two-Handled Jug, with Six Punch Marks*, detail. Stoneware with alkaline glaze. Virginia Museum of Fine Arts, Richmond. Floyd D. and Anne C. Gottwald Fund and partial gift of Dr. and Mrs. John E. Hoar, 2017.150. Photo © Travis Fullerton.

advanced and individual style of penmanship.[31] According to Thornton, the eighteenth century witnessed a separation between print and script by which print was alienated from "the hand" of the author and script was "endowed . . . with a unique set of cultural meanings and functions" that "necessarily referred back to the hand, the body, and the individual in new ways," not as a form of "self-expression" but as a medium of "self-presentation" within the public sphere.[32] As Dave's pots and jugs were transported to neighboring communities of Blacks and whites, enslaved and free, his hand and mind were likewise carried, trespassing on the lives of the wares' recipients in ways that potentially challenged oppressive preconceptions about the abilities of Black people while fueling aspirations of freedom among enslaved populations.[33]

It is unclear how Dave the Potter became literate.[34] However, it is speculated that, once literate, he honed his skills while performing tasks for Abner Landrum at his newspaper, the *Edgefield Hive*, a possibility that corresponds with the proposed timeline of the inscribed brick.[35] Landrum's pro-Unionist weekly, which operated from 1827 to 1830/31, would have exposed Dave not only to printed letters and words but its "Recommendation of Poetry," which was intended to mitigate the escalating tensions of the antebellum period.[36] But the six-stanza poem "My Pen," by the little-known poet Frank Addison Mowig Philom (n.d.), also extolls the liberating virtues of written expression.[37] Published in 1852, the poem's first, fifth, and final stanzas read:

My pen, my pen, my joy and my pride,
My idol I worship each day;
A gem which adversity giveth to me,

Shall speak of the shackles, the bond and the free,
And sound thy loud anthems o'er woodland and lea,
To echo forever and aye . . .

My pen, my pen, there is joy in thy name.
My heart shall be ever thine own;
While a Washington's banner round us shall wave,
Oh! Stretch forth thy hand like an angel to save
From deep tears of anguish a free country's slave,
That *the stain* be forever unknown.

My pen, my pen, when I leave this dark sphere,
And pass to another more blest,
'Tis now my fond wish that there I may be
Engaged in recording some virtues of thee,
Who hast in thy might caused the slave to stand free,
And at last reach a haven of rest.[38]

That the "pen" has "caused the slave to stand free" is one way of reading Dave's inscriptions. As a medium of quiet rebellion, Wallace Stevens suggests, "poetry affirms a violence from within that protects us from violence from without; it is the imagination pressing back against the pressure of reality."[39]

Recent scholarship has highlighted the inherent complications—and contradictions—in acquiring, interpreting, and celebrating objects produced by artisans under forced labor, and there is a particular risk to interpreting Dave's couplets.[40] Frederick Douglass's reference to the songs of enslaved folks cautions against simple readings. In January 1852, just one month before Philom's poem was printed in his newspaper, Douglass wrote: "I have often been utterly astonished, since I came to the north, to find persons who could speak of the singing, among slaves, as evidence of their contentment and happiness. It is impossible to conceive a greater mistake. Slaves sing most when they are most unhappy. The songs of the slave represent the sorrows of his heart; and he is relieved by them, only as an aching heart is relieved by its tears."[41]

Douglass's insight provides a compelling context for considering Dave's inscriptions. The potter's typographical marks recall music's vertical scores: rearranged, reconfigured as dots and dashes, or converted to the horizontal, they interrupt the composition, controlling its tempo almost like drumbeats. Babatunde Lawal has noted the "complicated marks" that appear on the multicultural colonoware found in the South during the seventeenth and early eighteenth centuries. These "Africanist influences" continued to infiltrate South Carolina with the importation of enslaved Africans even after the slave trade was banned in 1808.[42] Indeed, Lawal proposes, the African tradition of work songs may have inspired Dave to sing as he inscribed. If so, he writes, "each jar has . . . a sight and sound implication, resonating like the banjar . . . [a] genre [that] evolved from an attempt to find a musical outlet for the harrowing experience of enslavement."[43] Dave's circumstances and the rhythm of his couplets seem to recall this tradition:

> I wonder where is all my relations
> Friendship to all—and every nation
> *August 16, 1857*
>
> The forth of July is surely come
> To blow the fife = and beat the drum
> *July 4, 1859*
>
> I saw a leopard & a lions face
> Then I felt, the need of grace
> *August 7, 1860*

Like a slave's song, Dave's verses invite multivalent meanings: clever amusements, declarations of self-identity, a force of resistance, and tears of grief.[44]

Frederick Douglass (1818–95) published his famous autobiography, *Narrative of the Life of Frederick Douglass, an American Slave,* in 1845, concurrent with Dave the Potter's inscriptions. In the *Narrative,* Douglass recalls the moment he realized that "the white man's power to enslave the black man" was linked, in part, to literacy: "From that moment, I understood the pathway from slavery to freedom" and became determined "in learning to read and write."[45] Douglass was first taught to read by his Baltimore slaveholder Sophia Auld, whose efforts were reprimanded by her husband, Hugh Auld: "If you teach [him] how to read," he declared, "there would be no keeping him. It would forever unfit him to be a slave."[46] The overheard conversation was a turning point in Douglass's life. When further studies exposed him to *The Columbian Orator*'s "bold denunciation of slavery," in which "a dialogue between a master and his slave" covering "the whole argument in behalf of slavery" resulted in "the voluntary emancipation of the slave on the part of the master," Douglass began "to think . . . about the injustice of my enslavement, and the means of escape."[47] His success in 1838 via the Underground Railroad ultimately settled him in Rochester, New York, where he advanced the cause of the abolitionist movement through his newspapers, the *North Star* (1847–51) and *Frederick Douglass' Paper* (1851–60). Again, literacy became a medium of freedom; through "my pen as well as my voice," he writes, "I already saw myself . . . [engaging] in the great work of renovating the public mind, and building up a public sentiment which should, at least, send slavery and oppression to the grave, and restore to 'liberty and the pursuit of happiness' the people with whom I had suffered."[48]

Did Dave have his own moment of revelation? Perhaps. But at some point in his life, Dave the Potter lost his leg, limiting his ability to physically escape his fate or even join the slave community that traveled with Reuben Drake in 1836–37 to settle a Baptist colony in Mount Lebanon, Louisiana.[49] Instead, he published his thoughts in clay, thereby rescripting a destiny beyond the reach of slavery.[50] In this sense, the inscribed wares became a different means of flight.[51] As Jason Young has noted, in their transformation from the functional to the articulate, Dave's inscribed wares became not just "objects" but "things," which "act in the world, even as they are acted upon."[52]

Literacy as freedom in the inscribed works of Dave the Potter appears to operate on two levels. On one hand, Dave's scripted text transformed functional objects into mediums by which the artisan could project himself into the public sphere and impress his personality on the world in which he lived. On the other hand, literacy served as a means by which the enslaved Dave could imagine and craft a metaphorical free self—a body, mind, and spirit reborn—in present time, a circumstance made manifest in his inscribed dates. The bifurcated condition of Dave's physical and mental state finds parallel in Elisa Edwards' reading of Dave's couplets, which draws on the concept of "black consciousness" to unite the divided self's real (enslaved) and imagined (free) identity.[53] Dave the Potter's last known poetic inscription dates to May 3, 1862, just eight months before January 1, 1863, when President Abraham Lincoln issued the Emancipation Proclamation.[54] Borrowing on Luke 13:1–5, "A Call to Repent," it reads: "I, Made this jar, all of cross / If, you don't repent, you will be, lost =."[55] Thereafter, at least fourteen additional works were produced, the last known dated March 31, 1864, yet none with his signature couplets have been identified.[56] If Dave's verses served as a conduit for his proclamation of personhood and resistance to slavery, perhaps emancipation made them no longer necessary.

Notes

1. In 1866, while registering to vote, the enslaved potter "Dave" adopted the surname Drake, and "David Drake" is subsequently recorded in the 1870 US Census (as, ironically, illiterate). It is unclear why Dave chose Drake rather than, for example, Landrum or Miles—the other families who held him in bondage—or a trade name such as Potter or Turner that celebrated his skills. One possibility proposed by scholars is that Drake would have identified him to family and friends who departed South Carolina when he was enslaved by the Drake family, which might have allowed them to track him in the post-emancipation period. This essay uses the name "Dave" because it is concerned with the period before 1866. See "South Carolina Secretary of State, Abstract of Voter Registrations Reported to the Military Government, 1868, Edgefield County, Seventh Regn. Prect., Edfield Court House Elec. Prect.," 31, in South Carolina Digital Library, https://digital.tcl.sc.edu/digital/collection/voterreg/id/993/rec/1; and "1870 United States Federal Census, Shaws, Edgefield, South Carolina," s.v. "David Drake," Ancestry.com. For further discussion, see Leonard Todd, *Carolina Clay: The Life and Legend of the Slave Potter Dave* (New York: W. W. Norton, 2008), 160–61; Michael A. Chaney, "Introduction," in *Where Is All My Relation? The Poetics of Dave the Potter*, ed. Michael A. Chaney (New York: Oxford University Press, 2018), 1; and Ira Berlin, *Generations of Captivity: A History of African-American Slaves* (Cambridge, MA: Belknap Press of Harvard University Press, 2003), 105–6, 121, 260–66, cited in Vincent Brown, "The Art of Enslaved Labor," in *Hear Me Now: The Black Potters of Old Edgefield, South Carolina*, ed. Adrienne Spinozzi (New York: Metropolitan Museum of Art, 2022), 17n3. The issue of lost family and friends is considered by P. Gabrielle Foreman in "1857: Dave the Potter's August Pots, Sexual Imagery, and *Dred Scott*," in Chaney, *Where Is All My Relation?*, 146–69.

2. The historic Edgefield District (1785–1865) was carved out of the old Ninety-Six District (1769–85) and included present-day Edgefield County as well as parts of Aiken, Saluda, Greenwood, and McCormick Counties. For a concise overview of the development of the Edgefield pottery industry, see Corbett Toussaint, "Edgefield District Stoneware: The Potter's Legacy," *Journal of Early Southern Decorative Arts* 42–43 (2021–22), www.mesdajournal.org/2021/edgefield-district-stoneware-the-potters-legacy; Todd, *Carolina Clay*, 46–50; and Carl Steen and Corbett Toussaint, "Who Were the Potters in the Old Edgefield District?," in *The Words and Wares of David Drake: Revisiting "I Made This Jar" and the Legacy of Edgefield Pottery*, ed. Jill Beute Koverman and Jane Przybysz (Columbia: University of South Carolina Press, 2024), 141–50. See also "Old

Pottersville and Dr. Landrum" and "The Late Dr. Abner Landrum," *Edgefield (SC) Advertiser*, May 11, 1859. For the historiography of Edgefield stoneware, see Adrienne Spinozzi, "Edgefield District Potteries" and "Confronting, Collecting, and Celebrating Edgefield Stoneware," both in Spinozzi, *Hear Me Now*, 14, 27–49. For more information about Dave the Potter and the Edgefield community, see Cinda K. Baldwin, *Great and Noble Jar: Traditional Stoneware of South Carolina* (Athens: University of Georgia Press, 1993); Orville Vernon Burton, *In My Father's House Are Many Mansions: Family and Community Edgefield, South Carolina* (Chapel Hill: University of North Carolina Press, 1985); Jill Beute Koverman, ed., *I Made This Jar . . . : The Life and Works of the Enslaved African-American Potter, Dave* (Columbia: University of South Carolina, 1998); Jill Beute Koverman, "The Ceramic Works of David Drake, aka, Dave the Potter or Dave the Slave of Edgefield, South Carolina," *American Ceramic Circle Journal* 13 (2005): 83–98; Jill Beute Koverman, "Clay Connections: A Thousand-Mile Journey from South Carolina to Texas," in *American Material Culture and the Texas Experience: The David B. Warren Symposium*, ed. Bayou Bend Collection and Gardens (Houston, TX: Museum of Fine Arts, 2009), 118–45; and Todd, *Carolina Clay*, which is based on documents held by the author's ancestors.

3. The kiln at the Pottersville Stoneware Manufactory was 105 feet long, a scale unprecedented in the American ceramics industry. In 1860, the output at Lewis Miles's pottery was 50,000 gallons. Abner Landrum's plantation activities included cotton cultivation, a pottery, a blacksmith shop, a hotel, a tannery, and his newspaper, the *Edgefield Hive*. See George Calfas, "Shifted Perspectives on Dave: Implications of Archaeological Excavation at the Pottersville Kiln Site," in Chaney, *Where Is All My Relation?*, 58–77; George Calfas and Carl Steen, "There Once Was a Man Named Dave . . . ," in Koverman and Przybysz, *Words and Ware of David Drake*, 85–99; John Michael Vlach, "International Encounters at the Crossroads of Clay: European, Asian, and African Influences on Edgefield Pottery," in *Crossroads of Clay: The Southern Alkaline-Glazed Stoneware Tradition*, ed. Catherine W. Horne (Columbia: University of South Carolina Press, 1990), 24–27; Koverman, "Ceramic Works of David Drake," 86–87; and Todd, *Carolina Clay*, 78.

4. According to Jill Beute Koverman, Dave numbered among seventy-six enslaved people laboring in the Edgefield potteries. Dave was not the only potter to inscribe his work. Others included "Harry" (active ca. 1839–42), who inscribed "Harry July 18" on a stoneware jar now in the collection of the Greenville County Museum of Art, and F. E. Justice, who inscribed cemetery headstones. Brister Jones, who is listed in the 1870 US Census in the household of David Drake, also became a turner who inscribed his work. See Koverman, "Ceramic Works of David Drake," 84; Todd, *Carolina Clay*, 211; Toussaint, "Edgefield District Stoneware"; and "1870 United States Federal Census, Shaws, Edgefield, South Carolina," s.v. "David Drake," Ancestry.com.

5. In particular, the slave code of 1740 and the amendments legislated in 1800, 1821, 1834, and 1841. See Annie Campbell, "Excerpts from South Carolina Slave Code of 1740 No. 670 (1740)," U.S. History Scene, www.ushistoryscene.com/article/excerpts-south-carolina-slave-code-1740-no-670-1740.

6. In 1690, the population of Black people in South Carolina numbered about 1,500, or 40 percent of the colony's inhabitants. By the second generation, around 1710, it accounted for the majority. That growth is indebted to the introduction and consolidation of a rice trade, which pressured for the increase in enslaved Black laborers—possibly, Peter Wood speculates, because they were more successful with the grain's cultivation than their white or Native American cohabitants as well as more resistant to the region's challenging environmental conditions. Though Wood interprets the migration of Blacks and whites from Barbados to the mainland as having direct influence on the colony's culture and the "Negro acts" of 1691, Edward Rugemer has convincingly argued for the mediating influence of Jamaica on South Carolina's slave codes. For a history of the demographic development of Black people in the southern regions of the United States from their arrival with Spanish explorers in 1526 to the first generation of African American "pioneers" of the Revolutionary period, see Peter H. Wood, *Black Majority: Negroes in Colonial South Carolina from 1670 through the Stono Rebellion* (1974; repr. New York: Alfred A. Knopf, 2012), 3–9, 13–91, 143–66. See also Edward B. Rugemer, "The Development of Mastery and Race in the Comprehensive Slave Codes of the Greater Caribbean during the Seventeenth Century," *William and Mary Quarterly*, 3rd ser., 70, no. 3 (2013): 429–58, population figures, 452; *Governor Archdale's Laws* (1696), South Carolina Archives, Columbia, fol. 60–66, cited in M. Eugene Sirmans, "The Legal Status of the Slave in South Carolina, 1670–1740," *Journal of Southern History* 28, no. 4 (1962): 466; and Burton, *In My Father's House*, 20, table 1-1, cited in Spinozzi, "Confronting, Collecting, and Celebrating Edgefield Stoneware," 35.

7. In 1696, South Carolina made slavery hereditary. Until that point, Wood argues, the imperial project had not yet clarified the lines between indentured and enslaved labor. Moreover, social distinctions were more often blurred and conventional rules governing intimate relationships less rigidly followed on the frontier than in Europe, a point of concern for imperial stakeholders. Rugemer, "Development of Mastery and Race," 449–50; Wood, *Black Majority*, 14, 95–103.

8. In addition, it legislated against enslaved persons growing their own food, assembling together, and earning extra wages. See Campbell, "Excerpts from South Carolina Slave Code of 1740."

9. As described by the New York jurist and abolitionist William Jay (1789–1858). Executive Committee of the American Anti-Slavery Committee, *Slavery and the International Slave Trade in the United States of America* (London: Thomas Ward, 1841).

10. For a comprehensive examination of the history of the slave codes, see Paul Finkelman, ed., *Statutes on Slavery: The Pamphlet Literature* (New York: Garland, 1988).

11. The act of 1740 was prompted by the Stono Rebellion of September 9, 1739, when approximately twenty enslaved men and women marched from Stono River in Saint Paul's Parish toward Saint Augustine, Florida, stealing arms, recruiting rebels, and killing white

inhabitants until their ultimate capture. Subsequent revisions to the code were likewise reactions to slave insurrections, including Gabriel's Rebellion in Virginia (1800), the revolt led by Denmark Vesey in South Carolina (1822), and Nat Turner's Rebellion in Virginia (1831), which intensified fears in the slaveholding South while fueling the abolitionist movement. For a history of the period leading up to the Stono Rebellion, see Wood, *Black Majority*, esp. 271–326. See also F. Peter Charles Hoffer, *Cry Liberty: The Great Stono River Slave Rebellion of 1739* (New York: Oxford University Press, 2015); Mark Michael Smith, ed., *Stono: Documenting and Interpreting a Southern Slave Revolt* (Columbia: University of South Carolina Press, 2005); Philip J. Schwarz, ed., *Gabriel's Conspiracy: A Documentary History* (Charlottesville: University of Virginia Press, 2012); David Robertson, *Denmark Vesey: The Buried Story of America's Largest Slave Rebellion and the Man Who Led It* (New York: Vintage, 2000); and Kenneth S. Greenberg, ed., *Nat Turner: A Slave Rebellion in History and Memory* (New York: Oxford University Press, 2003).

12. A legal review by John Belton O'Neall in 1848 indicated that the measure against slave literacy passed in 1834 was a response to the abolitionist movement and was not enforced. See John Belton O'Neall, *The Negro Law of South Carolina* (Columbia, SC: John G. Bowman, 1848), 23. For additional information on the erratic nature of enforcement, see Janet Duitsman Cornelius, *When I Can Read My Title Clear: Literacy, Slavery, and Religion in the Antebellum South* (Columbia: University of South Carolina Press, 1991), 37–58, 63–64.

13. Michael Chaney notes that "Christian paternalists in the vein of Abner Landrum responded to the fear brought about by the Denmark Vesey revolt of 1822 with renewed conviction in the religious instruction of slaves." By contrast "secular proslavery" advocates such as Whitemarsh Seabrook and Edward Laurens opposed any medium that allowed communication among slaves. According to Orville Burton, in addition to the literate enslaved population, 72.4 percent of free black households included a literate adult. Chaney, "Introduction," 3; Burton, *In My Father's House*, 42. See also John W. Blassingame, ed., *Slave Testimony: Two Centuries of Letters, Speeches, Interviews, and Autobiographies* (Baton Rouge: Louisiana State University Press, 1977); Cornelius, *When I Can Read My Title Clear*, 11–36, 105–41; and Carla L. Peterson, "An Easter Prayer, 1859," in Chaney, *Where Is All My Relation?*, 173.

14. As Tamara Thornton notes, "Those in power were conscious of the subversive potential of being able to write, and they deliberately prohibited those under their power from learning. . . . Thus, literacy skills, like information, would be imparted on a 'need-to-know' basis, and some people, it was believed—African-Americans, Native Americans, humble whites, women—did not need to know how to write." Tamara Plakins Thornton, *Handwriting in America: A Cultural History* (New Haven, CT: Yale University Press, 1996), 17.

15. Beth Barton Schweiger, "The Literate South: Reading before Emancipation," *Journal of the Civil War Era* 3, no. 3 (2013): 337–38. To be "literate" in eighteenth-century terms was to be educated in Latin and Greek, a skill associated with the classical humanists and the academic education of the upper classes. This was distinct from the rudimentary skills of reading and writing of "the humbler sort," which also differed from the courses in penmanship deemed appropriate to the "industrious hand" of merchants, clerks, and traders. By 1850, an estimated 80 percent of southern whites could read and write, but that did not mean they were "educated" in the classical sense. Rather, "progress" was tied to commercial aspirations. See also Thornton, *Handwriting in America*, 6–15; and Cornelius, *When I Can Read My Title Clear*, 73–74.

16. The collateral was first noted on June 13, 1818, Edgefield County, South Carolina, Deed Book 35, pp. 237–38, Edgefield County Archives, Edgefield, SC. Dave was replaced as collateral later that year by Amos Landrum, who substituted the human collateral with his land on Shaws Creek. In 1830, Dave was listed in an agreement between Harvey and Reuben Drake as a servant. See Todd, *Carolina Clay*, 15–16, 19, 24; and "Appendix A," in Koverman and Przybysz, *Words and Wares of David Drake*, 162.

17. "Local Items," *Edgefield (SC) Advertiser*, October 30, 1873. Dave is mentioned in the *Edgefield Advertiser* on October 30, 1873 but not in the 1880 US Census, suggesting that he died sometime between 1873 and 1880.

18. To date, forty-two inscribed works by Dave have been identified, and an additional seven are attributed to him. Nineteen were produced during his most prolific period of 1858–59, and thirty reference his one-time enslaver Lewis Miles. James Witkowski, Arthur Goldberg, and Deborah A. Goldberg have identified additional works and sherds attributed to the pottery site. They have also made their inventory more exacting with a consideration of forms and glazes. See James Witkowski, Arthur Goldberg, and Deboral A. Goldberg, "Marking Time: The Dated Vessels of David Drake," and "Appendix C," both in Koverman and Przybysz, *Words and Ware of David Drake*, 122–35, 179–88.

In 1832, Harvey Drake died, and probate records dated January 30, 1833, administered by Harvey Drake's widow, Sarah Harlan Drake, document Dave's sale to the pottery firm of Reuben Drake & Jasper Gibbs for $400. The same probate record lists a woman named Lydia and her sons, John and George, as sold from the estate to Sarah Drake for $610. It has been speculated that Lydia was David Drake's sister or spouse. In 1836, Dave was again sold, this time to Reuben Drake's uncle, Rev. John Landrum, who owned a plantation and pottery on Big Horse Creek, just south of Edgefield Village. Around 1840, Landrum's daughter Mary wed Lewis Miles, who partnered with his father-in-law in the pottery. It is unclear how Dave came to work at the Horse Creek pottery or when exactly he became the property of Lewis Miles. It is possible that Dave came to Lewis Miles as part of his wife's dowry. We do know that Dave was working for him by 1837, when *Lm* is found on a dated vessel. In 1840, Dave inscribed a jar with the couplet: "Dave belongs to Mr. Miles / whir the oven bakes & the pot biles / 31st July 1840." However, following John Landrum's death in 1846, his son Franklin B. Landrum purchased Dave in 1847 for $800 at the estate sale. At the same time, he was made the administrator of his sister Mary Miles's portion of the estate. There are no known inscribed wares from the period of Franklin Landrum's enslavement of Dave. In 1849, Mary Landrum Miles successfully petitioned the court to replace her brother as administrator of her inheritance, and Dave seems again to have become the property of Mary and Lewis Miles. In 1850, Dave resumed inscribing his wares, this time, for the new and larger Stony Bluff Manufactory (ca. 1848–67). In 1865, Lewis Miles partnered with Lafayette Brenan Wever in a store where, in 1866, Dave is recorded as purchasing "a peck of meal 'for his wife.'" Wever's accounts for 1866 indicate that Dave held a short-term contract at the pottery for $5 per month. Around the same time, Lewis Miles contracted with several freedmen for use of the Stony Bluff Manufactory's kiln, houses, and wood source, probably while he was constructing his new Miles Mill pottery, grain mill, sawmill, and tannery, which he advertised in 1867. Miles died two years later, in 1869, when the South Carolina Census listed Dave Drake with "a colored female." She is not recorded in the 1870 census, which lists David Drake as a seventy-year-old turner living at "Dwelling Number 136" in Shaws Creek Township, just two houses away from the family of Lewis Miles. His household included the turner Mark Jones, age thirty-five, his wife, Caroline, age twenty-eight—possibly Dave's daughter—and five children ranging in age from two months to ten years. Caroline Jones's maiden name is listed as Miles on the death certificate of her and Mark Jones's daughter, Emma Long, which also states that Mark Jones was born in Charleston and Caroline Miles in Aiken County. David Drake does not appear in the 1880 census. See Jill Beute Koverman, "Searching for Messages in Clay," in Koverman, *I Made This Jar*, 20–22, 32; Calfas and Steen, "There Once Was a Man Named Dave," 86; "Verses by Dave," in Spinozzi, *Hear Me Now*, 180–81; Todd, *Carolina Clay*, 60–61, 78, 88–95, 115, 162–72, 181–82; "Edgefield, South Carolina, Slave Records, 1774–1866," 230–31, Ancestry.com; "1870 United States Federal Census, Shaws, Edgefield, South Carolina," s.v. "David Drake," Ancestry.com; and "South Carolina, U.S., Death Records, 1821–1971," s.v. "David Drake," Ancestry.com.

19. "Verses by Dave," 180.

20. The brick was found near the ruins of a Pottersville house dating to the 1820s. Todd, *Carolina Clay*, 43–45. Koverman speculates that a jug produced and marked 1821 may have been made by Dave. See Koverman, "Clay Connections," 126. The Tariff of 1828, also known as the Tariff of Abominations, protected northern manufactured goods by significantly increasing the taxes on foreign imports. Because the South's cotton trade depended on Britain's textile industry, the tax came at the expense of the southern economy: southern planters, who held credit with British banks and merchants, faced inflated prices; and British textiles made with southern cotton became more expensive, pressuring British textile manufacturers to look elsewhere for raw material. The tariff caused the Nullification Crisis, which pitted enraged Nullifiers, who advocated a state's right to veto federal law, against Unionists, moderates who believed that states should work to find compromise with the federal government. The crisis resulted in the South Carolina Ordinance of Nullification in 1832, which argued that the government's "application of Force . . . as inconsistent with the longer continuance of South Carolina in the Union." Though the Compromise Tax of 1833 temporarily resolved the issue, the tensions underscored the economic and social interests dividing the country. The tense conditions were compounded by the escalating abolitionist movement and its growing pressure for Bible literacy, which reinforced the sense of northern interference in southern interests. For more information about the Tariff of 1828 and related resources, see Julie Silverbrook, "The Nullification Crisis," Bill of Rights Institute, https://billofrightsinstitute.org/essays/the-nullification-crisis. For the involvement of the Edgefield community in the crisis, see Todd, *Carolina Clay*, 55–59.

21. According to Todd, typeset letters were found near the pottery and may have been used to imprint the side of vessels. See Todd, *Carolina Clay*, 49–50. According to a bill for its partition, John Landrum's estate consisted of more than 6,800 acres. See "South Carolina Edgefield District. In Equity," *Edgefield (SC) Advertiser*, October 27, 1847. This corresponds closely with observations made in 1930 by Laura M. Bragg, director of the Charleston Museum, whose archive includes a description of the Stony Bluff Manufactory (ca. 1848–67) and Miles Mill Pottery (1867–85): "Big plantation house. 50 negro houses. Had 250 slaves. About 5000 acres." See "'Pottery: Information Given by Mr. G. U. Flesher, 7/8/30,'" p. 2, typescript prepared by E. Burnham Chamberlain from handwritten notes taken by Laura M. Bragg, Director's Correspondence, Laura M. Bragg, Charleston Museum Records Collection, Charleston Museum Archives, cited in Spinozzi, "Confronting, Collecting, and Celebrating Edgefield Stoneware," 35n31; and Toussaint, "Edgefield District Stoneware."

22. For a discussion of the tradition of inscribing in clay and its relevance for our understanding of Dave's individual purpose in this regard, see John A. Burrison, "Talking Jars: Dave and Larger Traditions of Pot-Poetry," in Koverman and Przybysz, *Words and Ware of David Drake*, 52–60.

23. "Dave belongs to Mr. Miles / wher the oven bakes & the pot biles" appeared as a couplet on jar dated July 31, 1840.

24. Michael A. Chaney, "The Concatenate Poetics of Slavery and the Articulate Material of Dave the Potter," in Chaney, *Where Is All My Relation?*, 112–33, quoted at 130.

25. Harvey and Sarah Drake were Baptists and may have encouraged a passive level of reading among their enslaved persons. Sarah Drake was a charter member of the Edgefield Village Baptist Church. Harvey Drake's uncle, Rev. John Landrum, was a Baptist minister who allegedly instructed slaves in Bible literacy. A member of either family may have instructed Dave. Todd, *Carolina Clay*, 40.

26. See Miller, "Dave the Potter and the Origins of African American Poetry," in Koverman and Przybysz, *Words and Ware of David Drake*, 46–51.

27. David Gough, "The Resurrection Body," a sermon for Temple Hills Baptist Church, August 27, 2017, www.thbchurch.org/sermons/sermon/2017-08-27/the-resurrection-body. Carla L. Peterson notes that the "very materiality" of Dave's jug serves as "an embodiment

of the human body" and "standing empty before him" was also "a reminder of [Jesus's] divine resurrection." Jon Woodson also remarks on the parallel between Dave and God, the "divine potter." See Peterson, "Easter Prayer," 176; and Jon Woodson, "Beneath Notice: A Social Philology of the Poetry of Dave the Potter," in Chaney, *Where Is All My Relation?*, 179.

28. Thornton, *Handwriting in America*, xiii.

29. It is estimated that 10 percent of South Carolina's enslaved population could read and write at a basic level. The federal census for 1820 records 265,301 blacks, suggesting an approximate number of 2,500. See Schweiger, "Literate South," 331; and Cornelius, *When I Can Read My Title Clear*, 8–9.

30. Noah Webster's three-by-five-inch *Grammatical Institute of the English Language*—known as the "blue-back speller"—was published in 1783 and became the most common tool for learning to read. Subsequently titled *The American Spelling Book* (1786) and *The Elementary Spelling Book* (1829), it progressed the student from vowel-consonant combinations to single- and multisyllable words. The small size meant it could be tucked away in a hat or pocket to pull out at free moments. For the different ways in which enslaved people achieved literacy, see Heather Andrea Williams, *Self-Taught: African American Education in Slavery and Freedom* (Chapel Hill: University of North Carolina Press, 2005), 7–29.

31. Cornelius, *When I Can Read My Title Clear*, 72–73. On December 28, 1840, the Pottersville Academy advertised for a teacher to be paid according to the degrees of his learning, from the mechanical to the intellectual: $4.50 per quarter for "Spelling, Reading, Writing and Arithmetic"; an additional $6.00 per quarter for teaching "Geography, English Grammar, and Parsing [Syntax], with other branches usually taught in Academies"; and, finally, an additional $8.00 per quarter for "Latin, Greek and Mathematics." See "Pottersville Academy," in *Edgefield (SC) Advertiser*, January 14, 1841. Similar advertisements followed in 1847 and 1858. See "Pottersville School," in *Edgefield (SC) Advertiser*, February 17, 1847, and December 15, 1858.

32. As Tamara Thornton notes, "Quite apart from the sense of the text," writing "took as its subject the self." Thornton, *Handwriting in America*, xiii (quotation), 29, 33–41.

33. Peter Wood has argued for the greater sociocultural cohesiveness of enslaved people in South Carolina arising from the "critical mass" that was a condition of its intense plantation economy. Such conditions would have lent more impact to Dave's verse while fueling the escalating efforts to curtail slave literacy. This was not always the case. The eighteenth-century demand for skilled craftspeople meant that many Blacks operated in trades ranging from coopering to carpentry to printing. As the colonies became more settled, however, and racial tensions escalated, such opportunities became rarer, prompting the South Carolina plantation owner James Henry Hammond to claim, for example, that "whenever a slave is made a mechanic, he is more than half freed, and soon . . . the most corrupt and turbulent of his class." See Wood, *Black Majority*, 196–238; and James Henry Hammond, *An Address Delivered before the South Carolina Institute, at Its First Annual Fair, on the 20th November, 1849*, 32–33, quoted in Orville Vernon Burton, "Edgefield, South Carolina: Home to Dave the Potter," in Koverman and Przybysz, *Words and Ware of David Drake*, 38.

34. A descendant of Dave's enslavers, Leonard Todd reconsiders the facts, myths, and possibilities surrounding Dave in "'The Unknown Potter': Continuing the Search for Dave," in Koverman and Przybysz, *Words and Wares of David Drake*, 151–60.

35. In 1827, Abner Landrum began selling his share of the Pottersville operation to nephews Harvey and Reuben Drake. About the same time, he arranged for Dave, then the property of Harvey Drake, to assist at his newspaper, the *Edgefield Hive*. Dave's involvement with the paper was recalled in a notice in the *Edgefield Advertiser* in 1863: "One day in years gone by we happened to meet DAVE POTTERY (whom many readers will remember as the grandiloquent old darkey once connected with a paper known as the *Edgefield Hive*)." See "Buttermilk," *Edgefield (SC) Advertiser*, April 1, 1863.

36. See "Recommendation of Poetry," *Edgefield (SC) Hive*, March 12, 1830, cited in Michael Bramwell, "Potter's Field: Trauma and Representation in the Art of David Drake," in Chaney, *Where Is All My Relation?*, 203; and Faith Barrett, "Great and Noble Lines: Dave the Potter, George Moses Horton, and the Possibilities of Poetry," in Chaney, *Where Is All My Relation?*, 26–50.

37. Frank Addison Mowig Philom has not been found in a US census. However, a Frank Addison is listed in the 1863 Civil War Draft Registration Records as a Maryland-born, forty-four-year-old "Colored" laborer in the Fifth Election District, Anne Arundel County, Maryland, as well as in the 1870 US Census for District 2, Anne Arundel County, Maryland, as a fifty-five-year-old illiterate Black farm laborer. Curiously, a Frank Addison is also listed in the 1870 US Census as a South Carolina–born, fifty-year-old Black farm laborer living in the township of Saluda in Edgefield County. See "U.S., Civil War Draft Registrations Records, 1863–1865," and "1870 United States Federal Census," both at Ancestry.com.

38. First published in *Frederick Douglass' Paper*, February 5, 1852, reprinted in Erika DeSimone and Fidel Louis, eds., *Voices beyond Bondage: An Anthology of Verse by African Americans of the 19th Century* (Montgomery, AL: New South Books, 2014), 88–89.

39. Wallace Stevens, "The Noble Rider and the Sound of Words," in *Collected Poetry and Prose* (New York: Library of America, 1997), cited in Bramwell, "Potter's Field," 205.

40. Jill Beute Koverman considers the multivalent meanings of Dave's words in "Dave's Verse as Social Response," in Koverman and Przybysz, *Words and Wares of David Drake*, 69–76. While considering the historical correctives informing the practice of contemporary artists, P. Gabrielle Foreman highlights the risks involved in presuming *how* to read work produced by Black artists—what Theaster Gates terms "conversations about positionality or about the vantage point of the maker." See P. Gabrielle Foreman, "Black Artists as Cultural Historians: Jonathan Green, Carrie Mae Weems, and David Drake," 100–112, and Theaster Gates, "Embodying Dave: Performance and the Creation of an Artistic, Para-Historical Narrative," both in Koverman

and Przybysz, *Words and Wares of David Drake*, 113–21, quoted at 115. See also Brown, "Art of Enslaved Labor," 17–25; James A. Miller, "Dave the Potter and the Origins of African-American Poetry," in Koverman, *I Made This Jar*, 45–51; Michael J. Bramwell and Ethan W. Lasser, "Incidents in the Life of an Enslaved Abolitionist Potter Written by Others," in Spinozzi, *Hear Me Now*, 62–63; Jason R. Young, "'But Oh the Clay Is Vile': Edgefield Pottery in Life and Death," in Spinozzi, *Hear Me Now*, 75; Chaney, "Introduction," 12; Babatunde Lawal, "Signifying Jars, Resonating Like a Banjar: Influence, Politics, and Poetics in Dave's Pottery," in Chaney, *Where Is All My Relation?*, 92–98; and Elisa Edwards, "The Fourth of July Is Surely Come," in Chaney, *Where Is All My Relation?*, 108–11.

41. Frederick Douglass, *Narrative of the Life of Frederick Douglass: An American Slave* (Amazon Classics, Kindle, 2019), 33.

42. Lawal, "Signifying Jars," 87–90. In 1858, the slave ship *Wanderer* docked at Jekyll Island, Georgia, carrying more than 400 enslaved Africans who had survived the Middle Passage. Nearly half of the captives were sold to plantation owners in the Edgefield District. In one of many articles issued in 1858–59, the *New York Daily Herald* reported from the *Augusta (GA) Sentinel* on December 22, 1858: "Two hundred and seventy-seven of the cargo of Africans recently landed near Brunswick were brought up the Savannah River, and put ashore yesterday evening about 3 o'clock at the mouth of Horse Creek, three miles below this city, on the Carolina side. . . . It is quietly hinted that this is the third cargo landed by the same Company during the last six months." See "The Wanderer's Africans," *New York Daily Herald*, December 22, 1858.

43. The banjar was "an African lute now widely regarded as the ancestor of the American banjo . . . played in Africa by professional musicians as well as by the historians, poets, and social critics." Lawal, "Signifying Jars," 98.

44. It is what Glenda Carpio has called a "piercing tragicomedy, one in which laughter is disassociated from gaiety and is, instead, a form of mourning." Glenda R. Caprio, *Laughing Fit to Kill: Black Humor in the Fictions of Slavery* (New York: Oxford University Press, 2008), 7, cited in Brown, "Art of Enslaved Labor," 25n22.

45. Douglass, *Narrative*, 59.

46. Douglass, *Narrative*, 54.

47. Douglass, *Narrative*, 62, 128. But Douglass also highlights the physical and emotional challenges of escape, arguing "that thousands would escape from slavery, who now remain, but for the strong cords of affection that bind them to their friends. . . . The wretchedness of slavery, and the blessedness of freedom, were perpetually before me." Douglass, *Narrative*, 132.

48. Frederick Douglass, *My Bondage and My Freedom* (Amazon Classics, Kindle, 2013), 252–53.

49. Todd, *Carolina Clay*, 67, 74. For a discussion of the physical and familial arrangements of Edgefield's plantation community, see Burton, "Edgefield, South Carolina," 38–44.

50. Faith Barrett compares the nonconfrontational nature of Dave's text with that of the enslaved North Carolina poet George Moses Horton, who likewise won the favor of white patrons with his poetry. Barrett, "Great and Noble Lines," 28–36. See also Evie Shockley, "A Letter to David Drake from a Friend and a Relation," in Chaney, *Where Is All My Relation?*, 51; and Woodson, "Beneath Notice," 179.

51. The "runaway slave" was a consistent theme of slavery from the beginning. See Wood, *Black Majority*, 239–68.

52. Young, "'But Oh the Clay Is Vile,'" 74.

53. Elisa Edwards invokes W. E. B. Du Bois's notion of the "double consciousness" of black people in *The Souls of Black Folk* (1903), what the *Stanford Encyclopedia of Philosophy* defines as "a concept in social philosophy referring, originally, to a source of inward 'twoness' putatively experienced by African-Americans because of their racialized oppression and disvaluation in a white-dominated society." Borrowing on the writings of John Michael Vlach, Edwards also considers the symbolic meaning of the fife and drum as both African and revolutionary. Edwards, "Fourth of July Is Surely Come," 108–11. See also John Michael Vlach, *The Afro-American Tradition in Decorative Arts* (Athens: University of Georgia Press, 1978), 20, cited in Edwards, "Fourth of July Is Surely Come," 110; and John P. Pittman, "Double Consciousness," in *The Stanford Encyclopedia of Philosophy*, ed. Edward N. Zalta and Uri Nodelman, last modified February 16, 2023, https://plato.stanford.edu/entries/double-consciousness/.

54. Jill Beute Koverman describes the signed pot from 1864 as "approximately five to eight gallons," with a "drippy, deep olive-green alkaline glaze" and a "texture . . . very rough because the impurities in the clay body and glaze were not thoroughly removed. Bits of quartz and other particles are also evident on the vessel's surface." This description suggests that the conditions of production had deteriorated during the war, making successful production challenging. Koverman, "Searching for Messages in Clay," 30.

55. Luke 13:1–5 is part of the "Call to Repent." The King James Version reads: "There were present at that season some that told him of the Galileans, whose blood Pilate had mingled with their sacrifices. And Jesus answering said unto them, Suppose ye that these Galileans were sinners above all the Galileans, because they suffered such things? I tell you, Nay: but, except ye repent, ye shall all likewise perish. Or those eighteen, upon whom the tower in Siloam fell, and slew them, think ye that they were sinners above all men that dwelt in Jerusalem? I tell you, Nay: but, except ye repent, ye shall all likewise perish." At the cusp of the Civil War, Dave may have been comparing the slaveholders with the Galileans, a sect of political extremists and religious fanatics who violently opposed Roman rule. Frederick Douglass noted the hypocrisy of Christians such as Rev. Rigby Hopkins, who "could always find something . . . to justify the use of the lash" and "yet there was not a man anywhere round, who made higher professions of religion, or was more active in revivals, than this same reverend slave-driver, Rigby Hopkins." Douglass, *Narrative*, 29–30.

56. The possibility of a later work dated 1868 is considered by Carl Steen in "The Last Dave Pot?," in Koverman and Przybysz, *Words and Wares of David Drake*, 136–40.

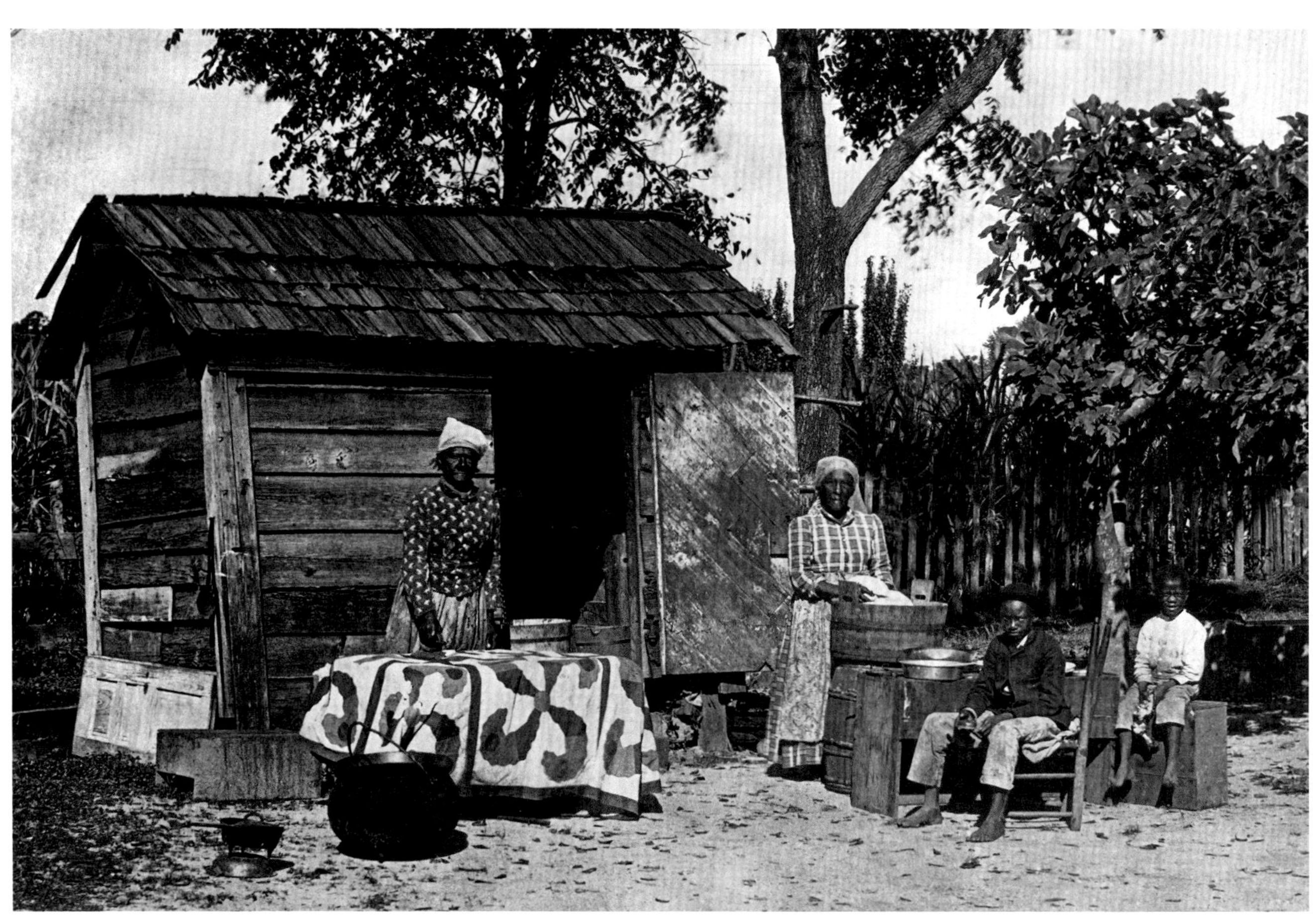

FIGURE 6.1. *Black Women Doing Washing*. State Library and Archive of Florida, Tallahassee.

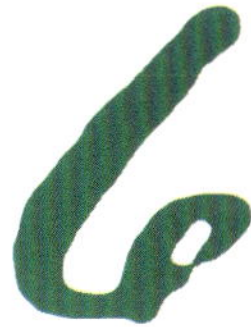

Considering the Black Laundress as Radical Crafter

ALEIA M. BROWN

Follow the cultural guides which African-American women have left us. . . . We will understand their world.

Elsa Barkley Brown, "African-American Women's Quilting"

They Sing the Blues, They Declare a General Strike

The women made their way through town rounding up laundry at the beginning of the week. The unpaved roads and poor drainage systems they traversed were evidence that the Atlanta that developers had dreamed up was still a dream not fully materialized. They returned to their own homes that were in need of cleaning and their own children that were in need of care, then they prepared the loads of clothes that they collected throughout the day to soak in warm water overnight. Sometimes there were loads of delicate materials that required more care and attention: fine lace dresses, chiffon gowns, quilts, and curtains.

They return to the laundry in the morning. The soak did good, lifting the detritus from the fabric's surface.

They started work with their main tools: lye soap, the washboard, an iron washpot, a row of sad irons, and a fire. The lye soap was effective for cleaning, but it burned and irritated the skin, leaving behind aged hands. The friction of running the clothes against the metal parts of the washboard was also effective, but the metal ridges sometimes snagged the flesh. They continued on to spot cleaning the pesky stains and soiled parts anyhow. Then, they stirred the clothes with big wooden sticks in the washpots with boiling water. Without enough force, the lye would settle into the fabric, causing yellow spots. The women then rinsed the clothes twice—the blue rinse whitened or clarified the fabric while the water rinse removed residual irritants to the skin. The clothes were left outside to dry for the night. They repaired any torn fabrics. Overall their position in the labor market was precarious, but the most dangerous part of the process

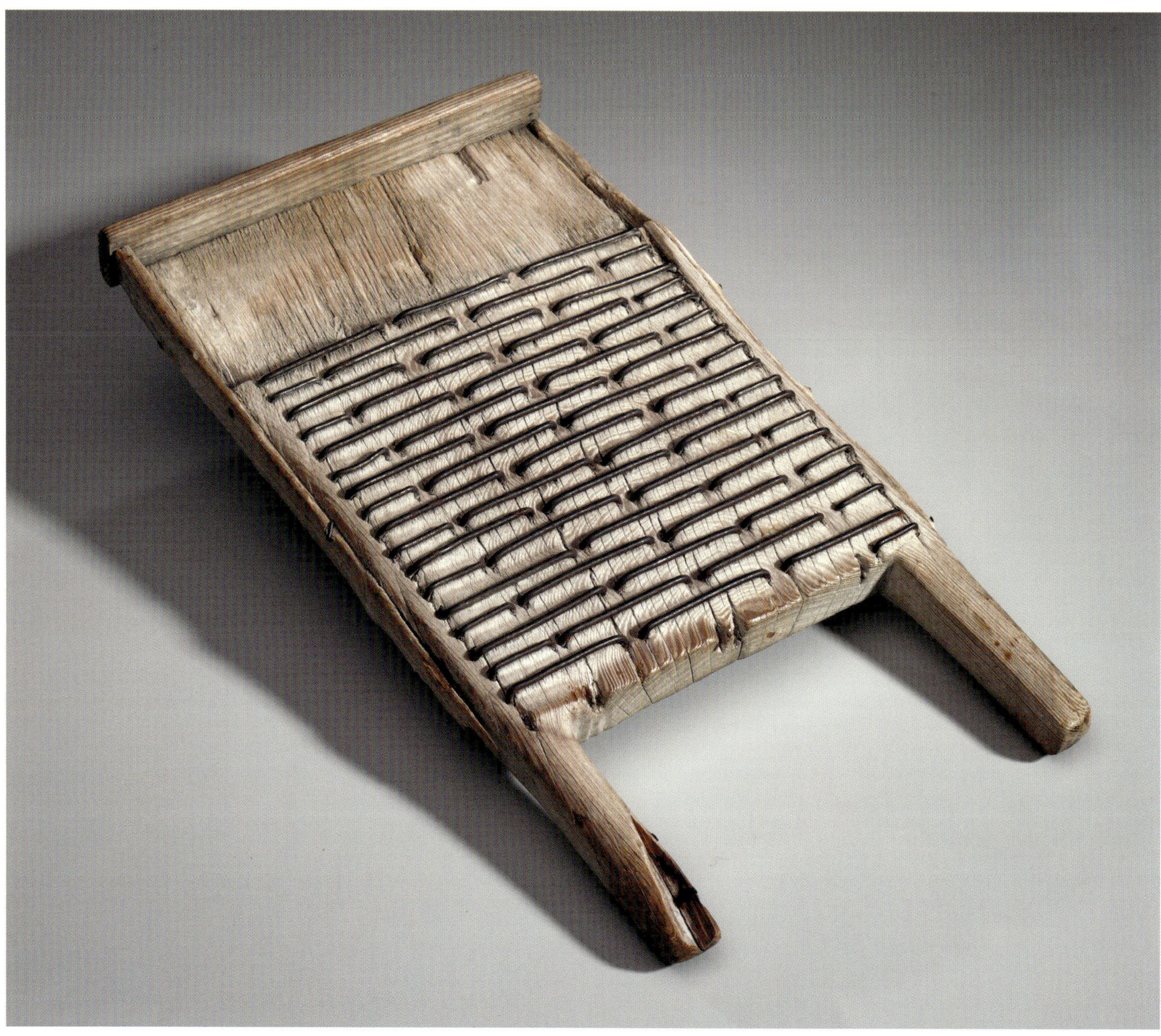

(*above*) FIGURE 6.2. *Handmade Wood and Metal Washboard*. Collection of the Smithsonian National Museum of African American History and Culture.

(*opposite*) FIGURE 6.3. *Sad Iron Owned by Members of the Ellis Family*. Library of Congress.

was pressing clothes with a sad iron. The heavy irons cooled quickly, requiring them to skillfully swap out the cooled irons for the blazing hot ones. Sometimes this process led to severe burns and disfigurements. They returned the loads of laundry at the end of the week.[1]

The grueling work schedule made the washerwoman a popular figure in blues culture. In "Washerwoman's Blues," Empress of the Blues Bessie Smith centered the plight of the washerwoman even as the rest of society refused to acknowledge that the prosperity of the country relied on Black women laboring below the base of subsistence.

All day long I'm slavin', all day long I'm bustin' suds
All day long I'm slavin', all day long I'm bustin' suds
Gee, my hands are tired, washin' out these dirty suds
Sorry I do washin' just to make my livelihood

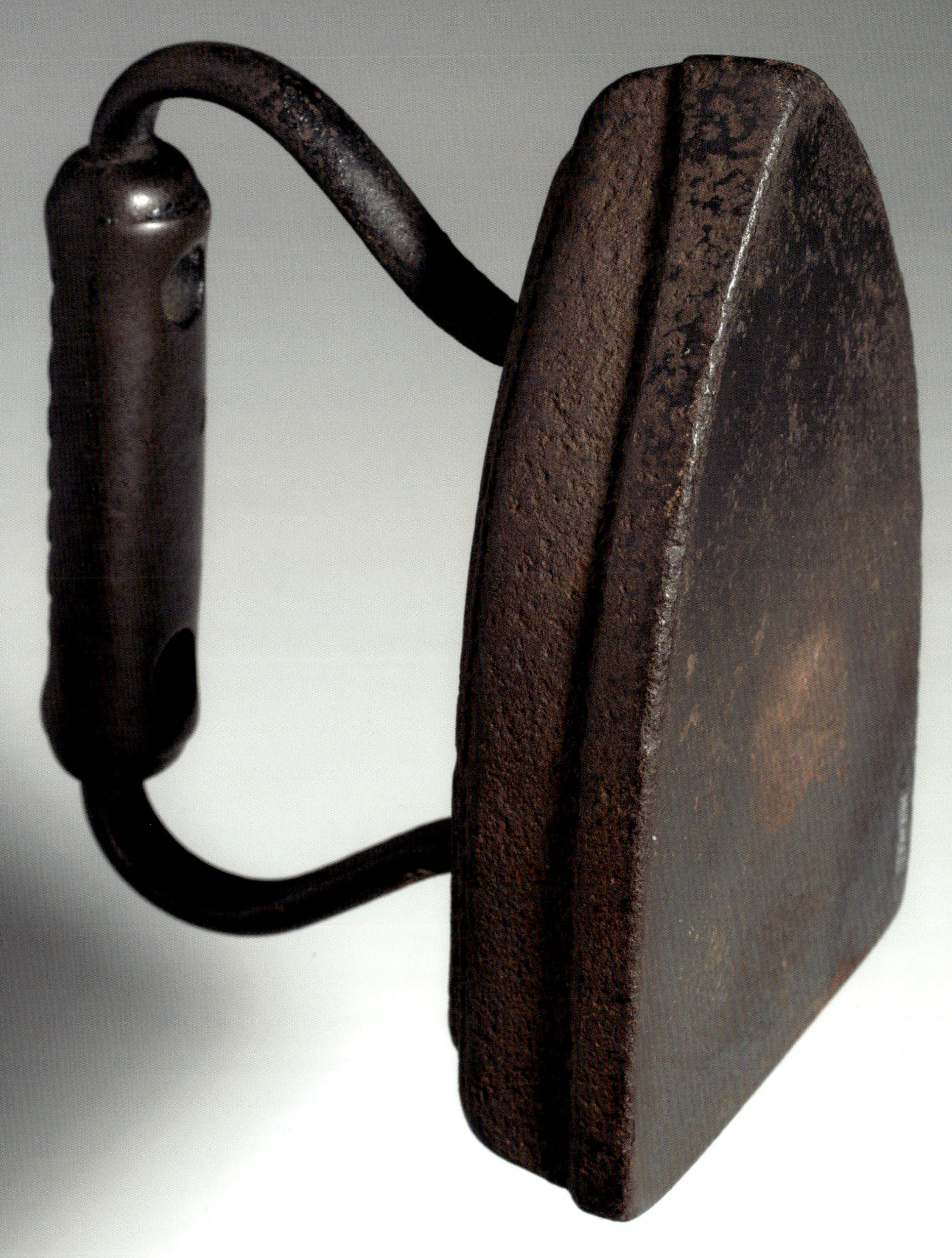

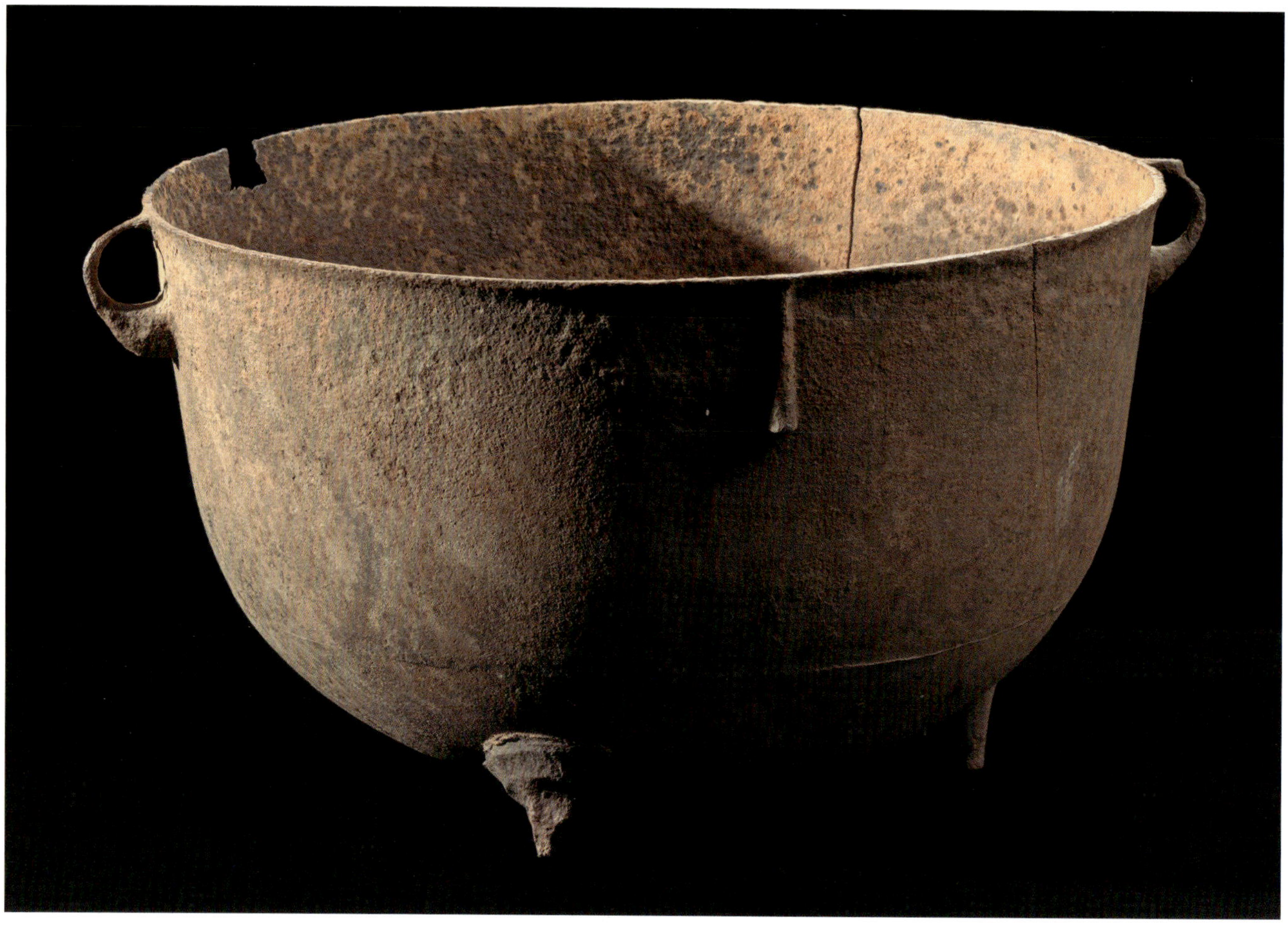

FIGURE 6.4. *Washpot Used by Manda Caldwell and Her Daughter Susan Caldwell McGill.* Collection of the Smithsonian National Museum of African American History and Culture. Gift of the Nichols Family.

Sorry I do washin' just to make my livelihood
Oh, the washwoman's life, it ain't a bit of good.[2]

For Black washerwomen in Atlanta, the laundry was not a site of hopelessness or finality. Instead, it was the impetus for a general strike. Though this labor provided more bodily and work autonomy than working as a live-in domestic, the low pay and conditional reprieve from the sexual violence did not align with how they conceptualized freedom in the post–Civil War South.[3] As they understood it, the laundry was a site that maintained the power relations of the plantation South, even as the emerging New South tried to evolve into a modern political economy with a progressive social landscape.[4] The general strike was the most effective modality for transforming Black women's relationship to the labor market and their craft while living in slavery's afterlife.[5] Their execution of a general strike demonstrated a radical commitment to liberation that pulses through Black textile traditions.

They Measure the Ingredients for the Laundry, They Organize the Strike

Foregrounding the history of the Washerwomen Strike of 1881 against the backdrop of the burgeoning New South demonstrates the labor implications behind Black craft, and more specifically Black textile traditions. While the laundresses' primary job did not include making textiles, their craft and care was apparent in their specialized skills of cleaning and repairing all sorts of textiles. Newly emancipated Black women were still bound in unfreedom where they were laundresses for white households. This position shaped not only their relationship to their craft but also the nature of their refusal to continue working at the base of subsistence.[6] Wealthy and working-class white families alike demanded washerwomen's services well into the 1930s even as labor-saving home appliances and industrialized technologies entered the market. It was not until the 1940s that washing machines became more affordable, leading to fewer opportunities for Black women working as washerwomen. In this decade of rapid industrialization, founder of African American historiography Carter G. Woodson encouraged Black communities not to be ashamed of work reminiscent of the plantation regime and implored them instead to remember and honor the Negro washerwoman.[7] Black women supported their families by taking on laundry loads when there were few options for employment. Historian Sharon Harley argues that Black women did these jobs but did not believe that their conditions reflected their worth as a person.[8] Navigating complicated gender and class aspirations, they also took on this work at a time when Black men preferred to be the breadwinner and have their wives take care of the home rather than work outside it. Not far removed from antebellum power relations in which Black women were forced into reproductive and domestic labor, Black men believed that it was the ultimate form of protection to earn enough income so that their partners and children did not have to encounter violence at work. Limited employment opportunities and inconsistent seasonal work often prohibited their dream from coming to fruition. The sociocultural landscape along with the continued exploitation created fertile ground for collectivizing and unionizing. The women's refusal to participate in their own exploitation, and therefore racial capitalism, also manifested in other Black textile traditions through abstract quilts that refuse to adhere to a regimented aesthetic and textiles as part of a gift economy. It was clear that they had a sense of freedom regardless of their station in life.

As early as 1877, Black women in Atlanta had organized and agreed on a standard rate of pay for laundry. They eventually acknowledged that they needed to form a trade union to increase their bargaining power for fair wages. So in July 1877, Matilda Crawford, Sallie Bell, Carrie Jones, Dora Jones, Orphelia Turner, and Sarah A. Collier met at a church in Atlanta's Summer Hill neighborhood to form the Washing Society.[9] Many of these six women were the sole income earners for their household. They canvassed, growing the society to 3,000 Black women, ultimately earning them the nickname "the Amazon Society." The

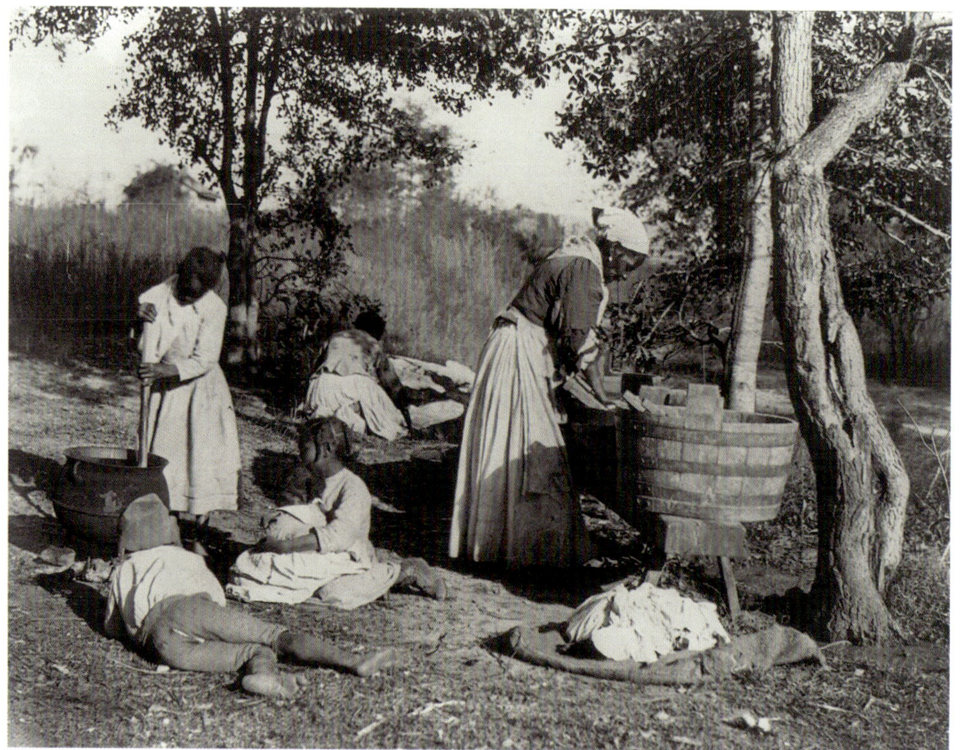

FIGURE 6.5. *African American Woman Doing Laundry with a Scrub Board and Tub.* Collection of the Smithsonian National Museum of African American History and Culture. Gift of Clara Ellis Payne.

support of local Black churches also swayed prospective members to join in the struggle. By then, Black women and some white and Irish washerwomen, in solidarity with them, went on strike. They held so much conviction that they were willing to risk their family's livelihood. The timing for striking was sophisticated in that the inaugural International Exposition of Cotton was slated to take place in Atlanta's Oglethorpe Park. This was the premier event to show the world the New South and the functionality of the city of Atlanta. The city's desperation to impress world leaders gave the strikers a strong advantage in negotiations. After much opposition, the city acquiesced to the washerwomen's demands for expanded autonomy and a pay rate of one dollar per twelve pounds of laundry.

The amount of women in the Washing Society combined with Atlanta's desire to be a progressive city likely led to the success of the strike of 1881. Beyond their material victory, the washerwomen's organizing proved that Black women had the will to organize and protest. Before this strike, Black women had organized smaller strikes in different parts of the South that yielded mixed results. Perhaps the most compelling strike organized by washerwomen occurred in 1866 in Jackson, Mississippi. Just a year after enslavement, these women demonstrated a commitment to autonomy and protest.[10] Laundresses in Galveston, Texas, organized a strike in 1877 after witnessing the success of strikes led by railroad workers.[11] Throughout the South, washerwomen often joined coopers, brickmakers, and other craftspeople in solidarity. Including the history of these strikes in interpretations of Black craft histories demonstrates that Black craftspeople were not solely creating for the benefit and under the direction of the white power structure.

The Strikers as Illegible in Craft History

The radical impulses in Black craft were illegible to mainstream history mostly because of a need for concealment: to make oneself legible runs the risk of the status quo sabotaging transformation at the root. For its own protection of members and strategy, the organization needed to operate in secrecy. Unlike the Drycleaning and Laundry Institute International, for example, which has documentation of its founding that dates back to 1883, the Washing Society's archive consists largely of journalistic stories and legal records, as documented and analyzed by historian Tera Hunter. There are no known extant records produced by the society itself, preventing us from analyzing detailed accounts of the women's process for cleaning and repairing fabrics, their detergent recipes and their application, or strategies for supporting the women in developing class consciousness and support for collective bargaining. We also do not have records of the society's membership outside of the times that some members appeared in newspaper articles and court or police records. This archive frames their freedom-seeking activities as criminal. What would it mean for those of us who are stewards of Black craft histories to confront how events such as the Washerwomen Strike of 1881 indicate an explicit resistance to racial capitalism among some craftspeople?

Early surveys of Black women's textile traditions describe their work mostly as a form of contrition, with enslaved Africans acquiring and then ultimately passing on a European skill set.[12] Between creating and maintaining a range of decorative arts that includes quilts, weavings, clothing, and bedding, scholars propagated the idea that Black women learned their skills, ideas, and techniques from white women without investigating Black women's material conditions, positionality, or how they pushed the craft beyond its traditional limits. Studying Black women, not as an extension of traditional material culture, but as an offshoot that diverges from it, brings forth their ability to create a trade union and strike in Georgia, Texas, and Arkansas in the late nineteenth and early twentieth centuries. Other surveys of Black women's textile traditions attempt to consider Africanisms or the retention of Afrocentric fabric manipulation techniques and styles but do not consider that the politics are inseparable from the culture. In the contemporary moment, there is a push to see that African American crafters are included in the canon of American craft and to argue for African American crafters to be acknowledged in their contributions to building the United States' infrastructure and wealth.[13] Recalling the Washerwomen Strike of 1881 breaks with the paradigm of inclusion of Black women in craft to consider the cohorts of women who refused to be useful or contribute to a racial capitalist order by not working and encouraging others to do the same. We cannot fully understand Black women's textile traditions if we solely study what they made and stewarded without considering how some craftspeople were also trying to undo the structure of a deeply exploitative system. Their jobs entailed making and repairing crafts, and their political lives entailed undoing systems.

Notes

1. This re-creation of the washerwoman's workflow in the late nineteenth century is drawn from a variety of sources that include photography of African American domestic scenes and manuscripts. See Tera W. Hunter, *To 'Joy My Freedom: Southern Black Women's Lives and Labors after the Civil War* (Cambridge, MA: Harvard University Press, 1998); and Elizabeth Clark Lewis, *Living In, Living Out: African American Domestics in Washington, D.C., 1910–1940* (Washington, DC: Smithsonian Institution Press, 2010).

2. Bessie Smith, "Washerwoman's Blues" (1929).

3. A chorus of Black women historians have written about the sexual violence that Black women domestics faced and the strategies that they used to protect themselves from this violence. These scholars include Darlene Clark Hine, Elizabeth Clark Lewis, and Sarah Haley.

4. Angela Davis, *Women, Race and Class* (New York: Vintage, 1981), 55.

5. Here, I am thinking with Saidiya Hartman where she identifies the general strike as radical opposition to slavery and its afterlives. See Saidiya Hartman, "The Belly of the World: A Note on Black Women's Labors," *Souls* 18, no. 1 (2016): 166–73.

6. Angela Y. Davis, *Blues Legacies and Black Feminism* (New York: Alfred A. Knopf, 1988).

7. C. G. Woodson, "The Negro Washerwoman, a Vanishing Figure," *Journal of Negro History* 15, no. 3 (1930): 269–77.

8. Sharon Harley, "When Your Work Is Not Who You Are: The Development of a Working-Class Consciousness among Afro-American Women," in *Gender, Class, Race, and Reform in the Progressive Era*, ed. Noralee Frankel and Nancy S. Dye (Lexington: University of Kentucky Press, 1991), 42–55.

9. Tera W. Hunter's groundbreaking work on Black women's culture and labor in the postbellum South provides the most comprehensive history of the strike. See Hunter, *To 'Joy My Freedom*.

10. Hunter, *To 'Joy My Freedom*, 75.

11. Hunter, *To 'Joy My Freedom*, 74.

12. Here, I am thinking with and challenging John Vlach's estimation that there is not "great possibility for a quilt to reflect anything more than the deliberate instruction of the slave owner." This estimation is serious when we consider the quilts –and other textiles– that enslaved women made and cared for but completely omits that enslaved women also made these crafts for their families and for their own pleasure. See John Michael Vlach, *The Afro-American Tradition in Decorative Arts* (Athens: University of Georgia Press, 1990), 43–45. Folklorist Gladys Marie Fry provides a thorough discussion of Black women making quilts to satisfy their own creative curiosities or share as gifts in *Stitched from the Soul: Slave Quilting in the Ante-Bellum South* (Chapel Hill: University of North Carolina Press, 2002).

13. Convenings such as Preservation North Carolina's We Built This provide an ongoing suite of programs and exhibitions that foreground the contributions of Black builders and other craftspeople and their impact today.

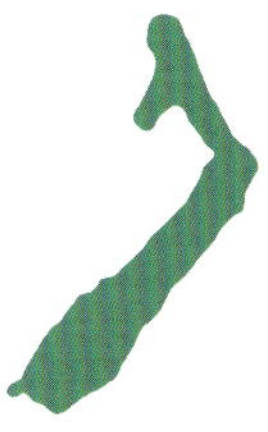

Bred to a Good Trade

Enslaved Furniture Artisans in Philadelphia, 1750–1800

ALEXANDRA ALEVIZATOS KIRTLEY

Enslaved people of African descent—farmers and artisans alike—created the prosperity of colonial and early national Philadelphia. This fact has long been overlooked but deserves to be foregrounded in any and all histories of Philadelphia and the Delaware Valley: Africans were both enslaved as laborers and artisans in colonial and early national Philadelphia and fueled the city's prosperity by being enslaved and toiling on the Caribbean plantations owned by the city's elite—specifically, Quaker merchants.[1] While the individual names of the master artisans or sole proprietors often dominate the art historical record, close examination of Philadelphia's legal and tax records makes it possible to learn the human makeup of artisans' shops: these documents not only reveal the existence of skilled enslaved workers but often name them. The use of enslaved labor in the intricately woven web of Philadelphia's Revolutionary-era furniture-making shops developed throughout the eighteenth century and can even be seen in the renowned shops of the upholsterer Plunkett Fleeson (1712–91) and the joiner-cabinetmakers Benjamin Randolph (1737–91) and Thomas Affleck (1740–95). Simply put, enslaved labor increased profitability for Philadelphia artisans, and Fleeson, Randolph, and Affleck depended on enslaved people who were, as manuscripts often describe, "bred to a good trade."

Background

Englishman William Penn (1644–1718) received a charter in 1681 from King Charles II to colonize 45,000 square miles of land flanking the Delaware River. Penn was a member of the Religious Society of Friends (commonly known as the Quakers), and he encouraged British, Irish, and European Quakers and members of all religions to colonize the lands inhabited by Lenape people (the Lenapehoking). Penn was an enslaver himself, and from the outset, he and his fellow colonials enslaved African and Indigenous people to clear the land and build the city of Philadelphia, the "greene countrie towne" that he designed as

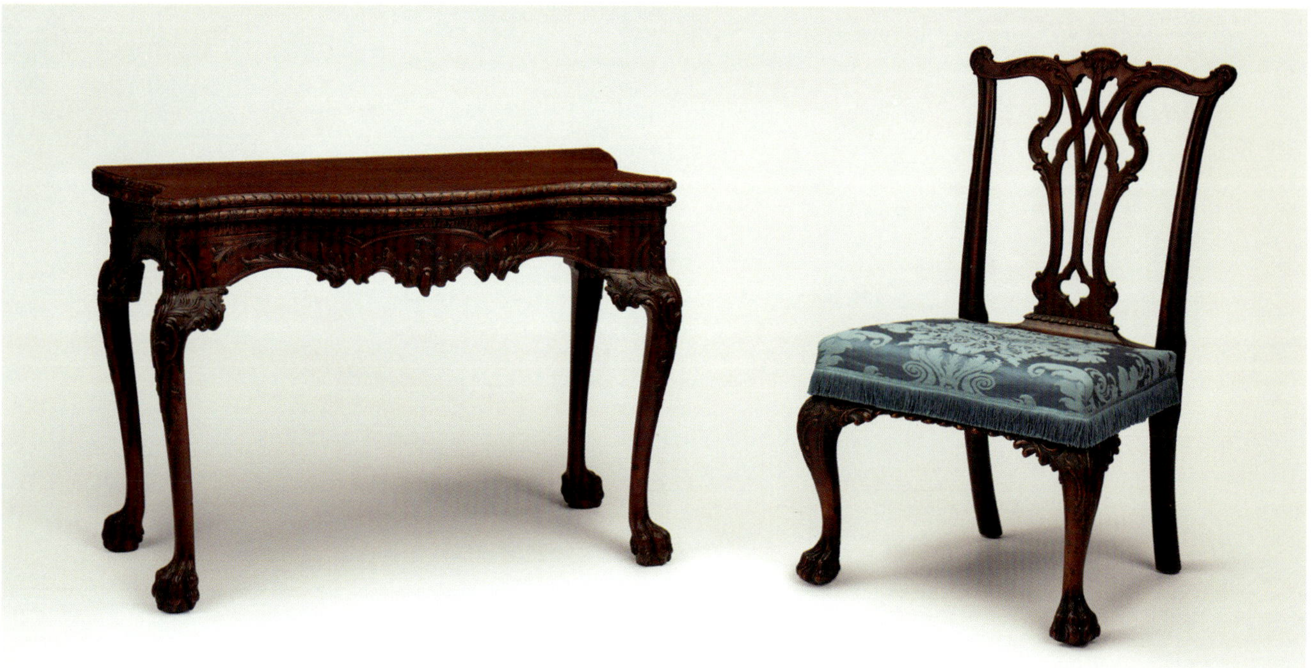

FIGURE 7.1. *Card Table*, by Thomas Affleck, Philadelphia, Pennsylvania, 1771. Mahogany, yellow pine, yellow poplar, oak. 1984-6-1. Philadelphia Museum of Art. Purchased for the Cadwalader Collection with funds contributed by the Mabel Pew Myrin Trust and with the gift of an anonymous donor, 1984.

Chair, by Benjamin Randolph, Philadelphia, Pennsylvania, 1769. Mahogany, white cedar; replacement upholstery. 2003-108-1. Philadelphia Museum of Art. Purchased with the Fiske Kimball Fund, the John T. Morris Fund, and with funds contributed by Marguerite and Gerry Lenfest, The Richard Chilton Foundation, H. Richard Dietrich Jr., Robert L. McNeil Jr., Fitz Eugene Dixon Jr., Mrs. E. Newbold Smith, Charlene Sussel, Anne H. and Frederick Vogel III, Andrew M. Rouse, and Dr. and Mrs. Robert E. Booth, 2003.

the market center of Pennsylvania, with streets laid out in a grid and punctuated by urban squares.[2]

Pennsylvania quickly became a prosperous colony that fulfilled Penn's vision (as well as creating his fortune) by supplying raw materials for Britain's mercantile economy and supporting a vigorous artisanal class: it boasted plentiful natural resources, fertile land, navigable waterways for flourishing inland, intercoastal, and international trade, and religious tolerance. By 1700, the majority of the colonial Philadelphia population were artisans, and chief among them were woodworkers, such as joiners, turners, carpenters, and shipwrights who found ready access to their materials in Pennsylvania—quite literally, *Penn's Woods*. While not governed by strict guilds, these artisans established loosely codified apprenticeships for white colonists and indentured servants but also forced enslaved people of African descent to learn their trade and work in their shops. Through their contributions to the artisanal trades, enslaved people profoundly contributed to the creative work and character of the arts of early Pennsylvania.

Enslaving people kidnapped from Africa or the Indigenous Lenape allowed Pennsylvania's colonial artisans and yeomen to become more prosperous, but they seemed tone-deaf to the fact that—beyond even its inhumanity—it created hierarchies and tension that ran antithetical to the stated rubrics under which Penn formed his colony. As historian Daniel Johnson explains, the acquisition and use of enslaved people beset the colony with conflict from its beginnings. Pennsylvania chief justice Nicholas More (d. 1689) wrote to Penn in England complaining "that the money supply was greatly depleted because of the rapidity with which labor-hungry Pennsylvanians purchased arriving African laborers." As Johnson writes, "Imperial economic policy, colonists' demand for cheap labor, and the resistance of an unfree labor force to the provincial work regime produced a unique form of conflict in the city from the founding."[3]

Wills and probate inventories from the 1690s through the 1760s detail the presence of numerous enslaved people in Philadelphia, and close examination reveals that the enslaved people were part of the labor force of an artisan's shop. The earliest enslaved people appear with yeomen and merchants, such as colonial justice and assemblyman Sven Svensson (1632–96), who had Jo and Betty and children Paul and Maria. Merchant James Metcalf (d. 1698) had a three-year-old Black girl named Clemena and "1 Indian Boy named Jack about 4 years old."[4] The first artisan whose enslaved people appear to be artisanal laborers is William Bevan, a cordwainer who died in 1706; his inventory enumerated a section of shop goods, followed by "One Negro young man named Hereford; one Indian boy Peter."[5] The frequency of enslaved people tied to an artisans' shop increased into the middle of the century: the saddler John Newman (d. 1715) had an unnamed "Negro woman"; the joiner and furniture maker John Crosswhit (d. 1715) listed among his tools, lumber, and coffin and upholstery furniture "A Negro girl named Hagar."[6] When the tanner Richard Preston died in 1729, his will stipulated that his minor daughter should inherit "a Negro Boy called by the name of Tom" but that, until the daughter reached majority, Tom should work in the tannery and "the yearly profits of the Negroes [*sic*] service" should be collected by the executors and put toward the care of the daughter.[7] Listed after the trade tools of house carpenter William Preston is "One Negroo [*sic*] Boy Name [*sic*] Cesar."[8] The joiner and furniture maker John Jones (d. 1744) enslaved a woman named Nan and a five-year-old boy named James as well as a boy named Scipio; at the time of his demise, Jones had bound Scipio to another joiner, and the administration papers account for the two years remaining for Scipio to serve as an enslaved journeyman.[9] Philadelphia's strong connection with the Caribbean trades helped establish enslavement as economically advantageous in artisanal shops: in 1750, Abraham Orpen, "late of Kingston in the Island of Jamaica at present residing in the City of Philadelphia in the Province of Pennsylvania, Mariner," directed in his will that his "Negro Man Dick" be manumitted but that his friend John Mifflin purchase "two Negro Boys who shall be put out to Trades" in order to support Dick.[10]

Throughout the 1750s, 1760s, and 1770s instances of enslaved Africans serving in artisanal shops increased, especially in businesses associated with Philadelphia's booming maritime trade that was often centered on the importation and sale of enslaved Africans: mariners (such as James Taylor, 1774), ship carpenters (Joseph Durburow, 1750), shipwrights (Gabriel Wilkinson, 1750), bakers (Wight Massey, 1762, and William Wallace, 1764), coopers (John Jackson, 1764), and carpenters (William Preston, 1740, and John Goodwin, 1775).[11] The tailor William Craddock enslaved five people in his shop in 1759 and peruke (or wig) maker Claudius du Bois—whose sole executor was Plunkett Fleeson and estate appraiser was Benjamin Randolph—enslaved one person in his shop in 1763.[12] London-born mariner William Lake—who had interests in Jamaica—died in

1765 and left to his son William, who was about to be "bound out Apprentices to" mahogany carving, "one half of a Negro called Quashay"; it is unknown if Quashay learned carving with William.[13] While the record is often unclear or obscured for lack of detail, legal documents left behind by three of the city's leading furniture makers expose an overlooked aspect of their work: their use of enslaved labor in their artisanal shops.

Plunkett Fleeson

Born in Philadelphia, Fleeson advertised from his shop "at the sign of the Easy Chair in Chestnut Street" in *The Pennsylvania Gazette* in 1739 as "upholsterer, lately from London and Dublin," calling out the capital cities where he had trained.[14] Fleeson took great advantage of intra-artisanal trade and kinship networks to broaden his ability to make his business thrive and be the upholsterer furnishing the increasingly elaborate houses of Philadelphia's mercantile elite. Fleeson worked with—and even shared space with—painters, joiners, turners, carvers, cabinetmakers, and blacksmiths, whose artisanal trades bolstered his chances of receiving upholstery commissions.[15] As the volume of commissions increased, Fleeson used enslaved labor to execute the upholstered seating and bedsteads and window treatments, which often included wooden cornices.

Urban artisans such as Fleeson may have seen the wealth generated by regional plantations that prospered only because of enslaved people.[16] He and Benjamin Randolph leased agricultural property from James Hamilton, and in 1769 that holding is listed in the Tax Exoneration for Hamilton in rural Northern Liberties along with five enslaved people.[17] By the 1770s, Fleeson owned his own meadowlands in Moyamensing and Passyunk, and while enslaved people are not listed there, "3 Negroes" are listed in 1774 at his dwelling and shop located on the east side of Water Street near Chestnut.[18] In the 1790 census, Fleeson had one enslaved person in his upholstery shop.[19] No record exists to track if any of these enslaved artisans continued on in the upholstery business, but up-and-coming upholsterers such as George Haughton (in 1776), and Hyns and Amelia Taylor (in 1787) advertised for apprentices—"a smart boy" for Haughton and "a Young Woman" for the Taylors.[20] Enslaved Africans working in Fleeson's upholstery shop would not have been unusual in the Chestnut Street area: cabinetmaker Richard Palmer (d. 1790), whose son John Jones Palmer married Fleeson's stepdaughter Deborah, lived nearby with enslaved Africans listed in his shop for the tax exoneration of 1782.[21] Fleeson's will was written in 1791, about two months before he died. In it, he outlined his bequest to his stepdaughter Margaret Linton Glentworth (1743–1815): "In Consideration of a promise made by me to her of a Mulattoe Girl, whom I have since disposed of, I do further Give and Bequeath unto the said Margaret Glentworth"; it is unclear if this is one of the enslaved people who worked in Fleeson's shop; she is not recorded in any of Glentworth's records.[22]

Randolph and Affleck

As talented as they were ambitious, cabinetmakers Affleck and Randolph were colleagues and competitors who had parallel careers. Both were born into stalwart Quaker families, but like many Quakers they married non-Quakers, which was described as "marrying out of meeting" or "being married by a hireling priest." Their most desirable material—mahogany—was the product of enslaved people in the Caribbean, where their wealthy clients all had commercial interests. Seeking to maximize their potential profits in the Caribbean mercantile trade, Affleck and Randolph chose to enslave Africans. While they also took on apprentices and journeymen of European descent, they clearly sought to expand their ability to operate profitable artisanal enterprises in the competitive landscape of 1770s and 1780s Philadelphia by having enslaved artisans in their shops.

Affleck's experience in and knowledge of the furniture trade was learned in his native Scotland and as a young journeyman in London. No doubt, it encouraged him to depend on allied artisans to make his Philadelphia shop more efficient and to adapt his shop practices to meet demand. When he arrived in Philadelphia in 1763, he sought and received commissions through a network of fellow Scots and Quakers, including his cousin, the turner John Elmslie (1733–1815), and the architect Robert Smith (1722–77). In a biographical study of Thomas Affleck, I noted that Affleck's wife, Isabella Gordon Affleck (1752–82), an Anglican, received in a bequest from her sister in 1774 "one Negro child named Cato" and assumed—incorrectly—that it "would certainly have been an unwelcome inheritance for Affleck as a Quaker": further research into Affleck's tax records reveals that he did have enslaved Africans working in this cabinetmaking shop.[23] By the 1770s, Quaker *Apologia*, or lifestyle strictures, had come out against slavery, but Affleck—who had already shown his ability to walk outside the bounds of Quaker beliefs by marrying an Anglican woman under the aegis of a "hireling" priest—paid no mind to that.[24] In 1786, the tax exoneration for Affleck's shop in the Dock Ward lists, "1 Servant . . . £12 / 1 Negro £50."[25] Three years later, that same tax names "Fiss, Negroe for Thomas Afflick's [*sic*] Est."[26] That the documentation of enslaved people in Affleck's shop is obscured in tax documents may speak to Affleck's obfuscation of his participation in the inhumane practice of slavery: he does not advertise enslaved people from his shop, and they do not appear in his estate inventory or will. The discovery not only of enslaved artisans in his shop but also of the name of at least one makes Affleck's participation a salient and integral part of his biography as an artisan.

Randolph (born FitzRandolph) was a native of Burlington County in western New Jersey, but his surviving output, the documentary evidence of his output, and a portrait miniature likeness of him (fig. 7.1) reveal him to be an upwardly aspiring aesthete—a man possessed of a keen ability to execute the finest in baroque and rococo style. When tastes changed toward the neoclassical, Randolph chose to leave furniture making behind and operate a lucrative iron forge—deepening his dependence on the enslaved labor he had used in his furniture-making shop. Randolph advertised as a joiner in 1765 and in 1770 as a cabinetmaker and carver, and he began his foray into forging iron at Speedwell Furnace in New Jersey by 1777. By 1778, he began to divest himself of his cabinetmaking tools and Philadelphia property, advertising for sale tools, property, and an enslaved woman and her young son, whom Randolph thought could be made use of immediately outside of the city for "country work."[27] In 1781, he advertised for a runaway "A Negro Man, named Mark, his hair remarkably long and black. . . . Whoever secures him, so his master may have him again."[28] And in 1782, he was taxed at his city shop location for one enslaved man.[29] By the time he died in 1791, Randolph was living full time in New Jersey and operating the Speedwell Furnace where it can be presumed that, like all iron furnaces and forges in the southeastern Pennsylvania region, many workers were enslaved.[30] His use of enslaved labor in his cabinetmaking shop in 1770s Philadelphia is more remarkable than his use of enslaved labor in the New Jersey iron forge, where enslaved people were commonly used; however, the skills of the cabinetmaking shop—such as forming and carving molds—would have translated to the forge. As with Affleck, no enslaved people are mentioned in Randolph's will or estate inventory, and that may or may not be because they died in the mid-1790s when attitudes toward slavery were shifting or because they were not willing to leave a record of their participation in their last will and testament.

Conclusion

Colonial and early national Philadelphia artisans trained enslaved people in their trades and used them in their shops with one Machiavellian goal in mind: to increase profitability, which in turn helped them rise within the social and economic hierarchy of Philadelphia. Evidence of their participation in the use of enslaved labor is not patently obvious, but rather it lays in obscure tax records and a few advertisements. The furniture makers Fleeson, Affleck, and Randolph participated in slavery through their use of enslaved shop help as well as use of luxury materials as mahogany and cochineal-dyed silks procured by enslaved labor and in assigning values to fellow humans who were enslaved in the numerous estates they appraised. Fleeson, Affleck, and Randolph translated their artisanal skills into an improved social status and personal wealth, all of which also allowed them to make advantageous marriages. They fraternized with wealthy merchants, became landholders, and acquired the material trappings of wealthy people, such as the fancy clothes Randolph wears in his portrait miniature or the substantial houses they built—often through barter with master builders such as Thomas Nevill (1721–91). Fleeson, Randolph, Affleck, and artisans like them achieved positions in colonial Philadelphia that would have been unattainable within the feudal strictures of the European, British, or Irish guild system, and enslaved artisans in their shops facilitated the prosperity that led to the rise. Many artisans seemingly shifted their position on enslaving, and only Fleeson left a record of it in his will. Perhaps they were like Benjamin Franklin (1706–90), who enslaved

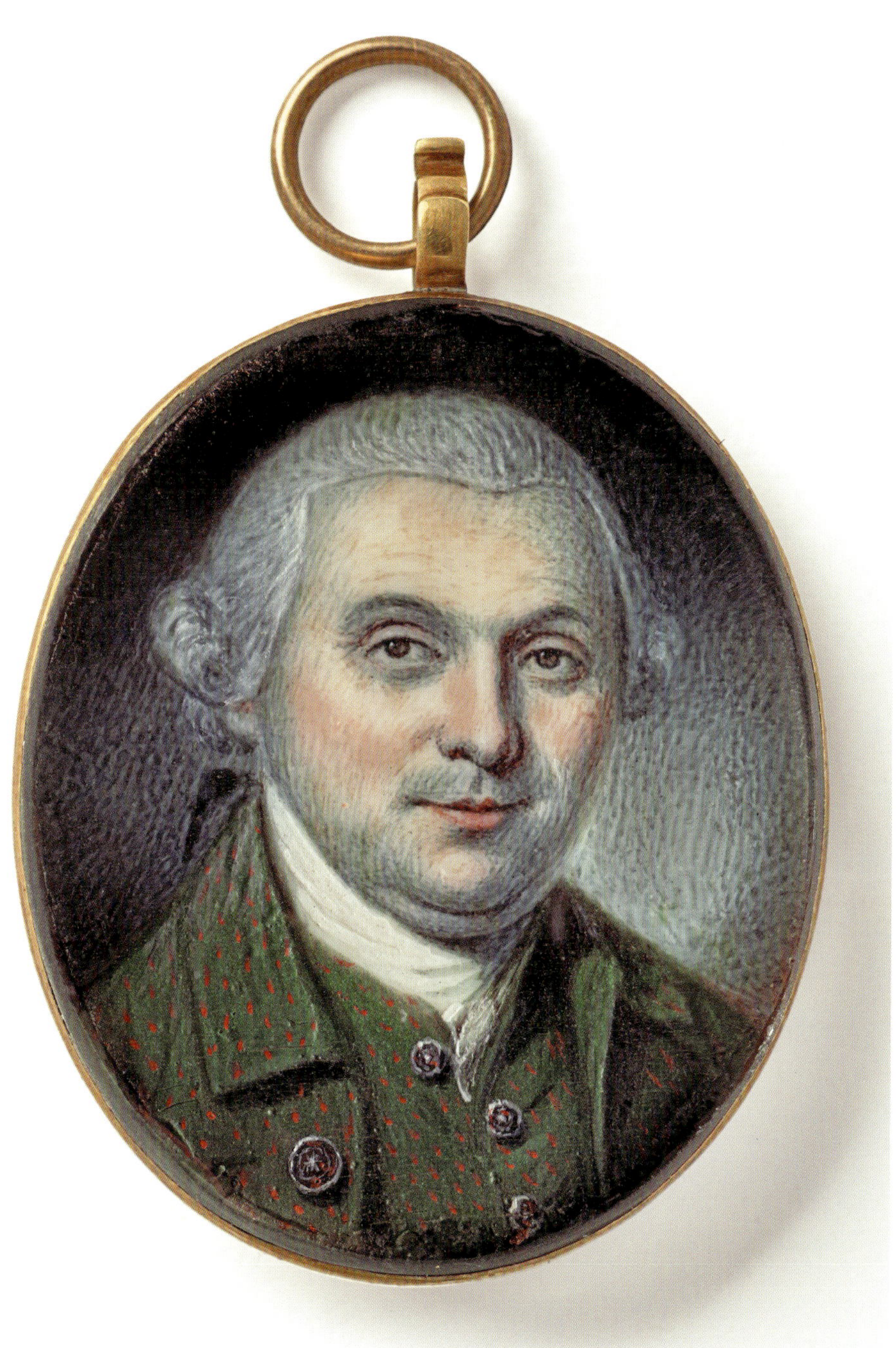

FIGURE 7.2. *Portrait of Benjamin Randolph*, by Charles Willson Peale, Philadelphia, Pennsylvania, ca. 1782. Watercolor on ivory. 1990-21-1. Philadelphia Museum of Art. Gift of Mr. and Mrs. Timothy Johnes Westbrook, 1990.

people in Philadelphia and sold and printed newspaper advertisements for the return of enslaved people who had run away before he shifted his thinking about the humanity of slavery late in his life and in 1785 became the first president of the Pennsylvania Society for the Abolition of Slavery.[31]

My intense and nearly comprehensive study of eighteenth-century Philadelphia wills and inventories reveals patterns of enslavement: artisans involved in woodworking (including cabinetmaking but most especially carpenters), shipping, and providing provisions for shipping ventures (such as bakers) were the most likely to enslave in their artisanal shops. In the 1790s, a vibrant free Black community began to take shape in Philadelphia, and the legacy of the enslaved artisans seemingly shaped that community: the forced artisanal training that many endured was translated into profitable, self-motivated work, such as that of Thomas Gross Jr. (1775–1839). Gross's father was a carpenter who was most likely forced to learn a trade in which he had no opportunity to choose or personally profit from; by the first decade of the 1800s, his son was able to choose to become an even more skilled (and therefore more lucrative) artisan—a cabinetmaker and undertaker who had a prosperous and independent career.

Notes

1. See Harriet Frorer Durham, *Caribbean Quakers* (Hollywood, FL: Dukane Press, 1972), 80, 81, 84, 87, 107, 115, 116. The commercial activity between Philadelphia and the Caribbean is evident throughout seventeenth- and eighteenth-century wills and inventories; see, for example, James Metcalf (1698), John Busby (1699), Thomas Budd (1699), Evan Jones (1708), Hugh Lowden (1723), Giles John Griffin (1760, no. 238), Daniel Steinmetz (1760, no. 13), Robert Tuite (1760, no. 261), and William Cooper (1770, no. 415). Philadelphia Wills and Inventories, microfilm, Joseph Downs Library, Winterthur, DE (hereafter, surname followed by date and will number).

2. For the reference and a history of William Penn's vision of Philadelphia as a "greene Country Towne which will never be burnt, and always be wholesome," see Inga Saffron's essay "Green Country Town," in *The Encyclopedia of Greater Philadelphia*, https://philadelphiaencyclopedia.org/themes/green-country-town/.

3. Daniel Johnson, "'What Must Poor People Do?': Economic Protest and Plebeian Culture in Philadelphia, 1682–1754," *Pennsylvania History: A Journal of Mid-Atlantic Studies* 79, no. 2 (2012): 121.

4. Svensson, 1696 (no. 145); Metcalf, 1698 (no. 189).

5. Bevan, 1706 (no. 38). The inventory of Andrew Rudman, 1708 (no. 105), a clerk, listed "1 Engen [Indian] woman and a Child."

6. Newman, 1715 (no. 41); Crosswhit, 1715 (no. 50).

7. Preston, 1729.

8. Preston, 1740.

9. Jones, 1744 (no. 79).

10. Orpen, 1750 (no. 156).

11. Taylor, 1774 (no. 381); Durburow, 1750; Wilkinson, 1750 (no. 183); Massey, 1762; Wallace, 1764 (no. 74); Jackson, 1764 (no. 58); Preston, 1740; Goodwin, 1775 (no. 80).

12. Craddock, 1759 (no. 176); du Bois, 1763 (no. 295).

13. Lake, 1765 (no. 220). See Thomas Lake, 1785 (no. 129), for reference to the junior William Lake as a mahogany carver.

14. *Pennsylvania Gazette* (Philadelphia), August 2, 1739.

15. The London-trained painter John Winter (d. 1783) advertised as a worker in Fleeson's shop in *Pennsylvania Gazette* (Philadelphia), March 20, 1740; by the 1770s, Winter was working as a painter and varnisher for cabinetmaker George Pickering (d. 1784). See Alexandra Alevizatos Kirtley, *American Furniture, 1650–1840: Highlights from the Philadelphia Museum of Art* (Philadelphia: Yale University Press, 2021), 128.

16. Fleeson was one of the bevy of artisans commissioned to fulfill incredible orders for extravagant bedecked and tasseled beds for John and Elizabeth Lloyd Cadwalader, whose own wealth was derived from the work of enslaved Africans on the Lloyd family's wheat plantations on the Eastern Shore of Maryland. See Nicholas Biddle Wainwright, *Colonial Grandeur in Philadelphia: The House and Furniture of General John Cadwalader* (Philadelphia: Historical Society of Pennsylvania, 1964), 39–45, which includes photographs of the detailed invoices. See also Kirtley, *American Furniture*, cat. nos. 86–91.

17. "U.S. Tax Exoneration for Pennsylvania, Philadelphia, 1769, Northern Liberties," s.v. "John Hamilton," Ancestry.com.

18. US Tax Exoneration for Pennsylvania, Philadelphia, 1774, Middle Ward, roll 332, p. 71, s.v. "Plunkett Fleeson," Ancestry.com. Fleeson's name appears in numerous records because he owned properties

throughout the city that he leased to painter George Rutter, his son-in-law George Glentworth, and the carver John Pollard, among others.

19. US Census, August 2, 1790, Water Street, East Side (at Chestnut Street), Philadelphia, p. 118, s.v. "Plunkett Fleeson," Ancestry.com.

20. George Haughton advertisement, *Pennsylvania Evening Post* (Philadelphia), March 18, 1776; the Taylors advertisement, *Dunlap and Claypoole's American Daily Advertiser* (Philadelphia), April 17, 1787.

21. Palmer, 1782 Middle Ward Tax Exoneration, Will and Inventory, 1790 (no. 176). Palmer lived next door to Affleck and Affleck's cousin, the turner John Elmslie, and very near the carver Martin Jugiez (d. 1815) and the joiner John Sustin.

22. Fleeson, 1791 (no. 89).

23. See Alexandra Alevizatos Kirtley, "The Ties That Bind: New Light on Philadelphia Cabinetmaker Thomas Affleck," *Antiques*, September–October 2010, 150–57.

24. It should also be noted that Quaker meeting minutes for the Philadelphia Monthly Meeting show that it took quite a while to repent after marrying out of meeting. See online Quaker records accessible through Ancestry.com; for example, Thomas Affleck to the Philadelphia Monthly Meeting, n.d., "U.S., Quaker Meeting Records, 1681–1935," s.v. "Thos Affleck," Ancestry.com.

25. "U.S. Tax Exoneration for Pennsylvania, Philadelphia, Dock Ward, 1786," roll 337, s.v. "Thomas Affleck," Ancestry.com.

26. "U.S. Tax Exoneration for Pennsylvania, Philadelphia, Dock Ward, 1789," roll 389, s.v. "Thomas Affleck," Ancestry.com. The high value for artisan-skilled enslaved people is obvious: in these same records, farmhands were usually £30 and women were usually £40.

27. *Pennsylvania Packet: or, The General Advertiser* (Philadelphia), January 20, 1781.

28. *The Freeman's Journal: or, The North-American Intelligencer* (Philadelphia), October 17, 1781.

29. "U.S. Tax Exoneration for Pennsylvania, Philadelphia, Middle Ward, 1782," roll 148, s.v. "Thomas Affleck," Ancestry.com.

30. Voluminous documentation survives for this. See, for example, John Bezis-Selfa, "Slavery and the Disciplining of Free Labor in the Colonial Mid-Atlantic Iron Industry," *Pennsylvania History: A Journal of Mid-Atlantic Studies* 64 (Summer 1997): 270–86.

31. The organization was founded in 1775 and reorganized after the Revolutionary War by Anthony Benezet in 1784.

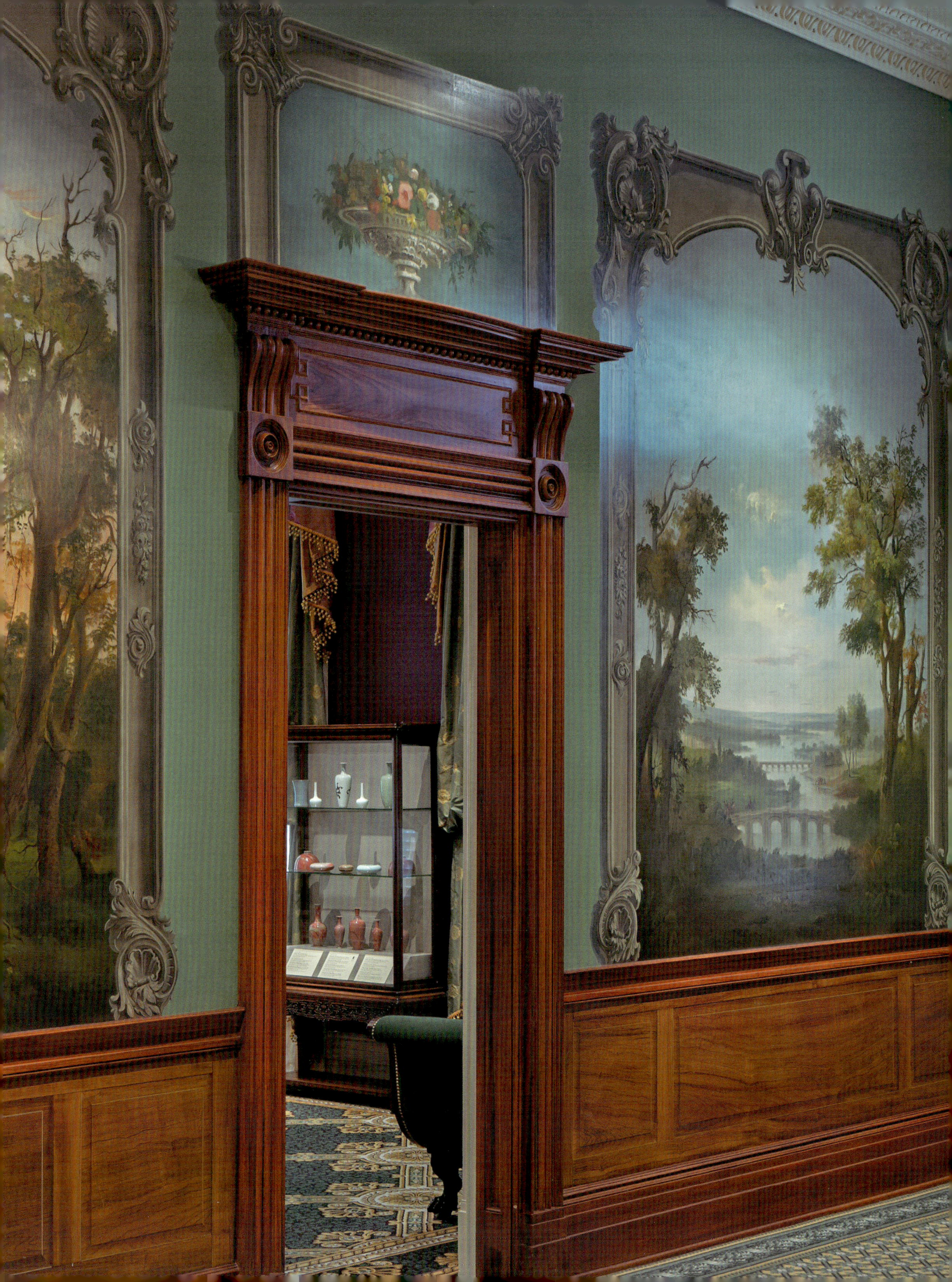

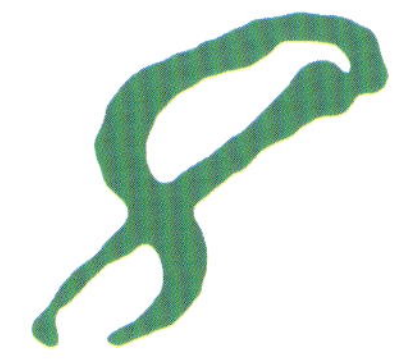

Robert Duncanson, Painter and Glazier

Enslaved and Free Black Men's Artistic Production in the Early United States

JENNIFER VAN HORN

Robert Seldon Duncanson (1821–72) is renowned for his landscape paintings. In many of his artworks, the African American artist presents a peaceful rural scene with mountains rising and rivers winding to the horizon before a luminous sky. Scholars have probed the meanings of Duncanson's landscape paintings—from his selection of locales, to the symbolic importance of water, to his engagement with American and European landscape traditions.[1] In this essay, I ask us to turn our attention from the represented landscape to the act of painting itself. Duncanson positioned his work in relation to the artistic practice of landscape painters who made sketches and small paintings *en plein air*. As a member of the Cincinnati Sketch Club (1858–64) and during his own extensive travels, Duncanson often undertook such sketching expeditions.[2]

Duncanson's artistic production activates another trajectory, however, that of enslaved and free Black house painters. Robert Duncanson trained and worked initially as a "painter and glazier," as he advertised in Monroe, Michigan, in 1838, when he opened a house painting firm with John Gamblin.[3] As Joseph Ketner has discussed, Duncanson learned to grind pigments, mix paints, prepare plaster, and paint interior and exterior surfaces from his father, John Dean (ca. 1777–1851), who likely learned from his father, Charles (ca. 1745–1828). Charles Duncanson was enslaved in Virginia before obtaining freedom and relocating his family to upstate New York.[4] In 1828, John Dean Duncanson moved his family to Michigan where eventually four of his sons (Nathan, John Dean, Robert, and Simeon) worked as house painters and carpenters. Duncanson's nephew (Simeon's son), Lucius, then became the fourth generation of Duncanson house painters.[5]

The Duncanson family's multigenerational transference of the skills of house painting spanned enslavement and freedom and facilitated Robert Duncanson's career as a landscape painter. Their story illuminates those of the many enslaved and free Black house painters across the eighteenth- and nineteenth-century United States, men whose work has been devalued historically and remains understudied.[6] In Duncanson's case, scholars have viewed his house-painting career as the staging ground for his meteoric rise, a view predicated on the presumed superiority of easel-based artists.[7] Duncanson's significant accomplishments as a Black landscape painter in the nineteenth-century United States where anti-Black racism, and—in many parts of the country—race-based enslavement, constrained and often eliminated Black makers' ability to be socially recognized as professionals, unquestionably deserves recognition. Yet by tracing the contours of the skilled artistic labor undertaken by enslaved and free Black men, this essay reclaims house painting as a fundamental part of Duncanson's artistic practice and begins to suggest the importance of house painters in American art history.

Scholars have yet to uncover much about Robert Duncanson's grandfather Charles beyond his training in house painting, thought to have happened during his enslavement in Virginia. Duncanson was one of a group of men who ground pigments, mixed them with a binder, and applied paints and varnishes for their enslavers across the early United States. At George Washington's Virginia plantation, Mount Vernon, three enslaved men worked as house painters. Stone and brick mason Tom Davis undertook "grinding of paint & Mixing of it" and painted the exterior of the main house and outbuildings. His fellow enslaved mason William (Billy) Muclus, completed interior work: "plastering weight-washing & painting at ye Mansion house." Davis also instructed enslaved butler Frank Lee in exterior painting. While Lee usually worked in a domestic context, when the family was away during the presidency Washington directed that Lee turn his hand to painting.[8]

So, too, did Burwell Colbert, the enslaved butler at Thomas Jefferson's Virginia plantation Monticello, receive training in house painting. Painter Richard Barry taught Colbert to paint, including perhaps decorative finishes such as "graining," which involved the application of layers of paint in different colors with special brushes. A surviving interior southern pine door at Monticello—painted to resemble mahogany panels with inlay (fig. 8.1)—indicates the kinds of trompe l'oeil painting that skilled house painters, including the Duncansons, accomplished.[9]

In urban areas, enslaved painters constituted a small but significant portion of skilled craftspeople.[10] The Museum of Early Southern Decorative Arts' Craftsman Database records forty-eight enslaved "painters," eight "plasterers,"

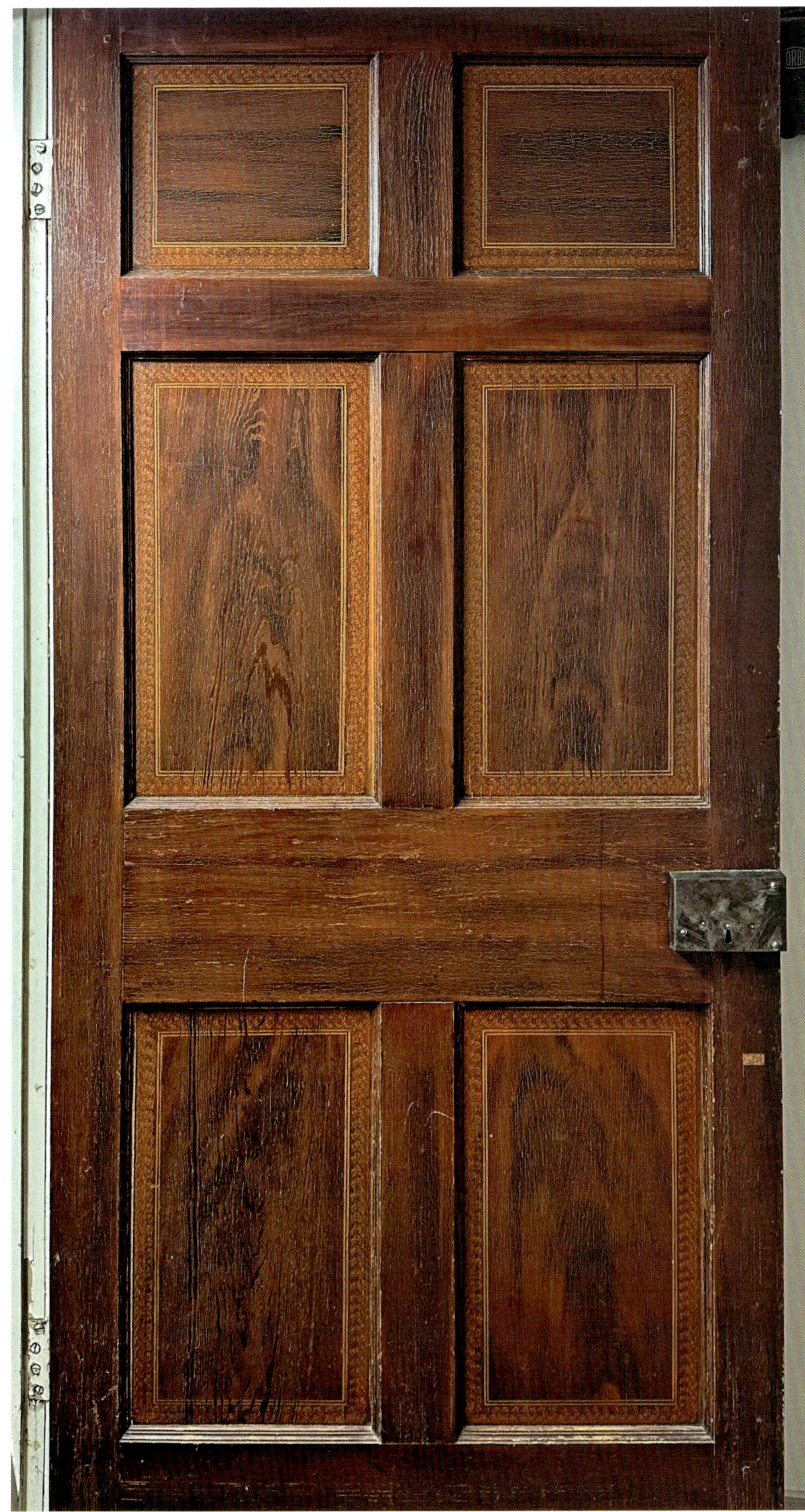

FIGURE 8.1. The North Attic door at Monticello, made from heart pine and grained to look like mahogany, 1805–8. Graining attributed to Richard Barry. Thomas Jefferson's plantation, Monticello, Virginia. Photograph by Lucy Midelfort. © Thomas Jefferson Foundation at Monticello.

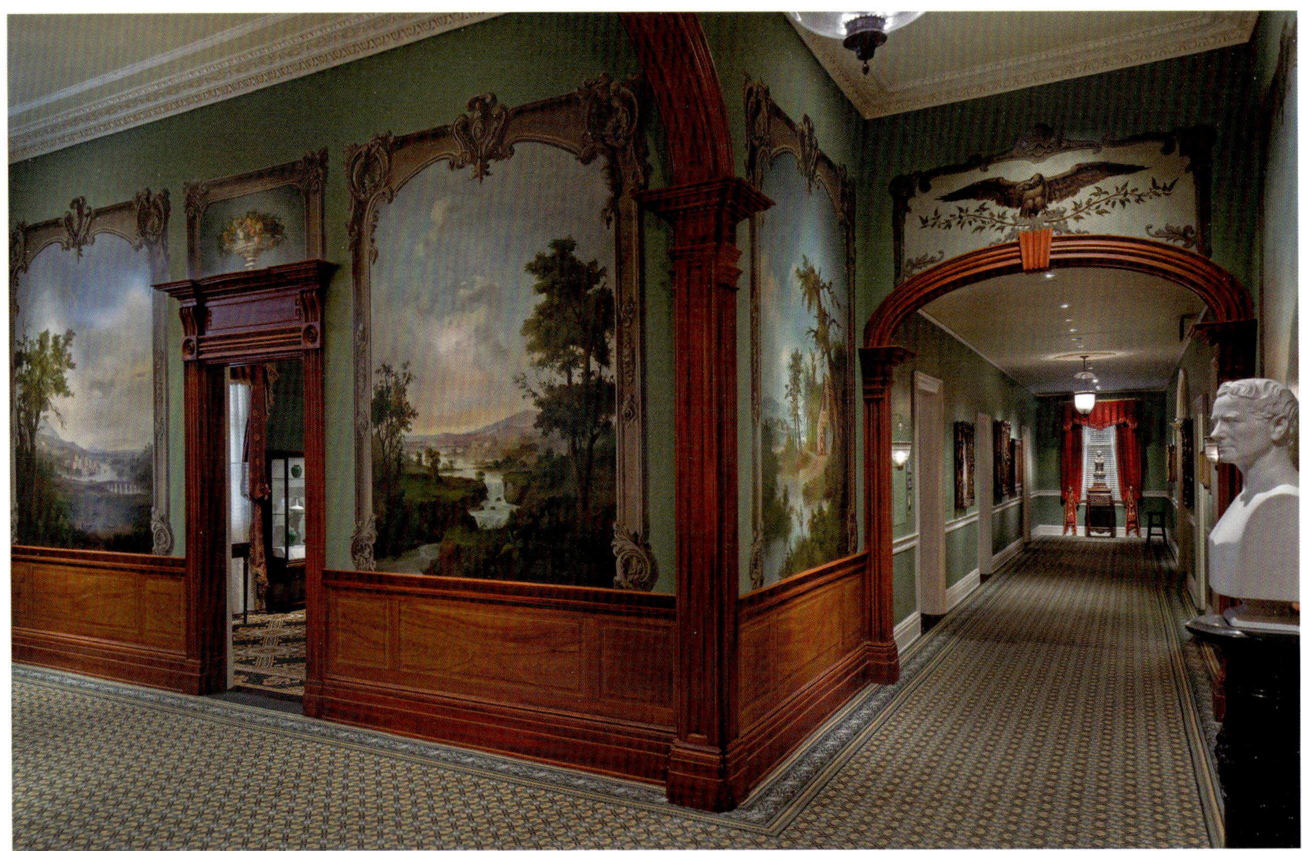

FIGURES 8.2 AND 8.3. *Landscape Murals*, by Robert S. Duncanson, ca. 1850–52. Oil on painted plaster. Taft Museum of Art, Cincinnati, Ohio. Bequest of Charles Phelps Taft and Anna Sinton Taft, 1932.233-35, 237-41, including *Floral Still-Lifes*, ca. 1850–52, oil on painted plaster, 1932.244, 1932.245; and *Eagles with Olive Branches*, by unknown artist, 1820–40s, oil on painted plaster, 1932.242, 1932.243. Courtesy of the Taft Museum of Art, Cincinnati, Ohio. Tony Walsh Photography.

and twelve "glaziers," who installed windows and glass, in major southern cities between about 1700 and 1820 (there were approximately 120 enslaved blacksmiths and 587 carpenters).[11] Urban enslaved painters worked for artisan enslavers, such as coachmakers and cabinetmakers, and on construction crews.[12] The eight enslaved persons whom Mark Morris of Charleston mortgaged in 1777 are representative: "David & John (Carpenters), Cheshire, Sam, Prince & Liberty (Painters), Isaac a brick layer & Will, a Labourer."[13] Many urban painters were rented out by their enslavers, whereas others self-hired and then paid their enslavers.

Like other crafts, house painting could be a route to freedom and the beginnings of a career as a free artisan; the commonality of enslaved painters "jobbing out" arguably made this one of the easiest trades for self-emancipated men to find employment.[14] To give one example of many, Jim and John (surnames unknown), "painters by trade" who self-emancipated in Charleston in 1817, were assumed to be "pass[ing] . . . as free" and hiring out in the city.[15] As with enslaved masons Tom Davis and William Muclus at Mount Vernon, house painting was often one of a set of allied crafts, meaning that self-emancipated painters mobilized multiple skills for support. Freedom-seeker Charles Harding, originally enslaved in Virginia, was identified in a *Maryland Gazette* advertisement as a "Carpenter and Joiner by Trade, and can paint." Harding likely leveraged all of these skills during the seven years he lived "as a Free Man" (1765 to 1772) moving among Philadelphia; Hanover, Pennsylvania; and Baltimore.[16] Harding's success

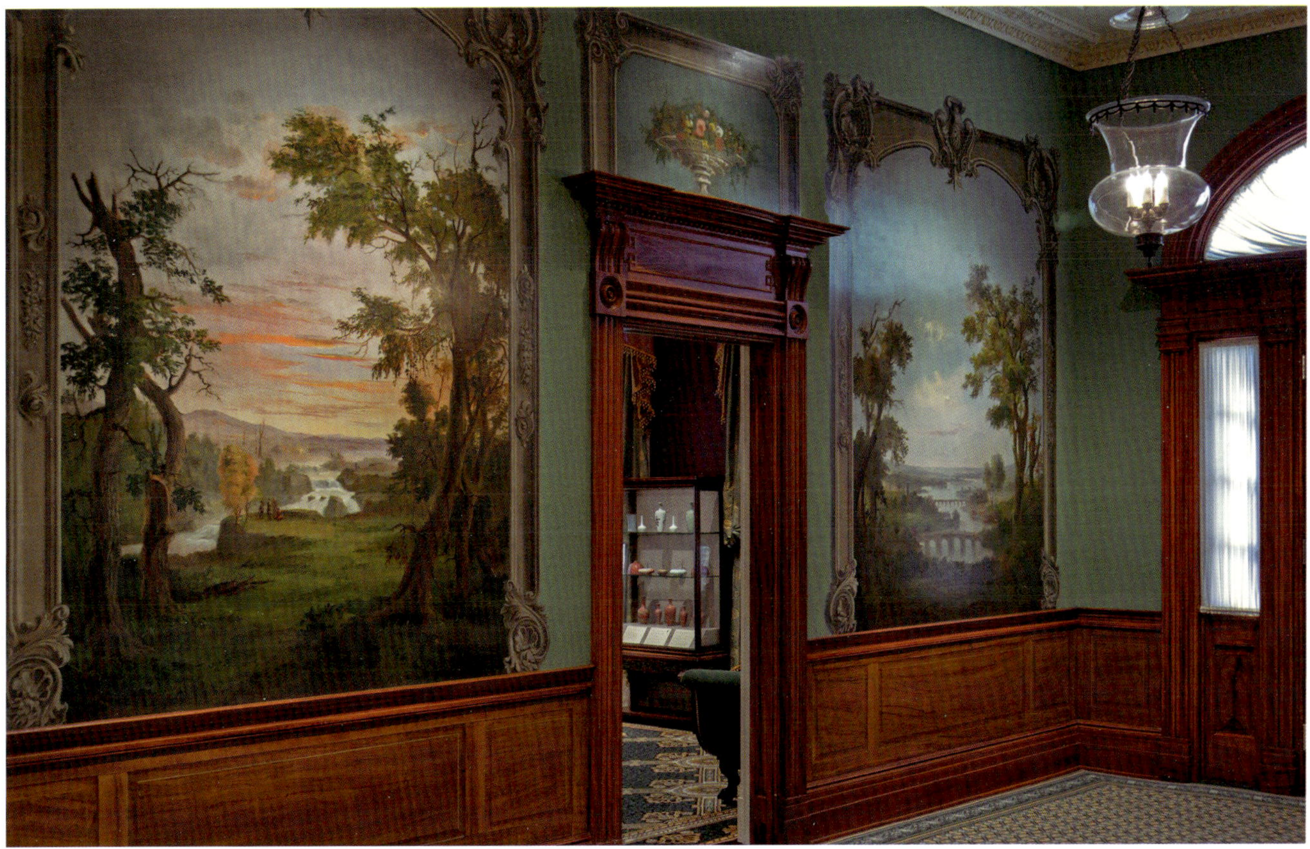

suggests the consistent desire for house painters in the early United States, as well as painters' constant search for new customers. Although established in freedom, the Duncanson family was similarly mobile, moving from Virginia to New York to Michigan and (for Robert) then to Ohio, as they sought the best markets and most welcoming environments to practice their trade. In Cincinnati, Robert Duncanson discovered a flourishing community of free Black craftspeople (proportionally more than in New York or Boston at that time) that included many house painters.[17]

While scholars have recognized Robert Duncanson as the beneficiary of a patronage network of white Cincinnati abolitionists, he also benefited from enmeshment in a network of Black house painters and from the skills that he mastered as a house painter.[18] The conjoining of house with landscape painting is most evident in the monumental landscape murals Duncanson completed between about 1850 and 1852 for wealthy white Cincinnatian Nicholas Longworth's house (now the Taft Museum of Art) (figs. 8.2, 8.3). Duncanson's murals in the entry and cross halls consisted of eight landscapes surrounded by decorative frames (each measuring roughly nine by seven feet), and five overdoor decorations. Duncanson likely activated a network of house painters, including perhaps his brothers or former business partner, to complete this commission; scholars have noted different hands. The artist certainly drew on his knowledge of house painting: the rococo-revival frames surrounding each landscape derive from French wallpaper, a common source for house painters, and the landscape murals, while complex, follow house painters' procedure of sketching onto a primed plaster surface before building up layers of oil paint, allowing for drying between.[19] Duncanson's famed rapidity, his ability to scale his work up and down, and his facility in painting on a variety of surfaces and at many sizes—from the daguerreotypes he chemically colored in James Presley Ball's studio to the Longworth murals and to the massive panorama (now lost) that he painted for Ball—were skills developed and honed through house painting.[20]

As Duncanson's oeuvre suggests, house painters and professional painters shared multiple materials and skills, as well as aesthetic connections. William Mullingar Higgins's guide of 1841 argued that house painting was "not confine[d] to the mere circumstance of covering the surface of wood or plaster with paint, but extend[ed] to the choice of suitable and harmonious colours, and the decoration of apartments in the highest style of art." Yet house painting's uneasy status as "both . . . a mechanical and a fine art" meant that the profession, as well as its practitioners (many of whom were Black), garnered a reputation as unskilled. Higgins's guide blamed house painters for their "degraded" reputation, chastising: "The house painter is not . . . conscious that he should occupy the rank of an artist, and is consequently satisfied with his knowledge . . . if he can . . . produce a tolerable imitation of ornamental woods and marbles." House painting, Higgins lectured, now required "only patient endurance of monotonous labour."[21] It also necessitated exposure to lead-based pigments and paints that had deleterious health consequences. Breathing in particles of toxic pigments was recognized to affect painters' mental health. For instance, guides advised artists to take care while grinding "Yellow-Arsenic" as "Fumes" could "offend the Brain in the Time of Grinding." Robert Duncanson's "dementia," which tragically cut short his career and resulted in his institutionalization and eventual death in 1872, has led to speculation that his years of exposure to dangerous paints were partly to blame.[22]

Duncanson was buried in Monroe's Woodland Cemetery near the graves of many in his family of house painters. Yet it was not until 2019 that a headstone was erected to mark Duncanson's grave. That headstone, the result of a grassroots fundraising campaign by Monroe residents, celebrates Duncanson as a landscape painter and includes an image of one of his landscape paintings *Ellen's Isle, Loch Katrine* (1871, Detroit Institute of Arts). Its long-delayed placement testifies to the exclusion of Black artists from the traditionally accepted canon of "American art," even as the headstone's focus on Duncanson's easel painting inadvertently reinscribes the distinction between Duncanson and those Black house painters with whom he worked.[23]

House painting's devaluation and the health risk its practitioners assumed conjoined with the anti-Black environment of the eighteenth- and nineteenth-century United States to ensure its common practice by enslaved and free Black men. White artists and patrons sought to sidestep the risks and lower reputation of this form of painting while ensuring that the white professional artist remained separate. Yet house painting was nevertheless a form of skilled artmaking that enslaved and free Black men grasped as a route to freedom and familial success, despite the health hazards. In the figure of Robert Duncanson these two lineages of art making, one applauded and one unacknowledged within art history, come together to reveal the racial power dynamics that shaped the development of art in the United States.

Notes

1. The scholarship on Robert Duncanson is considerable. See esp. Joseph D. Ketner, *The Emergence of the African-American Artist Robert S. Duncanson* (Columbia: University of Missouri Press, 1993); David Lubin, *Picturing a Nation: Art and Social Change in Nineteenth-Century America* (New Haven, CT: Yale University Press, 1994); and Kirsten Pai Buick, *Child of the Fire: Mary Edmonia Lewis and the Problem of Art History's Black and Indian Subject* (Durham, NC: Duke University Press, 2010), 31–76. Michael F. Meyer has argued for the importance of locations in Duncanson's work in relation to self-emancipation; see *Robert Duncanson and His Courageous Southern Travels*, exhibition, Meyer Fine Art Gallery, Fredericksburg, VA, 2023.

2. Wendy Katz, *Regionalism and Reform: Art and Class Formation in Antebellum Cincinnati* (Columbus: Ohio State University Press, 2002), 92–93; Peter Betjemann, "The Ends of Time: Abolition, Apocalypse, and Narrativity in Robert S. Duncanson's Literary Paintings," *American Art* 31, no. 1 (2017): 81–109.

3. "A New Firm," *Monroe (MI) Gazette*, April 17, 1838.

4. Much remains yet to be confirmed about Charles Duncanson. Some have suggested that he fought in the Continental Army and received his freedom (and land in New York) as a veteran, others that he was enslaved in Virginia then in New York, where he was manumitted, and others that he was at one time enslaved by George Washington's father, Augustine. See "Winterthur Acquires Rare Painting by Robert S. Duncanson," press release, June 4, 2019, Winterthur, https://pressroom.winterthur.org/pdfs/FINAL_press_release.pdf; Walter Gable, "Honoring Robert S. Duncanson," May 2021, www.co.seneca.ny.us/wp-content/uploads/2020/11/5-19-21-Honoring-Robert-S.-Duncanson_ADA.pdf; and Michael F. Meyer interviewed in Adele Uphaus, "19th-Century Black Landscape Artist's Work on Display in Downtown Gallery," *Free Lance-Star* (Fredericksburg, VA), September 10, 2023, https://fredericksburg.com/news/local/19th-century-black-landscape-artists-work-on-display-in-downtown-gallery/article_8e60f19a-4d88-11ee-a41f-27bf0d568106.html.

5. Ketner, *Emergence of the African-American Artist*, 12–13; James Ayers, *The Artist's Craft: A History of Tools, Techniques, and Materials* (Oxford: Phaidon, 1985), 87–94; Susan Buck and Willie Graham, "Paint," in *The Chesapeake House: Architectural Investigation by Colonial Williamsburg*, ed. Cary Carson and Carl R. Lounsbury (Chapel Hill: University of North Carolina Press, 2013), 353–75.

6. Jennifer Van Horn, *Portraits of Resistance: Activating Art during Slavery* (New Haven, CT: Yale University Press, 2022), 27–71.

7. See, for instance, Ketner, *Emergence of the African-American Artist*, 1.

8. "Tom Davis," May 23, 1786, July 29, 1797; "Muclus, A," August 10, 1793; "Frank Lee," "Database of Mount Vernon's Enslaved Community," all at www.mountvernon.org/george-washington/slavery/slavery-database/. George Washington to Anthony Whitting, October 14, 1792, February 10, 1793, Founders Online, National Archives, https://founders.archives.gov. For slavery at Mount Vernon, see esp. Mary V. Thompson, *"The Only Unavoidable Subject of Regret": George Washington, Slavery, and the Enslaved Community at Mount Vernon* (Charlottesville: University of Virginia Press, 2019).

9. Tessa Honeycutt, "Real or Faux: The Art of Imitation in Madison's Montpelier," November 30, 2021, https://storymaps.arcgis.com/stories/04ef8a454c184a1f8510eee0dacab26bf; Buck and Graham, "Paint," 348–75. For Burwell Colbert, see Lucia Stanton, *"Those Who Labor for My Happiness": Slavery at Thomas Jefferson's Monticello* (Charlottesville: University of Virginia Press, 2012), 181; and Thomas Jefferson to James Leitch, February 15, 1812, Founders Online, National Archives, https://founders.archives.gov.

10. This work builds from important scholarship on Black craftspeople and participates in a recent resurgence championed by Torren Gatson and Tiffany Momon. See esp. John Michael Vlach, *The Afro-American Tradition in Decorative Arts* (Athens: University of Georgia Press, 1990); Black Craftspeople Digital Archive, https://blackcraftspeople.org; and Torren Gatson, "Editor's Introduction," and essays in *Journal of Early Southern Decorative Arts (MESDA Journal)* 41 (2020), www.mesdajournal.org.

11. My thanks to Michael Hartman for assembling this data in summer 2019 using the MESDA Craftsman Database, https://mesda.org/research/craftsman-database (hereafter MESDACD). He searched the cities of Charleston, Columbia, Savannah, New Bern, Richmond, and Baltimore. Craftspeople were counted for each trade, so if individuals were listed as a "painter and glazier," they are represented twice. Although the Craftsman Database is an invaluable source, it includes only named individuals.

12. Catharine W. Bishir, *Crafting Lives: African American Artisans in New Bern, North Carolina, 1770–1900* (Chapel Hill: University of North Carolina Press, 2013).

13. Mortage Mark Morris of Charleston, March 10, 1777, Charleston County, SC, South Carolina Mortgages No. EEE 1777–1790, 247. Located through MESDACD.

14. Tiffany Momon, "John 'Quash' Williams, Charleston Builder," *Journal of Early Southern Decorative Arts* 41 (2020), www.mesdajournal.org/2020/john-quash-williams-charleston-builder/.

15. Jim "Runaway Advertisement," *Southern Patriot and Commercial Advertiser* (Charleston, SC), February 22, 1817; Jim and John "Runaway Advertisement," May 2, 1817, *City Gazette and Commercial Daily Advertiser* (Charleston, SC), May 2, 1817. Both located through MESDACD.

16. Charles Harding "Runaway Advertisement," *Maryland Gazette* (Annapolis), July 16, 1772. Located through MESDACD.

17. Katz, *Regionalism and Reform*, 105.

18. For a broader concept of networks in relation to Duncanson, see Anna Arabindan-Kesson, "From Poetry into Paint: Robert S. Duncanson and the Song of Hiawatha," in *Intermedia: Terra Foundation Essays*, vol. 6, ed. Ursula Frohne (Chicago: University of Chicago Press, 2022), 86–121.

19. Ketner, *Emergence of the African-American Artist*, 50–70, esp. 55–59. For decorative painting, see Nina Fletcher Little, *American Decorative Wall Painting, 1700–1850* (1952; New York: Dutton, 1972).

20. Ketner, *Emergence of the African-American Artist*, 60. Shana Klein highlights Duncanson's emergence as a still-life painter and related work as a portraitist, stressing the multiple aspects of his career, in Shana Klein, "Cultivating Fruit and Equality," *American Art* 29, no. 2 (2015): 64–85. Jill Vaum Rothschild similarly considers how Joshua Johnson's initial training as a blacksmith affected his later career as a portraitist. See Jill Vaum Rothschild, "Joshua Johnson: Black Craftsmanship and Artistry in Early National Baltimore," in *Unnamed Figures: Black Presence and Absence in the Early American North*, ed. Emelie Gevalt, R. L. Watson, and Sadé Ayorinde (New York: American Folk Art Museum, 2023), 148–81.

21. William Mullingar Higgins, *The House Painter; or, Decorator's Companion . . .* (London: Thomas Kelly, 1841), preface, 3, 41, available at Smithsonian Libraries Digital Collections, www.sil.si.edu/DigitalCollections/art-design/higgins/essay.htm.

22. R. Campbell, *The London Tradesman: Being an Historical Account of All the Trades, Professions, Arts* (London: T. Gardner, 1757), 107; Ketner, *Emergence of the African-American Artist*, 181–85. See also Van Horn, *Portraits of Resistance*, 38–42.

23. Ryan Patrick Hooper, "Pioneering Black Artist Robert S. Duncanson Will Finally Get a Tombstone," *Detroit (MI) Free Press*, September 30, 2018. For the painting, see https://dia.org/collection/ellens-isle-loch-katrine-42998. One of the first to research Duncanson was African American artist and art historian James Dallas Parks, *Robert S. Duncanson: 19th Century Black Romantic Painter* (Washington, DC: Association for the Study of Afro-American Life and History, 1980). For Parks, see the website Missouri Remembers: Artists in Missouri through 1951, https://missouriartists.org/person/morem271/.

9

State Craft

Robert K. Griffin and the Black American Artisans of the Liberian Senate

R. RUTHIE DIBBLE

The American Colonization Society (ACS) records at the Library of Congress contain many fascinating traces of the lives of nineteenth-century Black craftspeople who risked shipwreck and disease to experience freedom and opportunity in Liberia, the world's second Black republic. From the emigrant lists kept by the ACS, scholars believe that of the 16,000 men and women who emigrated, approximately 10 percent were craftspeople, including tailors, seamstresses, cobblers, brickmakers and -layers, masons, cabinetmakers, plasterers, and carpenters both free and enslaved and hailing from states throughout the Eastern Seaboard and the Midwest.[1] Bringing their artisanal expertise, tools, and even materials, these Black Americans physically transformed Indigenous land into a colony and ultimately a republic, work they and many of their ancestors had carried out in America with little reward for their labors. Precious little evidence remains of their creative output, however, and many physical traces have been destroyed.

The watercolor of the Liberian Senate in Monrovia drafted by the Yonkers-born artist Robert K. Griffin between 1856 and 1857 is a rare and precious exception (fig. 9.1).[2] Griffin intended this precise and colorful image of Black American men and women surrounded by the architecture and furnishings of the Liberian State House to be made into a popular print to promote the cause of Liberian sovereignty, which Liberia had declared in 1847 but remained unrecognized by the United States. Instead, his watercolor languished in the ACS records, and only in modern scholarship has it received recognition as a crucial and strategic representation of Liberian governance.[3] Viewed through the framework of this exhibition, Griffin's watercolor is also a window into the abundant trade skills that Black artisans brought with them in their journey to Liberia. In this essay, I explore how Griffin's watercolor tells us not only about Liberian statecraft but also about the craftspeople who shaped this new republic's identity as a site of Black American liberation in the Atlantic World.

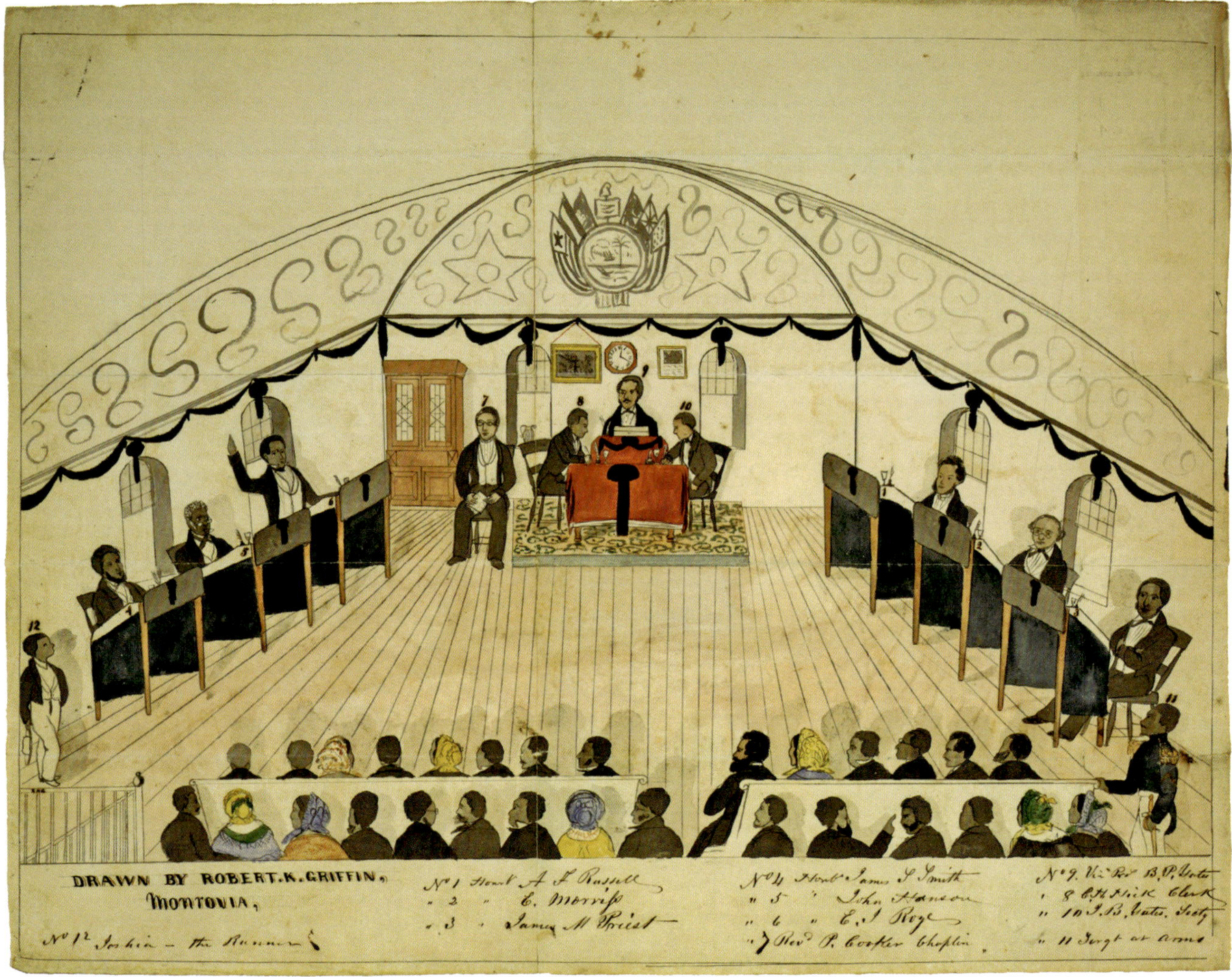

FIGURE 9.1. *Liberian Senate*, by Robert K. Griffin, 1857. Watercolor on paper. Library of Congress, LC-USZC4-4908.

When Robert K. Griffin arrived in Monrovia in January 1856, he found the daguerreotypist Augustus Washington working as a portraitist of middle- and upper-class Black settlers. Washington, whose *Boy with Books* is included in this exhibition (see fig. 31 in Exhibition Catalog of Objects), had emigrated from Hartford, Connecticut, in 1852, determined to work and live free from racial discrimination.[4] The record of these two men's meeting is lost to history, but together Griffin and Washington produced the image of the senate in chambers. Washington individually posed and photographed each of the six senators as well as the vice president (sitting at back, center), the senate chaplain, and supporting staff for the scene Griffin intended to depict: Senator Edward James Roye voting or swearing an oath as his colleagues bear witness.[5] Applying pen to nineteen-by-fifteen-inch paper, Griffin copied these men's likenesses—their haircuts, clothes, facial features—and populated the space with furnishings and men and women observing the proceedings.

The influence of a third artisan in the making of this image is more subtly present; Griffin copied the variations in each senator's dress from the daguerreotypes, but the women's dresses and head coverings are equally full of detail, showing variations of the low, deep collar neckline popular in the 1850s and distinct, beribboned bonnets in purple, green, and yellow. Robert Griffin's wife, Ellen E. Griffin, who emigrated with him and was also from New York City, was a mantuamaker, a term for dressmakers who cut and sewed the fitted style of dress worn by women in the mid-nineteenth century.[6] With her knowledge of fashion, she would have been well equipped to advise Griffin on these details of the watercolor. Many women in the textile trades in Liberia would have made similar clothes and accessories, including the milliner Harriet D. Brander, who emigrated with her husband at the age of forty-seven in 1824.[7] Indeed, Charles W. Thomas, who visited Liberia in the mid-1850s, commented on the "degree of refinement and taste" in Liberian Americans' fashions and society. Ellen E. Griffin, Harriet D. Brander, and other artisans of dress played a crucial role in Liberians' bodily refinement, which expressed their equality with Atlantic World nation-states and pronounced separateness from the Indigenous West African cultures whom Black Americans had colonized.[8]

Griffin drew around these figures a substantial and elegant chamber, the thirty-by-forty-foot-room on the second floor of the stone and brick State House built in Monrovia between 1839 and 1841. In 1848, Liberia's new constitution was framed and the declaration of independence signed in this building. This chamber was originally built to house the supreme court but became the senate chambers in the late 1840s when the court moved downstairs. We know from a speech made by President Anthony William Gardner in 1880 that it was a "stately edifice of exquisite beauty and worth," built of stone and featuring a balcony.[9]

The arched windows, barrel-vaulted ceiling, and smooth white walls depicted in Griffin's watercolor demonstrates that the tradespeople who built the State House created a coherent neoclassical design scheme. In the nineteenth-century United States, these features were often used in government buildings because they were viewed as a fitting expression of the representative government exemplified by the Roman Republic.[10] One particularly well known classical government structure was Benjamin Henry Latrobe's United States Senate chamber, built in 1808–10, designed so that a barrel vault rises over the vice president's chair just as it does in Griffin's image of the Liberian Senate chambers.

Men in the building trades who constructed the State House clearly knew not only the appropriateness of neoclassical architecture for government buildings but also how to build and decorate in this style.[11] Liberian emigrants such as the freeborn brickmaker Isaac James from North Carolina and the bricklayer James McGeorge from Louisiana arrived with the know-how to locate good clay, build kilns, and lay bricks to produce significant civic structures like the State House.[12] Carpenters—the most listed profession of craftsmen in Liberia—fitted out many details visible in Griffin's watercolor, including the sash windows, wood floors, and stairs visible in the left foreground.[13] The interior walls were plastered white, perhaps by Charles Guess, a Kentuckian who was offered emancipation by his enslaver on the condition that he leave his home for Liberia.[14]

In the arched wall at the end of the room is a representation of the Liberian coat of arms adopted at the constitutional convention of 1847, which depicts a scene of liberation that seems to redress the Middle Passage: a ship under sail arriving along the coast of Liberia with new emigrants. Whether this imagery was modeled in relief with the plaster or painted in grisaille is difficult to decipher. Perhaps Griffin, who also sent two watercolors of the Liberian coastline back to the ACS, contributed to the chamber's decorative program as well.[15] Despite the ideals represented in the room's construction and ornament, craftspeople who built the State House also benefited from unjust labor conditions by using members of Indigenous tribes to haul their materials.[16]

Griffin's watercolor also carefully limns the furnishings in the room. Many objects are imported, including the water pitcher and Hitchcock chairs, which were manufactured in the United States and shipped to Liberia by the dozens.[17] The senators' desks are unpainted, simply constructed, and not a form imported in large quantities, suggesting they were likely made in Liberia.[18] Here, they are draped with black crepe and are difficult to read fully. They have turned legs, slant tops for papers and writing, and flat surfaces to hold a drinking glass and inkpot with quill. Their legs, as well as the turned finial of the newel post, may have been made by Amos Herring, a literate turner who emigrated with his wife and five children from Virginia in 1833 at the age of thirty-nine.[19] As accessories to literacy and self-governance, they are a critical contribution to the room.

By far the most technically complex and aesthetically ambitious furnishing in Griffin's watercolor is the secretary and bookcase visible against the back left wall. Griffin captured its essence rather than precise construction; we see an abstracted cornice of exaggerated height, an approximated pattern of glass-paned cabinet doors, lopers—represented by the "X"s at left and right—placed beside rather than properly beneath the drop-down desk, and two framed cabinet drawers below. In the mid-nineteenth century, fine furniture was imported to Liberia, but it was also made locally by John Day Jr., the freeborn cabinetmaker, minister, and brother of Thomas Day, whose bureau is included in this exhibition.[20] Growing up in Dinwiddie County, Virginia, in the early nineteenth century, the brothers Day learned the trade of cabinetmaking from their father. As a young man, John Day Jr. experienced a religious awakening, entered the ministry in 1821, and immigrated to Liberia in 1830. While following his vocation in Grand Bassa County, Day also continued to make furniture; an ACS agent noted in 1835 that "two beautiful side-boards Mr. Day has made lately of African wood" equaled mahogany furniture made in the United States.[21] No pieces of his furniture are known to survive, but the secretary and bookcase in Griffin's watercolor shares intriguing similarities with the cabinetmaking of his brother, for example the mahogany veneered secretary and bookcase he made in the 1840s for the Giles family (fig. 9.2).[22] John Day was also intimately involved in the chambers of government that met at the State House, so the placement of his furniture here would have held personal and political significance. He signed the Liberian constitution in this very room in 1847 and, in the months that Griffin drew this watercolor, was serving as the second Chief Justice of the Supreme Court of Liberia in the chamber

FIGURE 9.2. *Secretary Desk and Bookcase*, by Thomas Day. Photo courtesy of the North Carolina Museum of History, Raleigh.

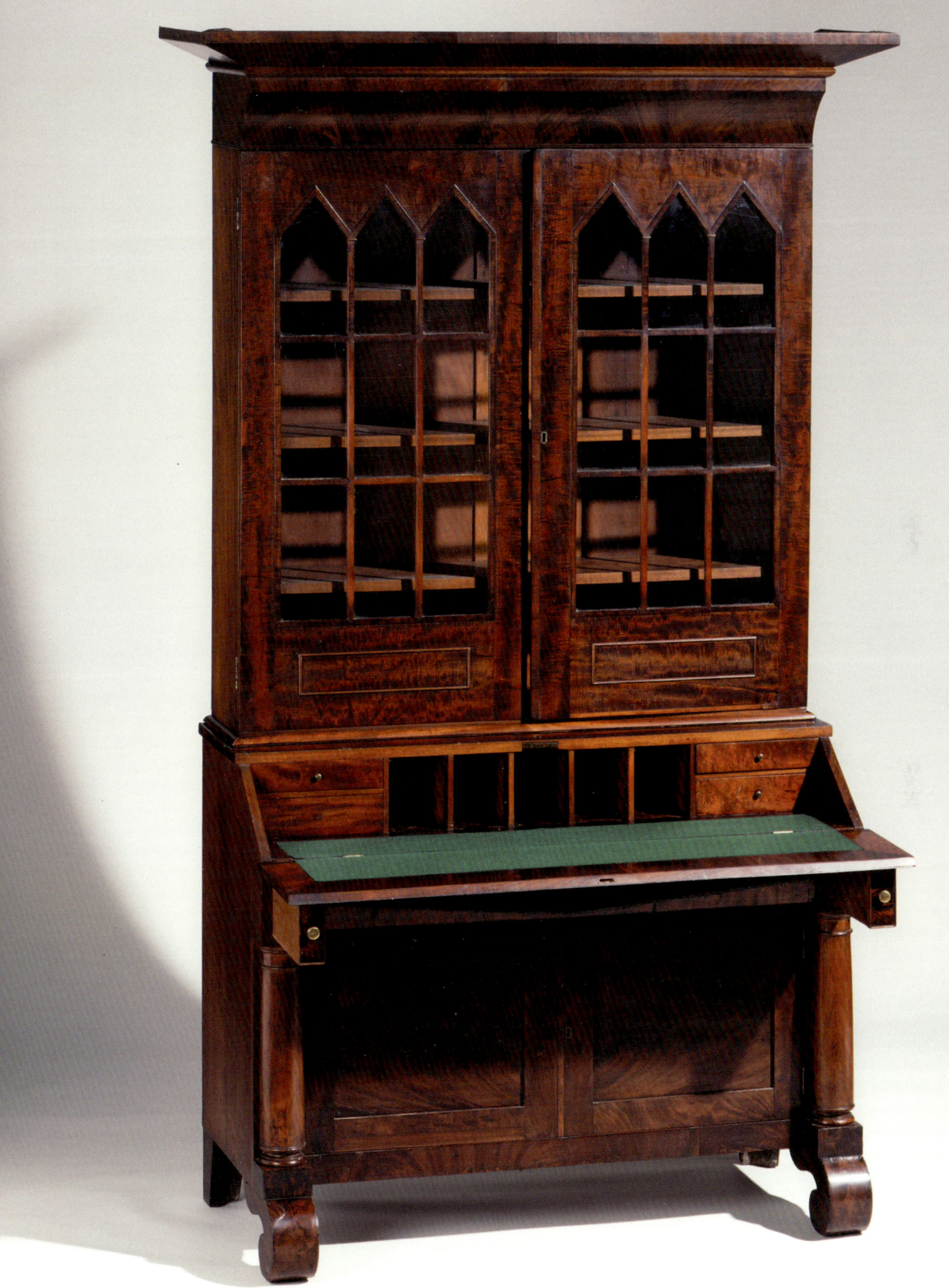

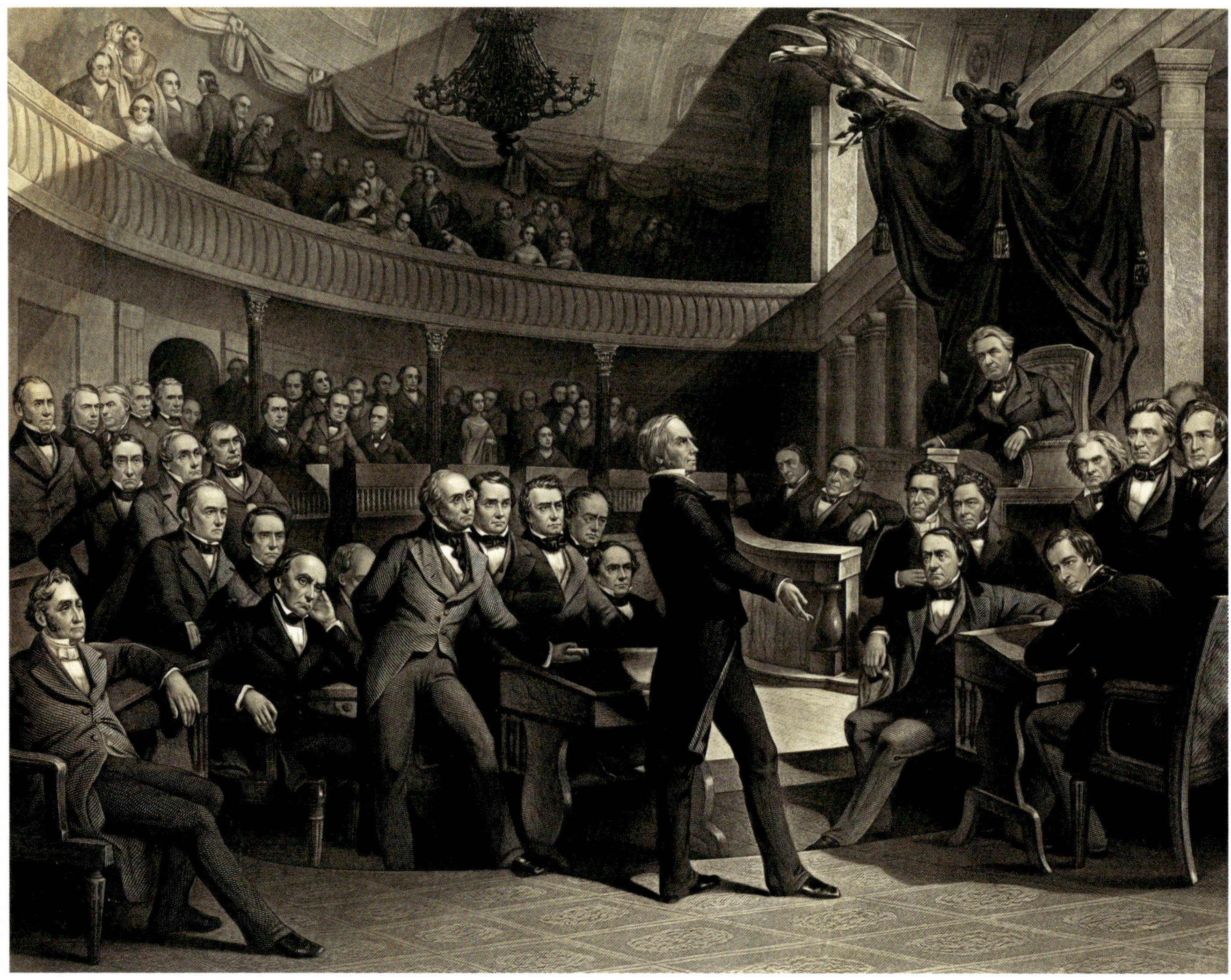

FIGURE 9.3. *The United States Senate, A.D. 1850*, by P. F. Rothermel, ca. 1855, engraved by R. Whitechurch. Library of Congress, LC-DIG-pga-05850 (digital file from original print).

downstairs.[23] Day's career exemplifies the opportunities Liberia could afford those with good finances and sound health; whereas his brother served members of the North Carolina legislature by producing their furniture, John Day served his government at the highest level.

The art historian Dalila Scruggs has identified one additional crucial detail in Griffin's painting. Hanging on the back wall is a gilt-framed lithograph by Robert Whitechurch of Peter Rothermel's painting *The United States Senate, A.D. 1850*. Remarkably, the artwork arrived in Monrovia on the same voyage that brought Robert and Ellen Griffin (fig. 9.3).[24] The print is set in Benjamin Latrobe's Old Senate Chamber; the barrel vaulting is visible in the upper right. The image shows the Kentucky statesman Henry Clay introducing the Compromise of 1850, which ultimately altered several laws related to slavery to preserve the Union. Inspired as Scruggs has shown by the Rothermel print, Griffin's watercolor emphasizes the shared republican ideals and legislative processes that connected Liberia and the United States.[25] But there is another fundamental commonality: the material worlds constructed in both images are indebted, in part or wholly, to Black craftspeople. Enslaved craftspeople built the US Capitol and grounds, including Latrobe's renovations, and indeed this practice did not end until 1862, when the District of Columbia Compensated Emancipation Act was passed. Neither of these senate chambers could exist without Black craftspeople. But in mid-nineteenth-century Monrovia, just as craftspeoples' work represents complex and hard-won free Black lives, so, too, did their senators.

Notes

1. Leigh Gardner has recently produced the most comprehensive listing to date of the people who migrated to Liberia in the nineteenth century, including their occupations when noted by colonization officers. Leigh Gardner, "African American Migration to Liberia, 1820-1906," Harvard Dataverse, V1, UNF:6:ul/DjU+oyb2X3ueqxNCNSA ==[fileUNF], accessed October 18, 2024, https://doi.org/10.7910/DVN/NJFNGY. For known occupations of North Carolina emigrants, 1825–93, see Claude A. Clegg, *The Price of Liberty: African Americans and the Making of Liberia* (Chapel Hill: University of North Carolina, 2004), 7.

2. Griffin identifies himself as an artist in the emigrant list. "List of Passengers and Immigrants per Barque Lamartine," *African Repository* 32, no. 2 (1856): 59. Dalila Scruggs, "'The Love of Liberty Has Brought Us Here': The American Colonization Society and the Imaging of African-American Settlers in Liberia." (PhD diss., Harvard University, 2010), 155.

3. Scruggs, "'Love of Liberty Has Brought Us Here,'" 196.

4. Shawn Michelle Smith, "Unredeemed Realities: Augustus Washington," in *Pictures and Progress: Early Photography and the Making of African American Identity*, ed. Maurice O. Wallace and Shawn Michelle Smith (Durham, NC: Duke University Press, 2012), 103.

5. Scruggs, "'Love of Liberty Has Brought Us Here,'" 193–94.

6. "List of Passengers and Immigrants per Barque Lamartine," 59.

7. "Roll of Emigrants That Have Been Sent to the Colony of Liberia, Western Africa, by the American Colonization Society and Its Auxiliaries, to September, 1843," United States Congressional Serial Set Vol. 458 (1844/45), 319. Textile artisans have also fashioned black crepe into bows, swags, and yardage around the walls and on the senators' desks, in commemoration of the deceased Liberian senator G. H. Ellis. Carol Johnson, "Faces of Freedom: Portraits from the American Colonization Society Collection," *Daguerreian Annual* (1996): 266.

8. Charles W. Thomas, *Adventures and Observations on the West Coast of Africa and Its Islands* (New York: Derby and Jackson, 1860), cited in Marie Tyler-McGraw, *An African Republic: Black and White Virginians in the Making of Liberia* (Chapel Hill: University of North Carolina Press, 2007), 151.

9. "Message of President Gardner," *African Repository* 56, no. 7 (1880): 119–20. See also "Annual Report of the American Colonization Society," *African Repository and Colonial Journal* 21, no. 1 (1845): 43.

10. Jocelyn J. Evans and Keith Gaddie, *The U.S. Supreme Court's Democratic Spaces* (Norman: University of Oklahoma Press, 2021), 13.

11. Bernard L. Herman, "Settler Houses," in *A Land and Life Remembered: Americo-Liberian Folk Architecture*, ed. Svend E. Holsoe and Bernard L. Herman (Athens: University of Georgia Press, 1988), 95–147.

12. "Roll of Emigrants," 210, 295.

13. "Roll of Emigrants," 152–299.

14. Guess is the only recorded plasterer living in Liberia in 1843. "Roll of Emigrants," 284.

15. Two watercolors depicting the Liberian coastline with a ship at sail in the foreground by Griffin also survive at the Library of Congress, *Fish Town at Bassua Liberia* and *Bassua Liberia*, both painted ca. 1856. Jill Schade, "Picturing Freedom's Shores: The Visual Culture of Liberian Colonization, 1821–1861" (MA thesis, University of Virginia, 2016), 320.

16. Alexander M. Cowan, *Liberia, as I Found It, in 1858* (Frankfort, KY: A. G. Hodges, 1858), 43–44.

17. For example, 200 chairs and 100 bedsteads arrived on the *Stevens* in 1856. "Second Emigrant Expedition by the Mary Caroline Stevens," *African Repository* 33, no. 6 (1857): 162.

18. Cowan, *Liberia*, 83.

19. "Roll of Emigrants," 241.

20. The best-known example is a massive mahogany dining table given to President Roberts by Queen Victoria. Schade, "Picturing Freedom's Shores," 360.

21. James Brown, "Letter to the Editor," *African Repository and Colonial Journal* 11, no. 6 (1835): 181. Edward W. Blyden, "Eulogy of the Rev. Edward W. Blyden, on the Rev. John Day, Monrovia, 1859," *African Repository* 37, no. 5 (1861): 154–58. For more on Thomas Day's politics, see Laurel C. Sneed and Patricia D. Rogers, "The Hidden History of Thomas Day," North Carolina Humanities Council (2017): 6–9, available via Crafting Freedom Institute, https://craftingfreedom.net/research/; and Patricia Dane Rogers and Laurel Crone Sneed, "The Missing Chapter in the Life of Thomas Day," *American Furniture, 2013* (Hanover, NH: Chipstone Foundation, 2013), 100–154.

22. Patricia Phillips Marshall and Jo Ramsay Leimenstoll, "An Assortment of Fine and Fashionable Furniture," in *Thomas Day: Master Craftsman and Free Man of Color* (Chapel Hill: University of North Carolina Press, 2010), 81–83.

23. Blyden, "Eulogy," 157.

24. "A Handsome Present," *New-York Colonization Journal* 6, no. 12 (1856), cited in Scruggs, "'Love of Liberty Has Brought Us Here,'" 159.

25. Schade, "Picturing Freedom's Shores," 321.

D'orphevre et tout ce dont je servir[illegible] ra[illegible]
ries cacher et outre le nourrir coucher [illegible]
et entretenir de raccommoder de tous ling[es]
chaussures a son etat suivant sa condition
doucement et humainement comme il app[artient]
promettant ledit françois Dominique appre[ndre]
qu'il luy sera possible tout ce qu'il luy sera
ledit sr Delzergue luy obeir en tout ce qu'il luy
de licite et honneste le servir fidelement faire
enter son dommage l'en avertir s'il vient a
et sans parle dit Dominique
s'en sans pouvoir s'absenter ni aller travailler ai[lleurs]
cas d'absence le dit ~~sieur Malzieu promet~~
françois Dominique consent d'etre pris et
au corps pour etre ramené chez ledit sieur
pour parachever ~~ces presentes~~ ce qui manque
expirer des presentes qui seront faites moye[nnant]
somme de cent cinquante livres que ledit
promet et s'oblige de bailler et payer au dit
Dominique a l'expiration desdites presentes et
vieilles hardes servantes a l'usage de luy dit fran[çois]
~~Dominique~~ ~~[illegible]~~ & estant d'ailleur[s]
convenu entre lesdites parties qu'il ~~sera lois~~
Loisible de se desister respectivement des d[ites]
au bout des six mois et meme ledit françois D[ominique]
au bout d'un mois quoy faisant icelles de[...]

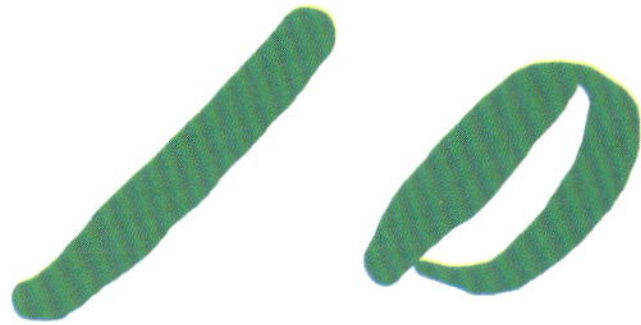

Mestre de luy mesme

François Mentor, Free Silversmith of Color in Colonial Canada

PHILIPPE L. B. HALBERT

In October 1773, British colonial officials in Montreal unveiled a slightly larger than life-sized marble bust of King George III on the Place d'Armes, the public square and parade ground in front of the church of Notre-Dame. Installed under a protective shelter, the royal likeness had been sent from London alongside two fire engines and £8,415 sterling to rebuild the town shortly after a disastrous fire in 1765. What had been intended as a philanthropic gesture and expression of benevolence toward the king's new francophone, largely Roman Catholic Canadian subjects quickly morphed into a political lightning rod. The month of May 1775 saw the monarch's white marble features smeared with black tar; one report described a rosary-like string of potatoes and a wooden cross bearing an anti-Catholic slogan hung around the neck. A radical contingent of disgruntled British and Anglo-American merchants was suspected of the vandalism, which foreshadowed the bust's decapitation during Montreal's occupation by the Continental Army in December of that year. Adding further insult to iconoclastic injury, the broken head was ultimately thrown down a well adjoining the square.[1]

A quarter-century earlier, and in a shop overlooking the same Place d'Armes, François Mentor (ca. 1723–73) began his career as Canada's earliest documented silversmith of color. Mentor did not live to witness the revolutionary desecration of George III's effigy. However, his story also stands to be reimagined as a bold fight for liberty and independence that transpired against an equally dramatic backdrop of art making, war for empire, and political upheaval. Mentor enters the historical stage not as a craftsman but as the enslaved property of Montreal merchant Dominique Nafréchoux (1681–1748). Putting pen to paper in September 1744, the Canadian-born Nafréchoux declared that on his death "my negro Jean Dominique François Mentor" be freed "in recompense for the good services that he has rendered me and for the devotion and loyalty that he has always shown in my service." He specified that Mentor "take with him all that he may require for his service. I leave him his own master [*mestre de luy mesme*], free to go with whomever he sees fit, continuing to live as an honorable man and taking care to pray to God for me."[2]

Canada's enslaved African population remained small under French and subsequent British rule. Colonial administrators first petitioned Versailles to transport African captives to the Saint Lawrence Valley in the late seventeenth century. "These types of negroes are adaptable to all sorts of work," wrote François Ruette d'Auteuil (ca. 1657–1737), attorney general of New France's Sovereign Council, in 1689, "and as their only cost is that of their purchase price, their clothing, and food, there is nothing to prevent one from doing great business with them."[3] Despite an ordinance from 1709 sanctioning slavery on Canadian soil and repeated requests for their importation by authorities, Africans were few and far between for the duration of the French regime.[4] The Swedish botanist Pehr Kalm, who took note of Pennsylvanians' preference for indentured servants and hired hands over enslaved laborers in 1748, observed that "to buy a Negroe or black slave, requires too much money at once."[5] He did not mention seeing any Africans when he visited Canada the following year, and although slavery would remain legal there until 1834, few Canadians possessed the means to effectively buy into the institution.

If the circumstances of Mentor's enslavement are not yet known, a majority of his peers lived and labored within the urban households of French colonial officials and civil servants, merchants, and more affluent tradespeople. Most were put to work as domestic servants, and boys and young men were particularly valued as valets and lackeys. A boy named Joseph-Marie (b. ca. 1721) may have served wealthy Québec (Quebec City) merchant and *seigneur*, or manorial lord, Joseph Fleury de La Gorgendière (1676–1755) in such a capacity before illness brought him to Québec's Hôtel-Dieu, established in 1637 and the first public hospital north of Mexico, in 1728; the then seven-year-old child was said to have been born and purchased in "Guinea."[6] If Mentor's birthplace is also a mystery, that he, too, was born in West Africa is not beyond the realm of possibility. He could just as easily have been born in Canada, and given the nature of French Atlantic trade and family networks, it is plausible that he made his way north via a Caribbean colony such as Guadeloupe, Martinique, or Saint-Domingue or even Louisiana.

Canadian laws governing the manumission of enslaved people were formalized in 1736 and mandated registry with the local court. As it was, Mentor became "master of himself" in 1748, setting his sights on a trade to support himself in newfound freedom.[7] An opportunity came in April 1749, when Mentor, then in his mid-twenties, apprenticed himself to the French immigrant silversmith Ignace-François Delezenne (1718–90). A native of Lille or its environs, Delezenne arrived in Montreal from Québec by 1743, whereupon he opened a shop on the Place d'Armes, producing everything from liturgical vessels to serving wares and dining equipage.[8] By the terms of their agreement, Mentor would receive room and board and 150 livres at the end of a six-year apprenticeship. The one-page contract, which Mentor signed as "François Dominicque," refers to him as "nègre de nation libre de sa personne," thereby reiterating both his race and status as a free man (fig. 10.1).[9] Delezenne returned to Québec in 1752, bringing Mentor downriver with him to the imperial capital. Four years later, he took his apprentice on as a *compagnon*, or journeyman. By the terms of this new agreement— which made no allusion to race or ethnicity— Mentor was to devote himself exclusively to working with silver and earn an annual wage of 200 livres for two consecutive years, with 300 if he chose to stay for a third.[10]

Mentor was neither alone in Delezenne's Québec shop nor the only individual of African birth or descent to labor under his direction. Delezenne, who also trained the prolific Canadian silversmith François Ranvoyzé (1739–1819), purchased a man named Pierre (b. ca. 1739) from Étienne Dassier (1711–after 1764), a sea captain from Bayonne; according to the bill of sale in 1757, Pierre was roughly eighteen years of age and identified as "nègre."[11] Delezenne's purchase of an enslaved bondsman mirrored his own rising success in the second half of the 1750s, and he bought a *seigneurie*, or manorial estate, outside of Québec in 1755. He soon entered the good graces of New France's notoriously corrupt intendant François Bigot (1703–78), who entrusted him with large-scale production of silver jewelry, including brooches, crosses, and other shimmering trinkets intended as trade items and diplomatic gifts for First Nations peoples. This lucrative enterprise was to occupy a great deal of Delezenne's time, although he continued to receive commissions from the Catholic church and aspiring laypeople before and after the British conquest of Canada.

Early Canadian silver by Delezenne is marked with variations of his initials *IF* over *D*, surmounted by an elaborate crown. The irregular arrangement of this mark, or *poinçon*, is comparable to that seen on contemporary Parisian silver. Delezenne appears to have changed his mark to the crowned letters *DZ* beginning around the year 1764. The linear *DZ* poinçon resembles simpler, more standardized British hallmarks, and Delezenne was possibly imitating newly arrived British silversmiths. Mentor himself may have been likewise influenced, and a silver incense boat and flared trifid spoon marked *FM* are the sole objects currently attributed to him (fig. 10.2). The *FM* mark and a small crown are prominently positioned atop the oblong incense boat's hinged lid, just below the buttonlike knop. These same elements appear on the underside of the spoon's flat-stemmed handle, which also features a reeded rattail on the reverse of the ovoid bowl. Each piece is engraved *HD* for the Hôtel-Dieu of Québec; they may have been supplied directly to the Augustinian canonesses who ran the institution until 1962 or offered as gifts by a faithful donor.[12] Incense boats held incense that was spooned over red-hot coals contained within censers, as in an ornately chased and pierced silver thurible made for the Hôtel-Dieu and triply marked *DZ* (fig. 10.3). Traditionally made from aromatic resins such as frankincense and myrrh that were sourced in East and sub-Saharan Africa, incense evolved into a potent symbol of Christian prayer and spirituality by the eleventh century. It was burned to both purify and sanctify sacred spaces such as the altar, and the

22 avril 1749 Engagement de frois Dominique avec le sr Delzene

n° 3978

Exped

Fut present francois Dominique dit mentor nègre de nation libre de
sa personne demeurant en cette ville lequel pour faire
son bien et avantage et se procurer les moyens de gagner sa
vie s'est volontairement obligé et alloüé de cejourdhuy
jusques et pour six années entieres consecutives finies et
accomplies avec sieur Ignace Delzene orphevre demeurant
en cette ditte ville sur la place darmes ace present et acceptant le
dit francois pour son apprenti et alloüé auquel durant le
dit temps il promet montrer et enseigner sa profession
d'orphevre et tout cedont il se mesle en jcelle sans luy en
rien cacher en outre le nourrir coucher chauffer blanchir
et entretenir de raccommoder de tous linges hardes et
chaussures a son etat suivant sa condition et le traitter
doucement et humainement comme il appartient,
promettant ledit francois Dominique apprendre de son mieux
qu'il luy sera possible tout cequi luy sera enseigné par
ledit sr Delzene luy obeir en tout cequ'il luy commandera
de licite et honneste le servir fidelement faire son profit
eviter son domage + et avertir s'il vient a sa connoissance ‡
et sans par le dit dominique
pouvoir s'absenter ni aller travailler ailleurs auquel
cas d'absence le dit ~~sieur malhiot promet et s'oblt~~
francois Dominique consent d'etre pris et apprehendé
au corps pour etre ramené chez ledit sieur Delzene
pour par ~~luy~~ ~~ces presentes~~ cequi manquera lors de l'
expirer des presentes qui seront faites moyennant la
somme de cent cinquante livres que ledit sr Delzene
promet et s'oblige de bailler et payer audit francois
Dominique a l'expiration desdites presentes et luy donnera ses
vieilles hardes servantes a lusage de luy dit francois
~~Dominique~~ ... & etant d'ailleurs expressement
convenu entre lesdites parties qu'il ~~sera loisible~~ leur sera
loisible de se desister respectivement desd presentes
au bout des six mois entiers ledit francois dominique
au bout d'un mois quoy faisant jcelles demeureront
nulles comme non faites ni avenues sans aucuns depens
domages et jnterests de part et d'autre car ainsy & promet &
oblige & renonce & fait et passé aud montreal Etude de
Danré l'un desd notaires le vingt deux avril de relevée mil
sept cens quarante neuf et ont lesd parties signé lecture faite faite
en la presence de sieur Jean francois malhiot son parrain lieutenant
particulier en ce siege. ‡ sans cependant que ledit sr delzene puisse
l'employer a d'autres choses qu'a celles auxquelles les apprentis sont
sujets. onze mots rayes nuls

Malhiot   francois Dominique

Delezenne   Adhemar   Danré de Blanzy

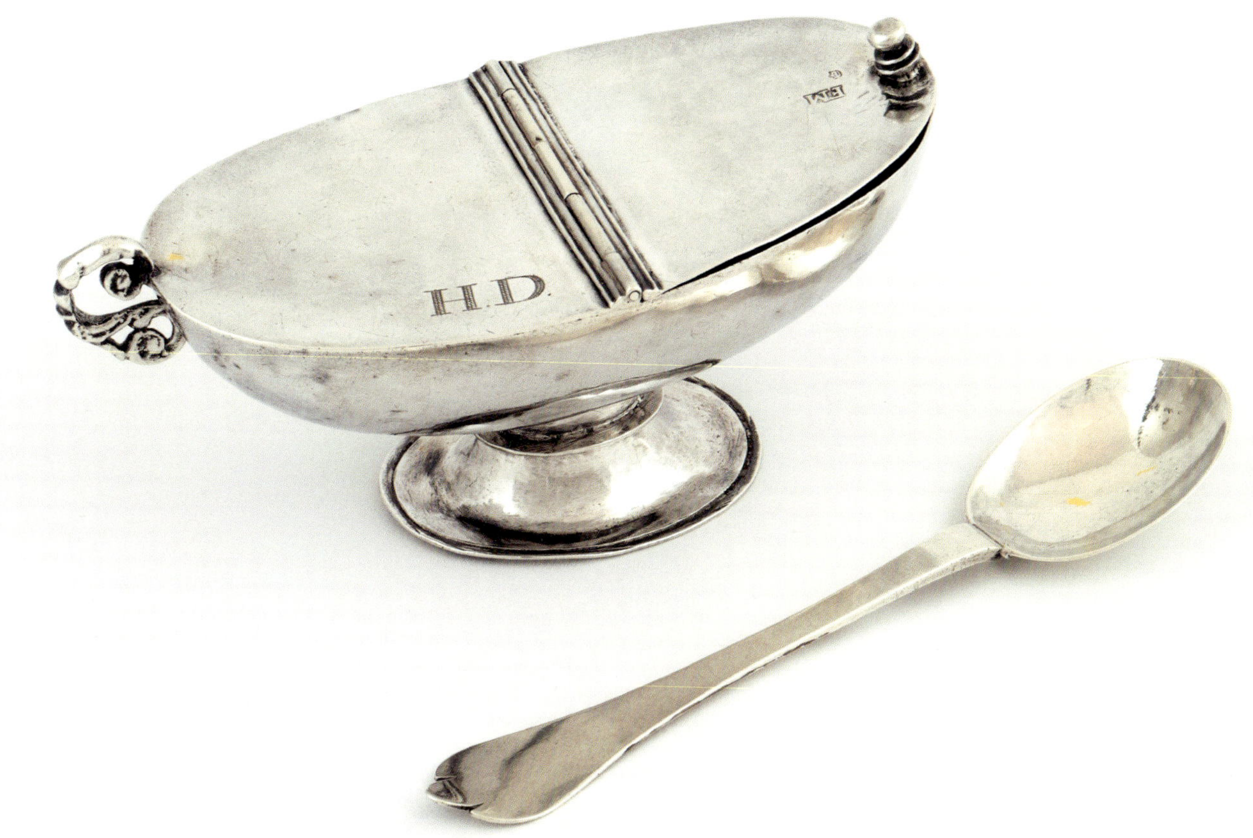

combined olfactory and visual qualities of holy smoke contributed to the ritual experience of the Mass.

Practical and elegant in its simplicity, the *FM* incense boat is equipped with a single auricular scroll handle that recalls the pair seen on a baroque-style presentation cup bearing a *DZ* mark.[13] On the one hand, this shared ornamental repertoire might be interpreted as Delezenne's influence on his apprentice-turned-journeyman. Just as intriguing to consider, however, is whether Mentor came to have a more direct hand in his master's larger artistic output. Such a tantalizing hypothesis is in keeping with typical patterns of production and divisions of labor whereby apprentices, journeymen, and others were called on to assist at various stages of creative and reparative processes.[14] The paper trail suggests that there was much work be done in the Delezenne shop. In November 1756, the parish priest of Saint-Antoine-de-Tilly, Jean-Baptiste Noël (1709–97), took legal action against the silversmith for failing to deliver a large personal order that comprised a pair of candlesticks, a candle snuffer and stand, six coffee spoons and a coffeepot, a tureen, and a pair of shoe buckles; Delezenne blamed his thirteen-month delay on Bigot's perpetual need for trade goods.[15] With his attention turned toward the scandalous intendant's demands as well as development of his seigneury, might he have at times relied on Mentor to manage other areas of his business?[16] The record is silent for now, but Mentor was

(opposite) FIGURE 10.1. *Apprenticeship Contract Signed by "François Domincque" and Ignace-François Delezenne, Montreal, April 22, 1749.* Bibliothèque et Archives nationales du Québec.

(above) FIGURE 10.2. *Incense Boat and Spoon,* by François Mentor, Québec, Canada, mid-eighteenth century. Silver. Le Monastère des Augustines, collection du Monastère de l'Hôtel-Dieu de Québec.

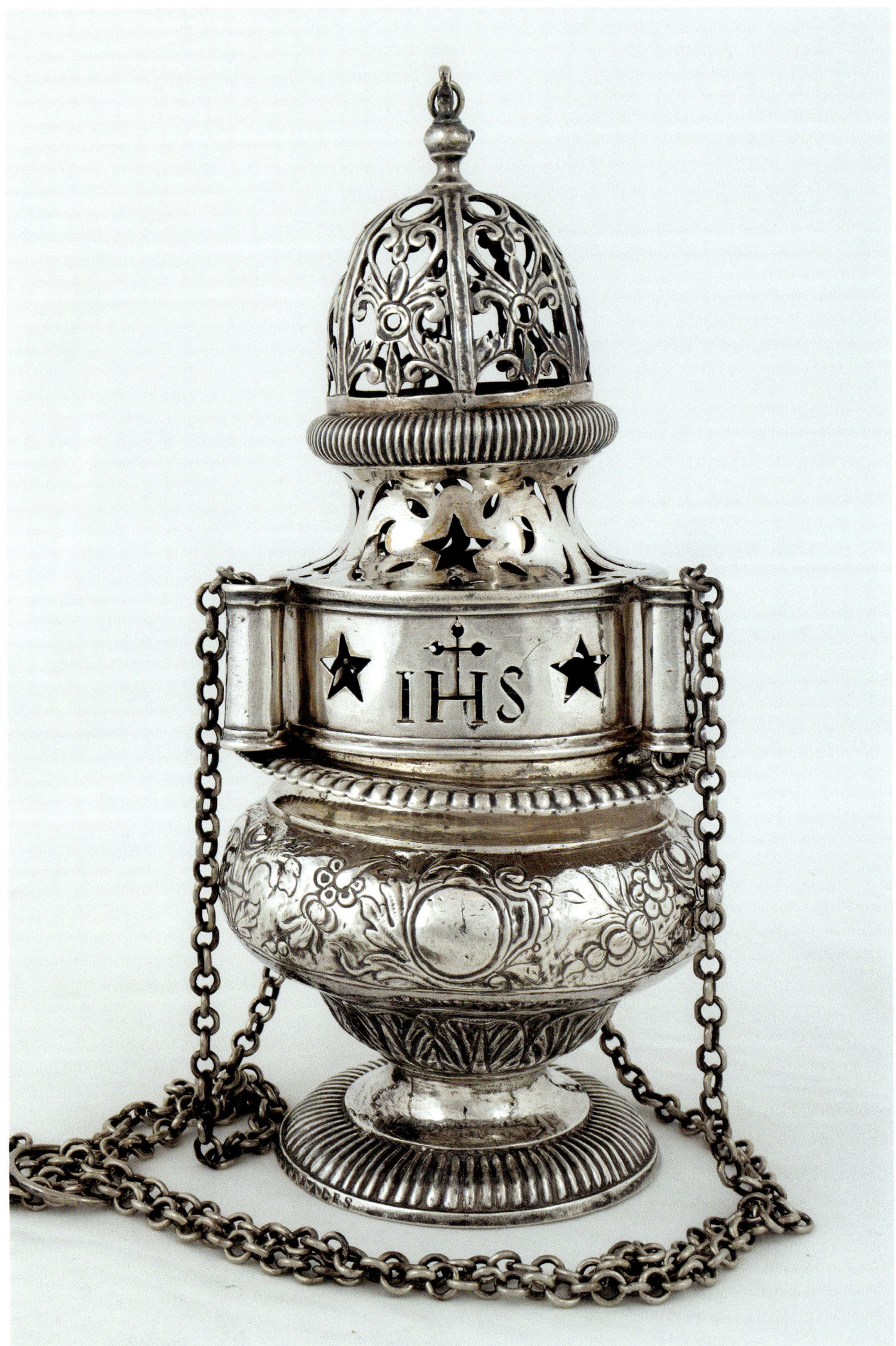
IHS

more than familiar with a variety of silver forms. Certainly, the skill and talent of a seasoned silversmith are apparent in the incense boat and spoon marked *FM*.

As indicated by his signed apprenticeship and journeyman contracts, Mentor was at least semiliterate and capable of writing his name. Taken as a whole, he was a valuable asset to the Delezenne shop in the period leading up to its destruction during the British bombardment of Québec in 1759. Having reached the end of his formal training at a decisive moment in the Seven Years' War, Mentor may have continued to seek employment in Québec, perhaps continuing to work for or in partnership with Delezenne and receiving commissions from the likes of the Hôtel-Dieu before returning to Montreal, where he drew his last breath on May 8, 1773. If virtually nothing has yet come to light regarding his professional activities at the onset of British rule, that Mentor was still identified by his trade ("orpheivre") as well as race ("Neigre") and approximate age at the time of his death is telling. For whatever reason, his burial record also alludes to his former enslavement by the long-dead Nafréchoux. Yet "Francois dit Mentor" had clearly put slavery behind him long before.[17] Notwithstanding archival lacunae and a dearth of surviving objects, Mentor's example underscores the potential of a more expansive, hemispheric approach to recovering traces of African and Afro-diasporic craftspeople across North America. Indeed, the cross-section of verbal and nonverbal evidence presented here transcends geography as well as language, constituting a surprising narrative of freedom that is no less compellingly reflected in silver.

FIGURE 10.3. *Thurible*, by Ignace-François Delezenne, Québec, Canada, ca. 1764–75. Silver. Le Monastère des Augustines, collection du Monastère de l'Hôtel-Dieu de Québec.

Notes

1. Now in the collection of the McCord-Stewart Museum, the bust was sculpted by Joseph Wilton (1722–1803) and accidentally rediscovered in 1834. See Joan Coutu, "Philanthropy and Propaganda: The Bust of George III in Montréal," *RACAR: Revue d'art canadienne / Canadian Art Review* 19, no. 1/2 (1992): 59–67. This iconoclasm anticipated the more famous destruction of an equestrian statute of the king on New York City's Bowling Green in 1776. See Wendy Bellion, *Iconoclasm in New York: Revolution to Reenactment* (University Park: Pennsylvania State University Press, 2019).

2. Emancipation deed, September 30, 1744, Greffe de Louis-Claude Danré de Blanzy, Bibliothèque et Archives nationales du Québec (hereafter BANQ), no. 2376. This and all other translations of original French-language texts are my own.

3. François Ruette d'Auteuil, *Mémoire*, April 1689, Archives nationales d'Outre-mer, C11A 10, fol. 344–45v. Of the roughly 4,200 enslaved people known to have lived in the Saint Lawrence Valley between 1671 and 1834, two-thirds were Indigenous; 1,443 people of African birth or descent make up an approximate third, most of whom cannot be documented before 1770. See Marcel Trudel, *L'esclavage au Canada français: Histoire et conditions de l'esclavage* (Quebec: Presses Universitaires Laval, 1960); and Marcel Trudel, *Dictionnaire des esclaves et de leurs propriétaires au Canada français* (Montreal: Hurtubise, 1990). See also Daniel Gay, *Les noirs du Québec, 1629–1900* (Quebec: Septentrion, 2004); Frank Mackey, *Done with Slavery: The Black Fact in Montreal, 1760–1840* (Montreal: McGill-Queen's University Press, 2010); Brett Rushforth, *Bonds of Alliance: Indigenous and Atlantic Slaveries in New France* (Chapel Hill: University of North Carolina Press, 2012); and Charmaine A. Nelson, *Slavery, Geography and Empire in Nineteenth-Century Marine Landscapes of Montreal and Jamaica* (London: Routledge, 2016).

4. Jacques Raudot, *Ordonnance*, April 13, 1709, Archives nationales d'Outre-mer, C11A 30, fol. 334–35. This law also threatened a fine of fifty livres for aiding and abetting runaway or fugitive slaves.

5. Pehr Kalm, *Travels into North America*, vol. 1, trans. John Reinhold Forster (London: T. Lowndes, 1771), 389.

6. Joseph-Marie's hospitalization is documented in Trudel, *Dictionnaire des esclaves*, 328. By the end of his life, Fleury's enslaved property included twelve Africans and five Native Americans. Brian Young counted sixty slaves owned by four generations of the Fleury family; ranging in age, forty-five were identified as "negro" or "mulatto." See Brian Young, *Patrician Families and the Making of Quebec: The Taschereaus and McCords* (Montreal: McGill-Queen's University Press, 2014), 38–39.

7. See *Ordonnance*, September 1, 1736, BANQ, E1, S1, P2855, fol.

99. Mentor's emancipation deed of 1744 was signed by Jacques-Joseph Guiton de Monrepos (1708–89), lieutenant general for civil and criminal affairs in Montreal.

8. On Delezenne and silversmithing in French colonial Canada more generally, see Jean Trudel, *L'orfèvrerie en Nouvelle-France / Silver in New France* (Ottawa: National Gallery of Canada, 1974); Robert Derome, *Les orfèvres de Nouvelle-France: Inventaire descriptif des sources* (Ottawa: National Gallery of Canada, 1974); Robert Derome, "Delezenne, le maître de Ranvoyzé / Delezenne, Ranvoyzé's Master," *Vie des arts* 2, no. 83 (1976): 56–58, 94–95; Robert Derome, "Delezenne, Ignace-François," in *Dictionnaire biographique du Canada*, vol. 4: *1771–1800* (Quebec: Presses de l'Université Laval, 1980), 220–24; and Laurier Lacroix, ed., *Les arts en Nouvelle-France* (Québec: Publications du Québec, 2012), 177–91.

9. Apprenticeship contract, April 22, 1749, Greffe de Louis-Claude Danré de Blanzy, BANQ, no. 3978.

10. Journeyman contract, July 23, 1756, Greffe de Jean-Baptiste Decharnay, BANQ, no. 95. In this document, the journeyman signed his name simply as "Mentor."

11. Pierre had cost Delezenne 1,192 livres, a sizable sum, although slightly less than what he had paid for a large amount of silver specie in 1748. Weighing 27 marcs, 2 onces, and valued at 1,553 livres, 5 sols, the coins were purchased from the estate of Montreal merchant Pierre Guy (1701–48). Cited in Derome, *Inventaire descriptif*, 46.

12. The incense boat and its then-unidentified mark were first published in Ramsay Traquair, *The Old Silver of Quebec* (Toronto: Macmillan of Canada, 1940), 62, 146, pl. 5. See also Derome, *Inventaire descriptif*, 130–32.

13. Associated with the Canadian noble Tarieu de Lanaudière family, the cup belongs to the Musée national des beaux-arts du Québec.

14. See Francis Puig and Michael Conforti, eds., *The American Craftsman and the European Tradition, 1620–1820* (Minneapolis, MN: Minneapolis Institute of Arts, 1989); and Maarten Prak and Patrick Wallis, eds., *Apprenticeship in Early Modern Europe* (Cambridge: Cambridge University Press, 2020).

15. Noël versus Delezenne, November 23, 1756, Fonds Prévôté de Québec, BANQ, fol. 37v–38.

16. A similar situation may have occurred in colonial South Carolina, where circumstantial evidence points to Charleston silversmith Alexander Petrie (ca. 1707–68) leaving some if not all business operations in the hands of the enslaved Abraham in 1765. The fact that rival Charleston silversmiths competed against one another over Abraham's purchase in 1768 implies that much of his value lay in skills that he undoubtedly learned from Petrie and continued to hone over time. See Culp, "Mr. Petrie's 'Shop on the Bay,'" 250–55. For additional treatment of enslaved labor in relation to early American trades and workshops, see Glenn Adamson, *Craft: An American History* (London: Bloomsbury, 2021).

17. Burial record, May 10, 1773, Registre des baptêmes, mariages et sépultures, Hôpital général de Montréal, BANQ, fol. 149. The use of *dit* (literally "called" or "said to be") before Mentor suggests that the origin of the surname originated with the deceased himself. Often functioning as a kind of alternate surname or nickname, dit names were widespread in early modern France and New France. They often referred to an individual's profession, a personal attribute, or some other distinctive characteristic.

Exhibition Catalog of Objects

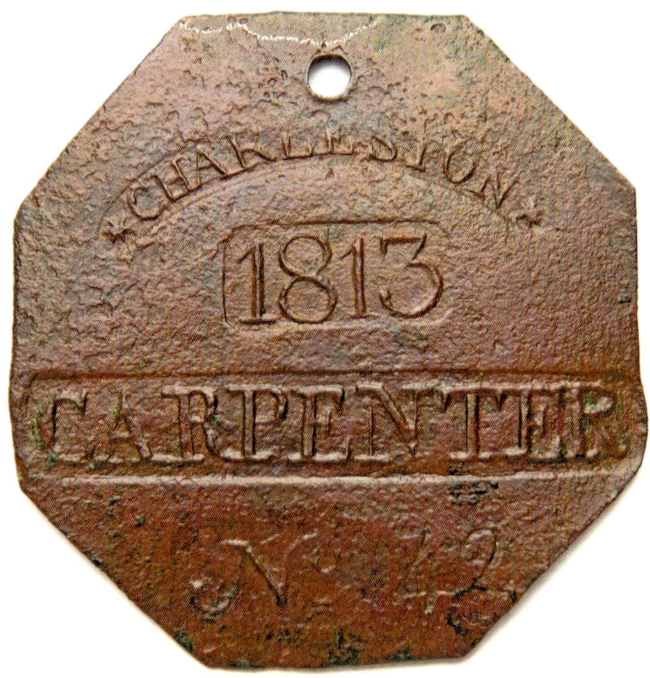

FIGURE 1
Shop of John Joseph Lafar
Slave Badge, 1813, Charleston, South Carolina
Copper
Loan courtesy of The Charleston Museum, Charleston, South Carolina, MG 175

In 1764, the Charleston city council passed a law requiring hired-out enslaved people to wear a badge identifying their trade, skill, identification number, and year. Composed of copper, the geometric tags were either pinned to clothing or worn around the neck. This yearly process of hiring out enslaved skilled labor offers a dimensional glimpse into the economic realm of the institution of enslavement. Not only did hired-out enslaved people wear these badges, but in certain cases, they were also forced to use their skills to make these badges. To create an object directly supporting your bondage cements the sinister nature of the institution of slavery.

(opposite) FIGURE 2
John Hoban
Monthly Payroll for Laborers at the President's House, December 1794, Washington, DC
Facsimile
Records of the Commissioners of the City of Washington, Record Group 217, National Archives, Washington, DC

The hallmark of performed skilled labor for service, this monthly payroll identifies the Black craftspeople who participated in building the White House. In 1791, Pierre L'Enfant leased enslaved skilled laborers listed as "Negro Hire" to clear the land for the erection of the White House and Capitol buildings. From 1795 to 1800, the record lists 122 enslaved workers who received pay for their skill. Initially, Washington city commissioners envisioned hiring white American and European laborers to build both structures. When the commissioners' attempt proved unsuccessful, enslaved skilled labor filled the void. Enslaved workers hauled materials, sawed lumber, and participated in bricklaying, carpentry, and stone cutting. Although little is known of the enslaved craftspeople's experiences, what does survive are their names and their contribution to the building of democracy in the nation's capital.

Time Role for December		1794	Monday 1	Tuesday 2	Wednesday 3	Thursday 4	Friday 5	Saturday 6	Monday 8	Tuesday 9	Wednesday 10	Thursday 11	Friday 12	Saturday 13	Monday 15	Tuesday 16	Wednesday 17	Thursday 18	Friday 19	Saturday 20	Monday 22	Tuesday 23	Wednesday 24	Thursday 25	Friday 26	Saturday 27	Monday 29	Tuesday 30	Wednesday 31	
Bennett Mudd Overseer	27	90/	1	1	1	1	1	1	1	1	1	1	1	1	1	1	1	1	1	1	1	1	1	1	1	1	1	1	1	27
Thos Smith Cook	27	52/6	1	1	1	1	1	1	1	1	1	1	1	1	1	1	1	1	1	1	1	1	1	1	1	1	1	1	1	27
John D Doran M scow	29	60/	1	1	1	1	11	1	1	1	1	1	1	11	1	1	1	1	1	11	1	1	11	a	a	a	1	1	1	29
Wm Bateman M scow	24	Do	1	1	1	1	1	1	1	1	1	1	1	1	1	1	1	1	1	1	1	1	1	a	a	a	1	1	1	24
John Bradman Do	22	Do	1	1	1	1	a	1	1	1	1	1	1	1	1	1	1	1	1	1	1	1	1	a	a	a	s	1	1	22
John Doran Labn	23	45/	1	1	1	1	1	1	1	1	1	1	1	1	1	1	1	1	1	1	1	1	a	a	a	a	1	1	1	23
Francis Smith Do	32	Do	1	1	1	11	1	1	1	1	1	1	1	11	1	1	1	1	1	11	1	1	1	a	1	11	1	1	1	32
Enoch Bryon Do	24	Do	1	1	1	1	1	1	1	1	1	1	1	1	1	1	1	1	1	1	1	1	1	a	1	1	s	1	s	24
Michl Crain Do	24	Do	1	1	1	1	1	1	1	1	1	1	1	1	1	1	1	1	1	1	1	1	a	a	1	a	1	1	1	24
Richard Hazel Do	23	Do	1	1	1	1	1	1	a	a	a	1	1	1	1	1	1	1	1	1	1	1	a	a	a	1	1	1	1	23
Henry Bateman Do	25	Do	1	1	1	1	1	s	1	s	1	1	1	1	1	1	1	1	1	1	1	1	a	a	a	a	1	1	1	25
Geo Love Do	20	Do	1	1	1	1	a	s	1	1	1	1	1	1	1	1	1	1	1	1	1	a	a	a	a	a	1	1	1	20
Joseph Rock Do	23	Do	1	1	1	1	a	1	1	1	1	1	1	1	1	1	1	1	1	1	1	1	a	a	a	a	1	1	1	23
Albin Fenewick Do	23	Do	1	1	1	1	1	1	1	1	1	1	1	1	1	1	1	1	1	1	1	1	a	a	a	a	1	1	1	23
John Leatch Do	12	Do	a	a	a	a	a	a	a	a	a	a	a	a	1	1	1	1	1	1	1	1	a	a	a	a	1	1	1	12
Wm Long with Mr Fenewick	21	60/	1	1	1	1	a	1	a	1	a	1	1	1	1	1	1	1	1	1	1	1	a	a	a	a	1	1	1	21
Richd Bannister Labr	13	45/	a	a	a	a	a	1	1	a	a	a	a	1	1	1	1	1	1	1	1	a	a	a	a	1	1	1	1	13
James Crook with the Serveyor	12	60/										Com		1	1	1	1	1	1	1	1	a	a	a	a	1	1	1	1	12
N Newton Wm D Meall			1	1	1	1	1	1	1	1	1	1	1	1	1	1	1	1	1	1	s	1	a	a	a	a	s	1	1	
N Davy Do			1	1	1	1	1	1	1	1	1	1	1	1	1	1	1	1	1	s	s	s	s	a	a	1	1	1	1	
N Jim Allen [illegible]			1	1	1	1	1	1	1	s	1	1	[illegible]	[illegible]	[illegible]	[illegible]	[illegible]	1	1	1	a	a	a	a	a	a	a	1	1	
N Dick Do			1	1	1	1	s	s	1	1	1	1	1	1	1	1	1	1	1	1	a	a	a	a	a	a	a	a	1	
N Richard Do			1	1	1	1	s	s	1	1	1	1	1	1	1	1	1	1	1	1	1	a	a	a	a	a	a	a	1	
N [illegible]			1	1	1	1	1	1	1	1	1	1	1	1	1	1	1	1	1	1	a	a	a	a	a	a	a	a	1	
N Charles John Cleare			1	1	1	1	1	1	1	1	1	a	a	a	a	a	a	a	a	a	a	a	a	a	a	a	1	1	1	
N Stephen Do			1	1	1	1	1	1	1	1	1	a	a	a	a	a	a	a	a	a	a	a	a	a	a	a	a	a	a	
N Charles Igns Boon			a	1	1	1	1	1	1	1	1	1	1	1	1	1	1	1	1	1	a	a	a	a	a	a	a	a	a	
N Jacob Do			1	1	1	1	1	1	1	1	1	1	1	1	1	1	1	1	1	1	1	a	a	a	a	a	a	a	a	
N Moses Do			1	1	1	1	1	1	1	1	1	1	s	s	1	1	1	1	1	a	a	a	a	a	a	a	a	a	a	
N Moses Edwd Plowden			1	1	1	1	1	1	1	1	s	s	1	1	1	1	1	1	1	a	1	a	a	a	a	a	a	a	a	
N Len Do			1	1	1	1	1	1	1	1	s	s	1	1	1	1	1	1	1	1	a	a	a	a	a	a	a	a	a	
N Jim Do			1	1	1	1	1	1	1	1	1	1	1	1	1	1	1	a	1	a	a	a	a	a	a	a	a	a	a	
N Arnold Do			1	1	1	1	1	1	1	1	1	1	1	1	1	1	1	1	1	1	1	1	1	a	a	a	1	1	1	
N Gin Do ⊗																														
N Anthony Joseph Queen			1	1	1	1	1	1	1	1	1	1	1	1	1	1	1	1	1	1	a	a	a	a	a	a	a	a	a	
N Jack Miss A Diggs			1	1	1	1	1	1	1	1	1	1	1	1	1	1	1	1	1	1	a	a	a	a	a	a	a	a	a	
N Jacob Geo Fenewick			s	1	s	s	1	1	a	a	a	a	a	a	s	a	a	a	a	a	a	a	a	a	a	a	1	1	1	
N Jack Middleton Belt Monthly			1	1	s	1	s	s	1	1	a	a	a	a	a	a	a	a	a	a	a	a	a	a	1	1	a	1	a	
N Gusp Barnard O Neall			a	1	1	1	1	1	1	a	a	a	a	a	a	a	a	a	a	1	a	a	a	a	a	1	1	1	1	
N Harry Do		Do	1	1	1	1	1	1	1	1	1	1	1	1	1	1	1	a	1	1	a	a	a	a	a	a	1	a	1	
N Geo Mr Clegett		Do	a	1	1	1	1	1	1	1	1	1	1	1	1	1	1	1	1	1	a	a	a	a	a	a	a	a	a	
N Dick Capt. H Boucher		Do 30/	1	1	1	1	1	1	1	1	1	1	1	1	a	a	a	a	a	a	a	a	a	a	a	a	a	a	a	
N Bob Gustavous Scott			1	1	s	s	1	1	1	1	1	1	1	1	1	1	a	a	a	1	a	a	a	a	a	a	a	a	a	
N Kitt Do			a	s	a	s	s	s	s	s	s	1	1	1	1	1	a	a	a	a	a	a	a	a	a	a	a	a	a	
N Bob Barnard O'Neall Monthly			a	s	a	a	a	a	1	1	1	1	a	a	a	a	a	a	a	a	a	a	a	a	a	a	a	a	a	

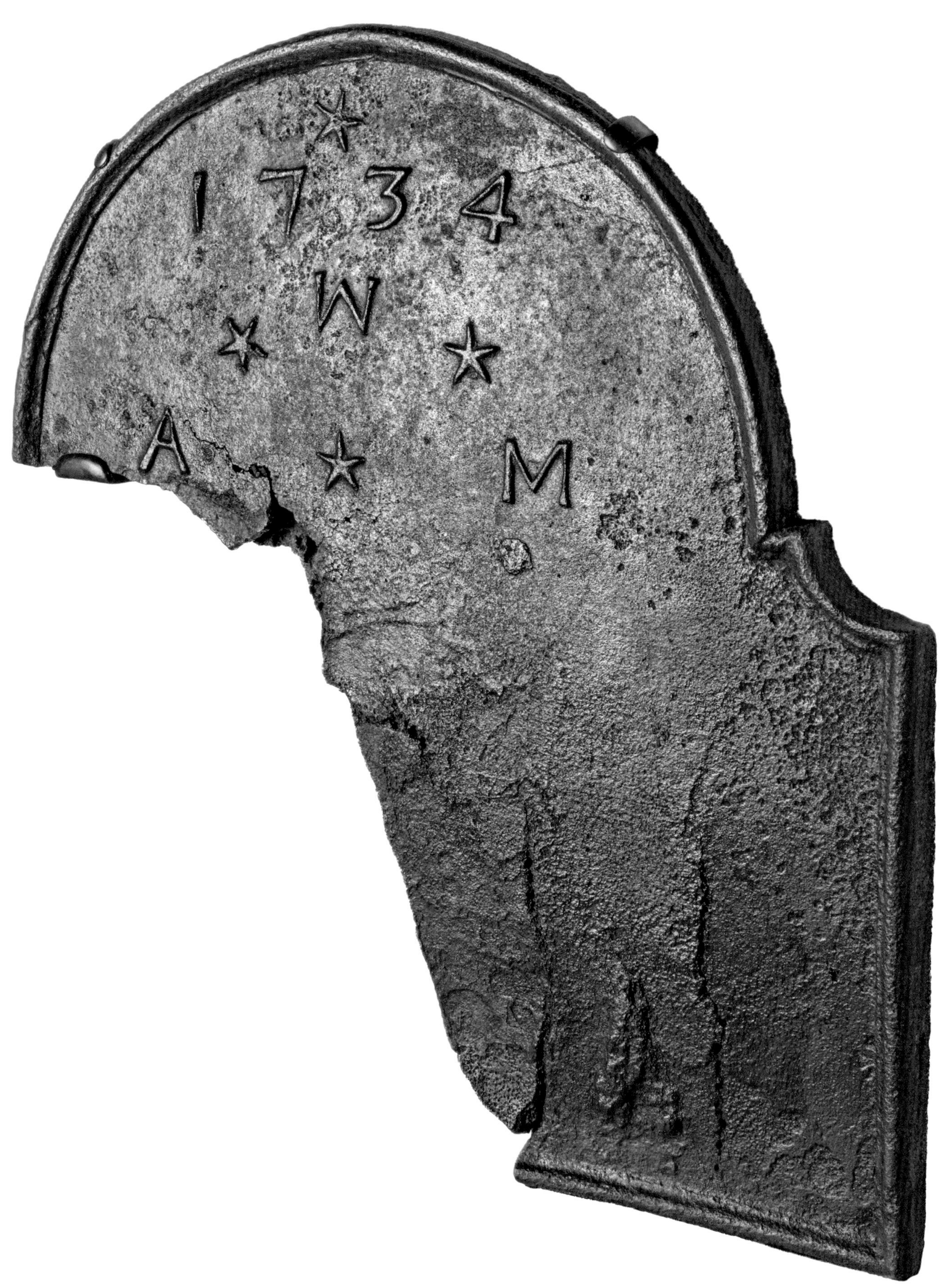
1734
W
A
M

(*opposite*) FIGURE 3
Unidentified craftspeople
Fireback, 1734, Accokeek Iron Furnace, Stafford County, Virginia
Iron
DAR Museum Collection. Gift of the Kate Waller Barrett Chapter, National Society Daughters of the American Revolution, 5286

I have seen tradesmen go throughout the city followed by a negro carrying their tools—Barbers who are supported in idleness & ease by their negroes who do the business.
—TIMOTHY FORD, DIARY, 1785

This fireback once resided at Mount Vernon and was created at Augustine Washington's Accokeek Iron Furnace. While this object is decorative in design, a fireback's creation opens a deeper discussion into the work at an iron furnace plantation, one of the most dangerous occupations for enslaved craftspeople. Enslaved people faced the dangers of potential furnace explosions if not carefully managed, sometimes resulting in death. It took a variety of enslaved craftspeople, including woodcutters and teamsters, to produce iron ore. Although roles such as ironmasters, clerks, and founders were generally reserved for white men, without the knowledge of enslaved iron furnace workers, the foundry could not function. To create objects such as this fireback, enslaved craftspeople were permitted to travel farther from their worksite or living quarters to create the goods for which they were hired. In some cases, skilled enslaved laborers were allowed to hire themselves out and earn income that could be used to self-emancipate or purchase goods to help ease their enslavement.

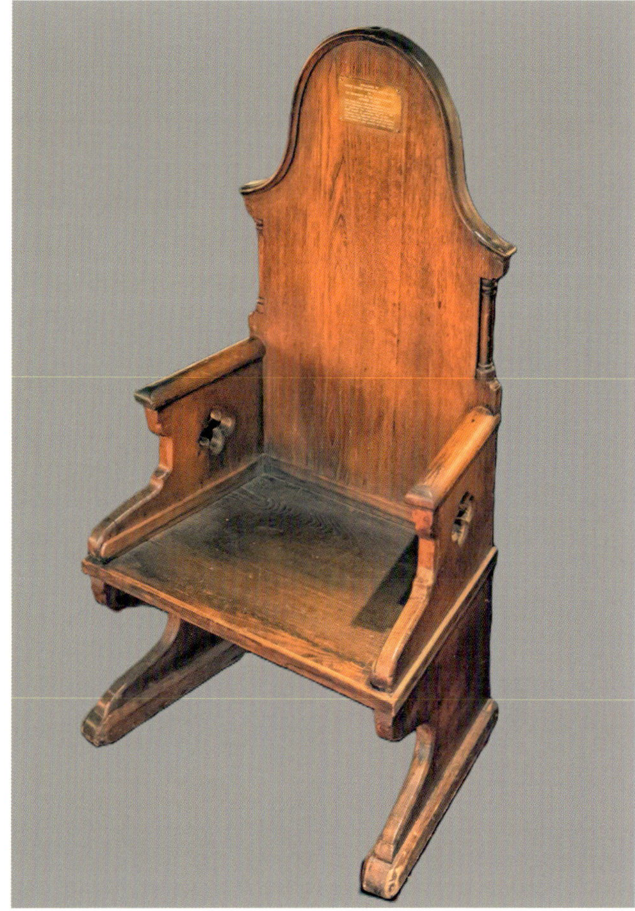

FIGURE 4
Altimore and Taylor McKeethen
Ceremonial Chair, 1841–64, Louisiana
Cypress
Loan courtesy of the University of the South, Sewanee, Tennessee

Made of Louisiana cypress wood, this chair is a piece of Leighton Place Plantation, home of Leonidas Polk, Episcopal bishop of Louisiana and the founder of the University of the South (Sewanee). Enslaved carpenters, father and son Altimore and Taylor McKeethen likely constructed this chair between 1841 and 1864. This chair not only symbolizes the connections between slavery in Louisiana and the Episcopal church, it also signifies the relationship between slavery and higher education. The wealth and stability of the University of the South rested on the backs of an estimated 40,000 enslaved people enslaved by the first 295 donors of the university. Their labor ensured that the university would be successful as it sought to educate white men of the South. After emancipation, Altimore and Taylor McKeethen continued to work as carpenters in New Orleans. Owing to Polk's founding of the university, this chair became an essential part of university ceremonies until recent years.

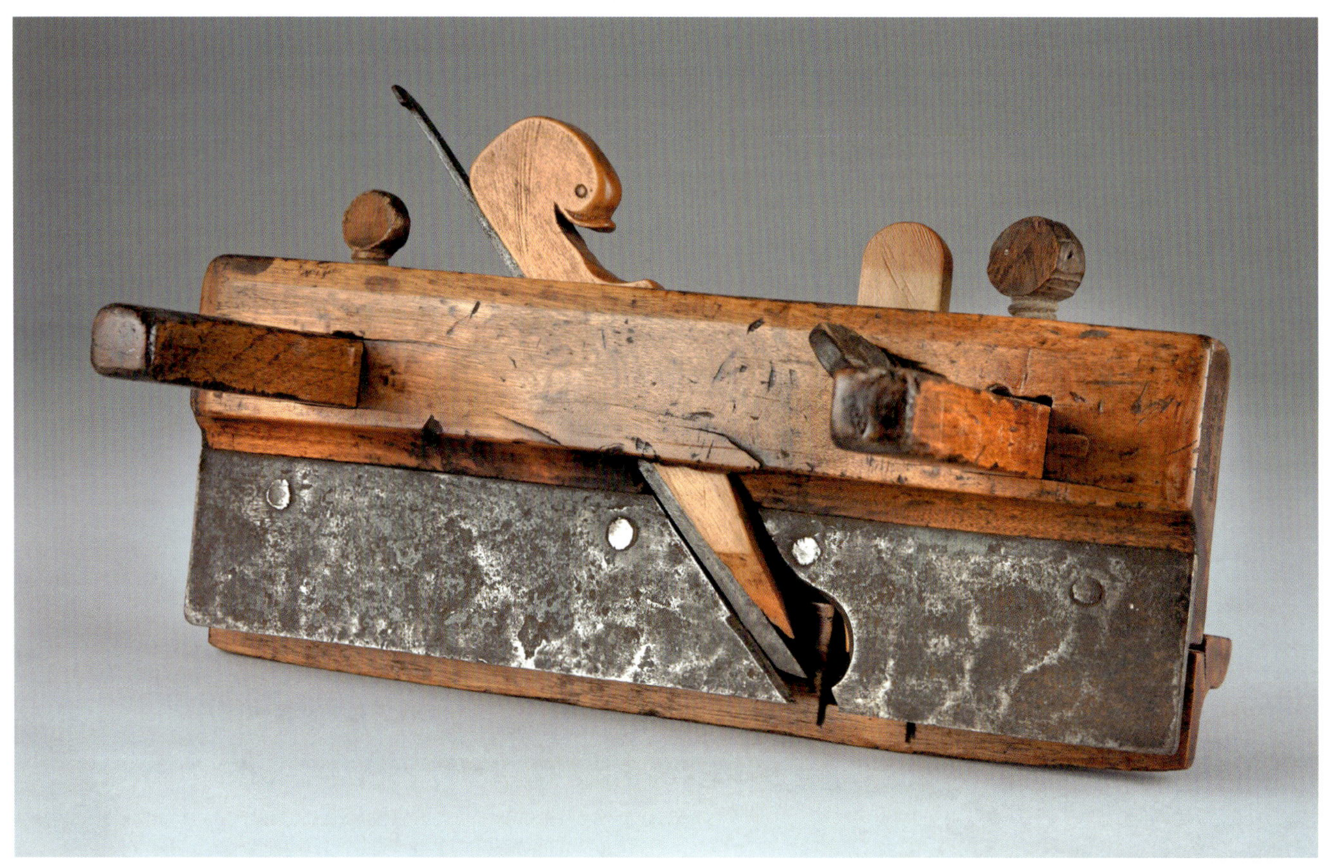

FIGURE 5
Cesar Chelor
Plow Plane, Yankee (NC-727), ca. 1753–84,
Wrentham, Massachusetts
Wood, iron, and steel
Loan courtesy of The Colonial Williamsburg Foundation,
bequest of David V. Englund, 2016-343

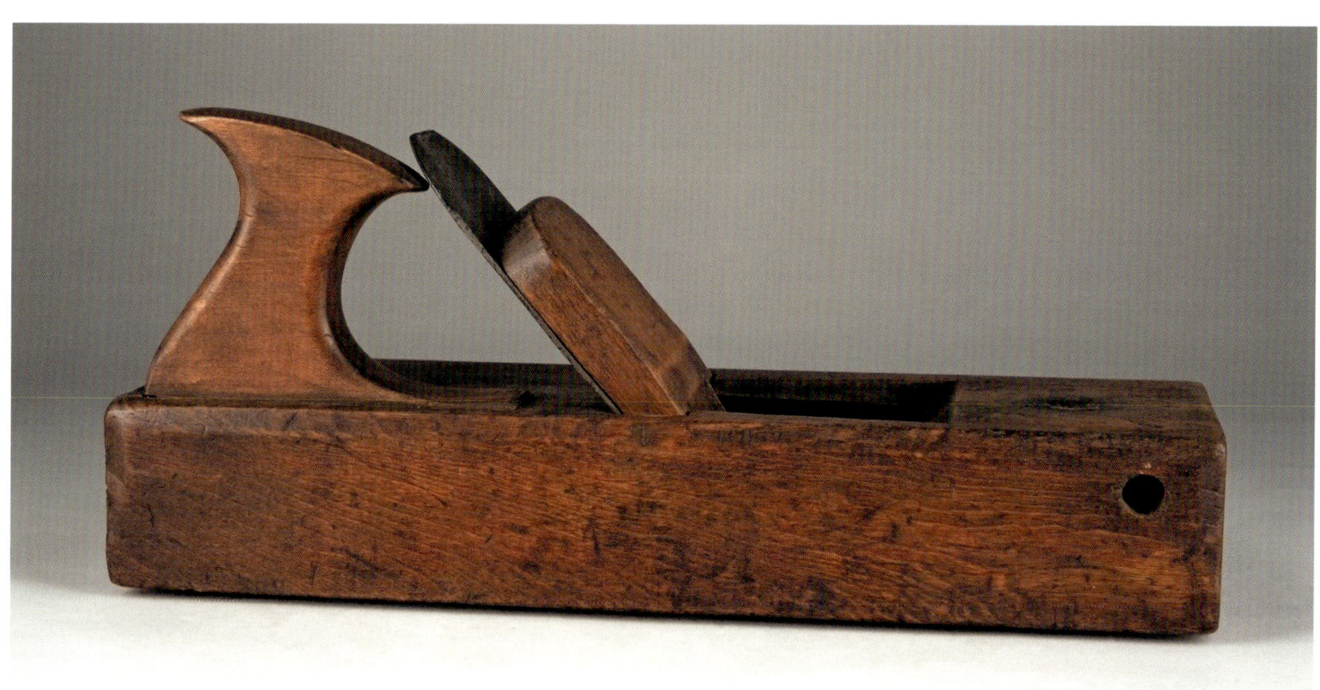

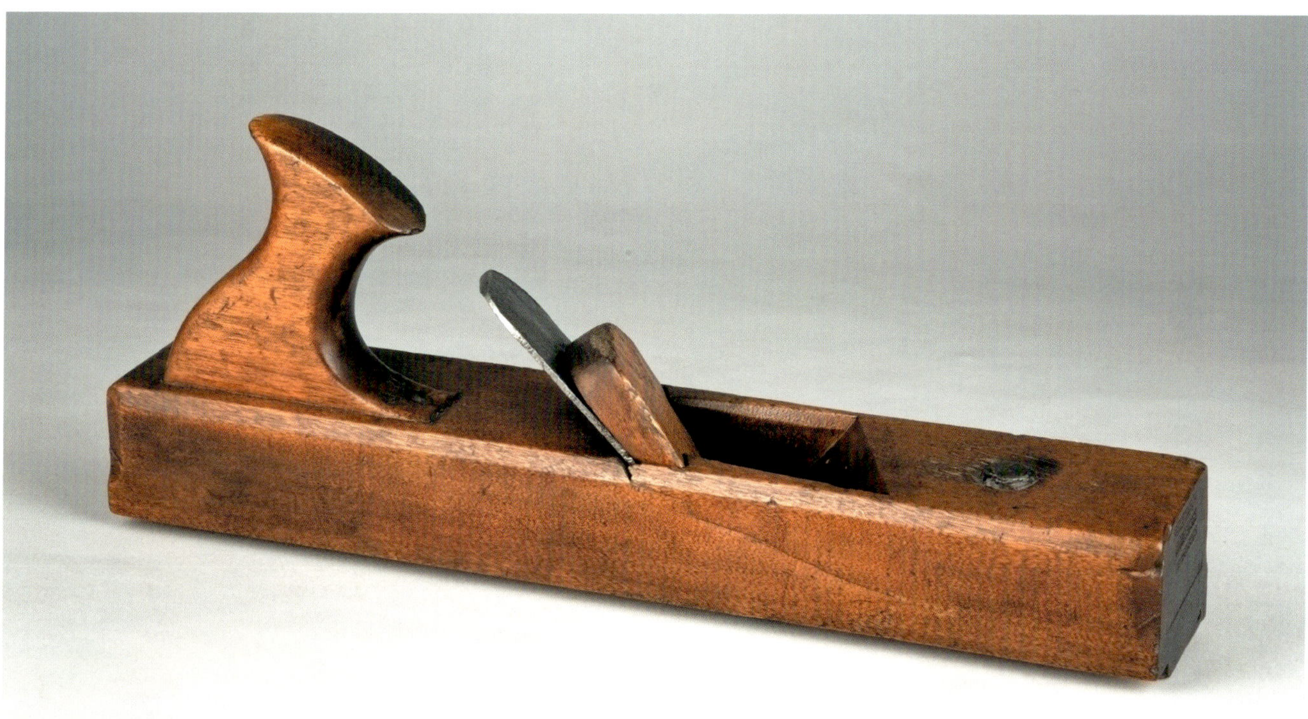

(top) FIGURE 6
Cesar Chelor
Cornice Plane, Ovolo/Ogee, ca. 1753–84,
Wrentham, Massachusetts
Wood, iron, and steel
Loan courtesy of The Colonial Williamsburg Foundation,
bequest of David V. Englund, 2016-347

(bottom) FIGURE 7
Cesar Chelor
Panel Raising Plane, ca. 1753–84,
Wrentham, Massachusetts
Wood, iron, and steel
Loan courtesy of The Colonial Williamsburg Foundation,
bequest of David V. Englund, 2016-351

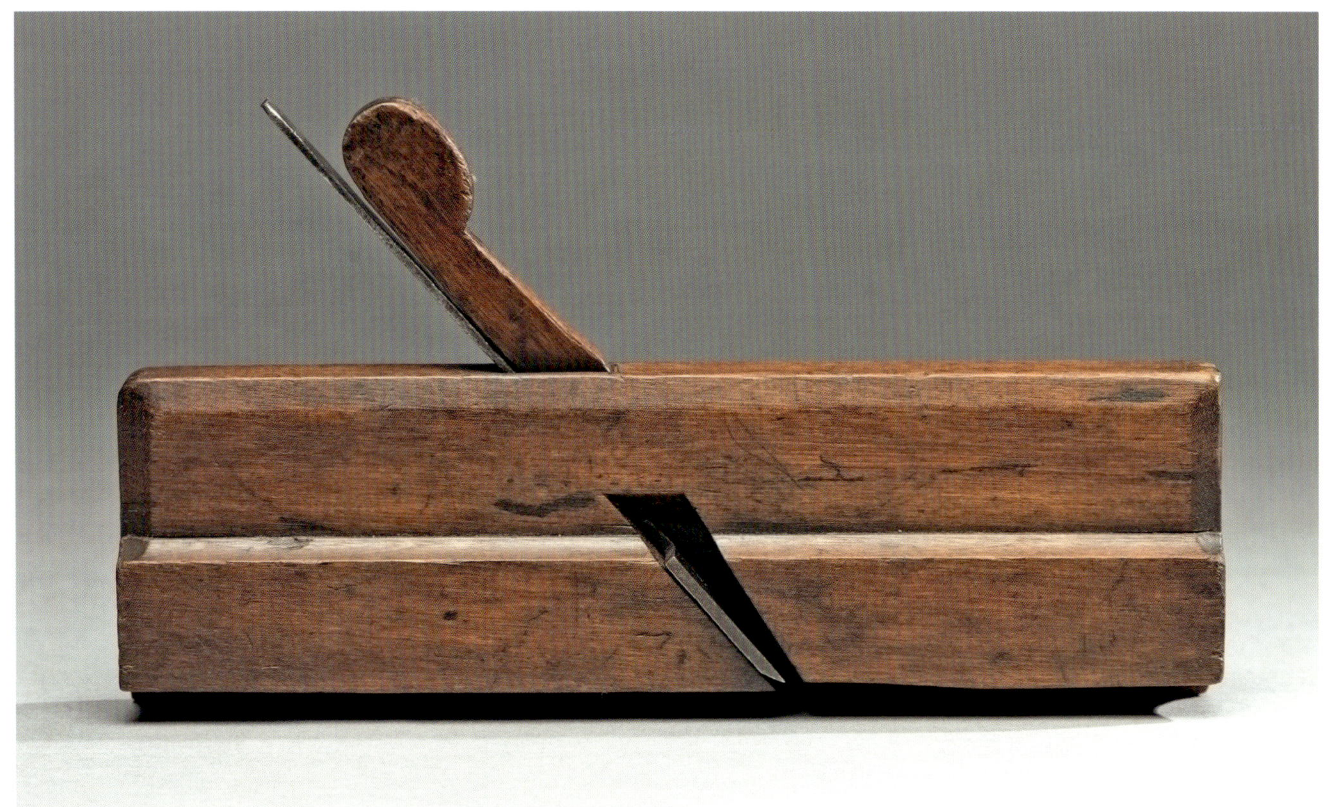

FIGURE 8
Cesar Chelor
Molding Plane (NC-853), ca. 1753–84, Wrentham, Massachusetts
Wood, iron, and steel
Loan courtesy of The Colonial Williamsburg Foundation, bequest of David V. Englund, 2016-392

Figures 5–8. Eighteenth-century carpenters built homes and furnishings using a variety of tools and knowledge. Their training prepared them to create using their hands and, at times, custom tools. Cesar Chelor, enslaved by Wrentham, Massachusetts, toolmaker Francis Nicholson, made wood planes by trade. When Nicholson died in 1752, Chelor was freed and continued to make and sell planes in Wrentham. Initially, Nicholson's name was marked on the wood planes as the creator, but when Chelor gained independence his name could be found on the planes he created. Throughout his lifetime, Chelor created thousands of wood planes used by Black and white hands in the forging of a new style of architectural and decorative arts used across New England.

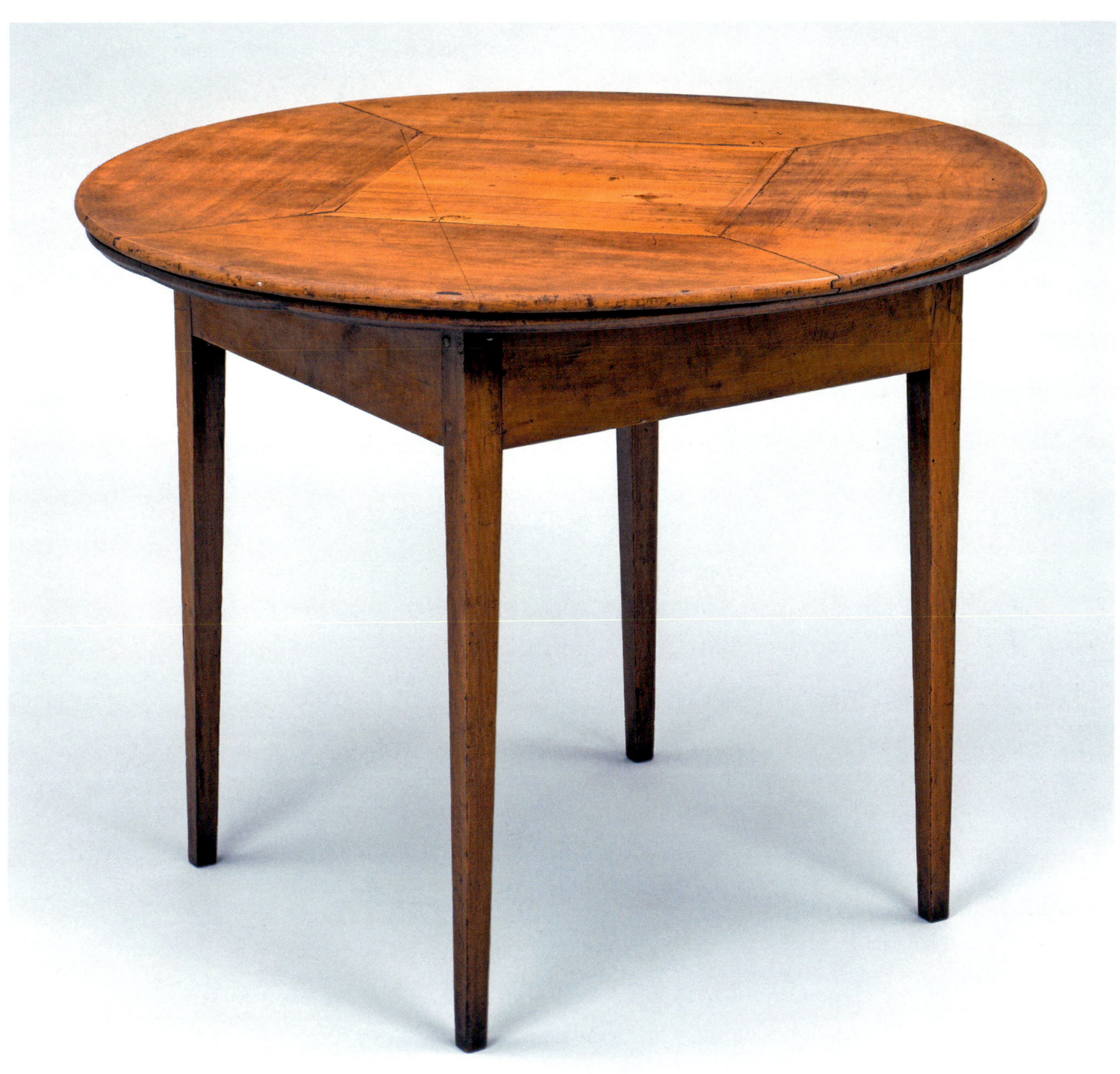

FIGURE 9
John Hemmings
Revolving Table, 1811, Monticello, Charlottesville, Virginia
Cherry, yellow poplar, walnut, southern pine, and brass
Loan courtesy of the Thomas Jefferson's Monticello Foundation, Thomas Jefferson Foundation Purchase, 1976-34

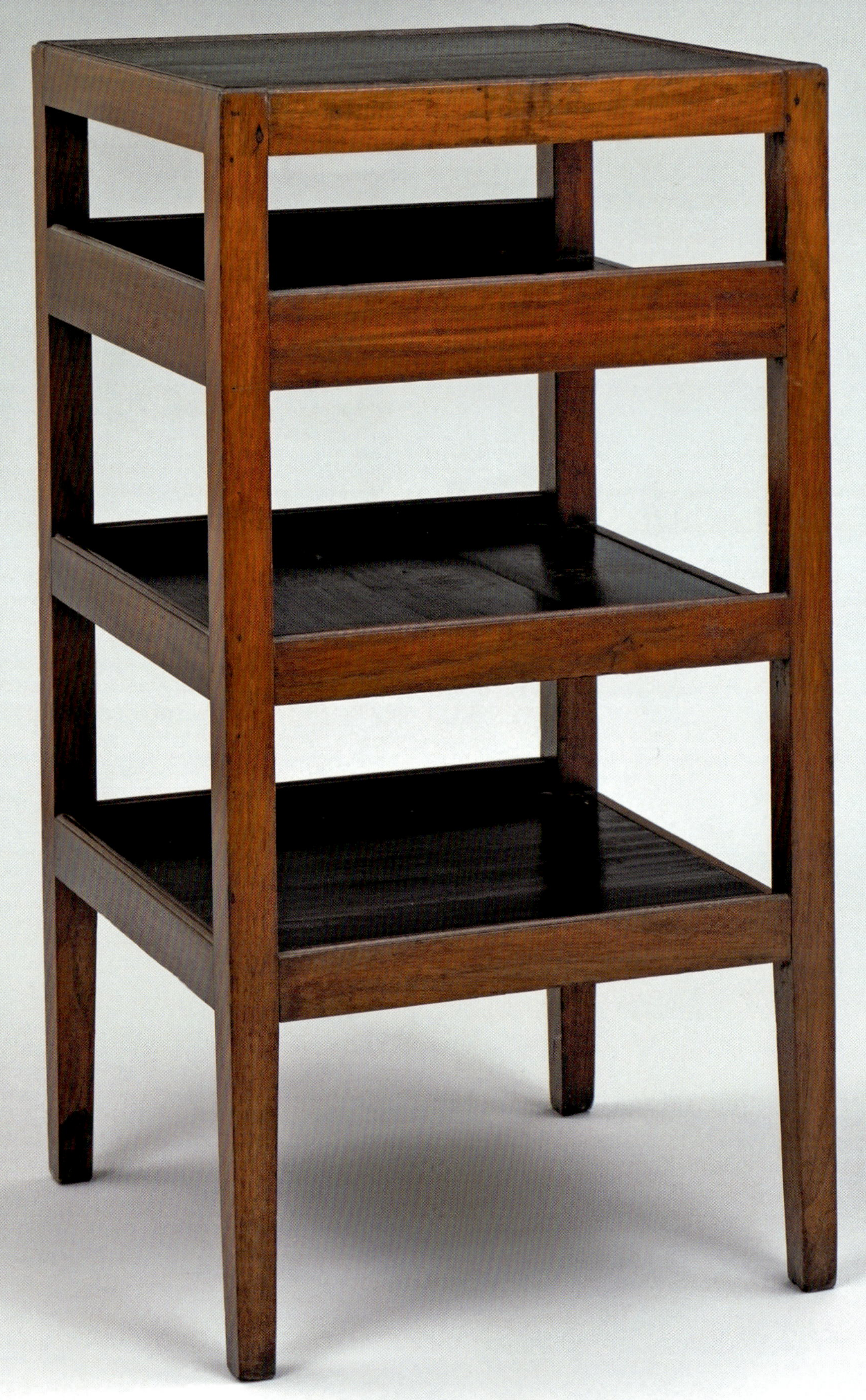

FIGURE 10
John Hemmings
Dumb Waiter, ca. 1815, Monticello, Charlottesville, Virginia
Walnut and pine
Loan courtesy of the Thomas Jefferson's
Monticello Foundation, Thomas Jefferson
Foundation Purchase, 1975-45

[King George III] has waged cruel war against human nature itself, violating it's most sacred rights of life & liberty in the persons of a distant people who never offended him, captivating & carrying them into slavery in another hemisphere, or to incur miserable death in their transportation thither. this piratical warfare.

—THOMAS JEFFERSON, DRAFT OF THE *DECLARATION OF INDEPENDENCE*, 1776

But, as it is, we have the wolf by the ear, and we can neither hold him, nor safely let him go. Justice is in one scale, and self preservation in the other.

—THOMAS JEFFERSON TO JOHN HOLMES, APRIL 22, 1820

Figures 9–10. When discussing the future of slavery, Thomas Jefferson openly favored "self preservation" over "Justice" despite the bold claims he made more than fifty years earlier in the draft of the Declaration of Independence. Listing the perpetuation of slavery as a grievance with King George III, Jefferson eventually leaned on the enslaved people of Monticello more than the hired-out white tradespeople for work at his Charlottesville, Virginia, home. Irish-born James Dinsmore was Jefferson's joiner and manager at Monticello from 1798 to 1809. While overseeing Monticello, Dinsmore trained enslaved carpenter John Hemmings in the trade of joinery. On Dinsmore's departure from Monticello, Jefferson did not hire another white joiner to take his place but used Hemmings as his lead joiner. Hemmings remained enslaved at Monticello until Jefferson's death, at which point he was freed with all of his tools.

John Hemmings was born into enslavement on the Monticello Plantation in Albemarle County, Virginia, in 1776, on the eve of the adoption of the Declaration of Independence. The child of a Black woman and a white joiner, Hemmings was raised in the trade of carpentry. He demonstrated a clear ability to work with wood and by his teenage years was tasked with helping white woodworkers enlarge the main house. Once James Dinsmore left Monticello, Hemmings became the chief joiner on the plantation. Over the years, many pieces have been attributed to Hemmings despite adequate documentation. These two pieces can definitively be ascribed to him because they were documented in Jefferson's shop accounts and were made after Dinsmore's departure. Both pieces were made for Poplar Forest, Jefferson's retreat in Bedford County, Virginia.

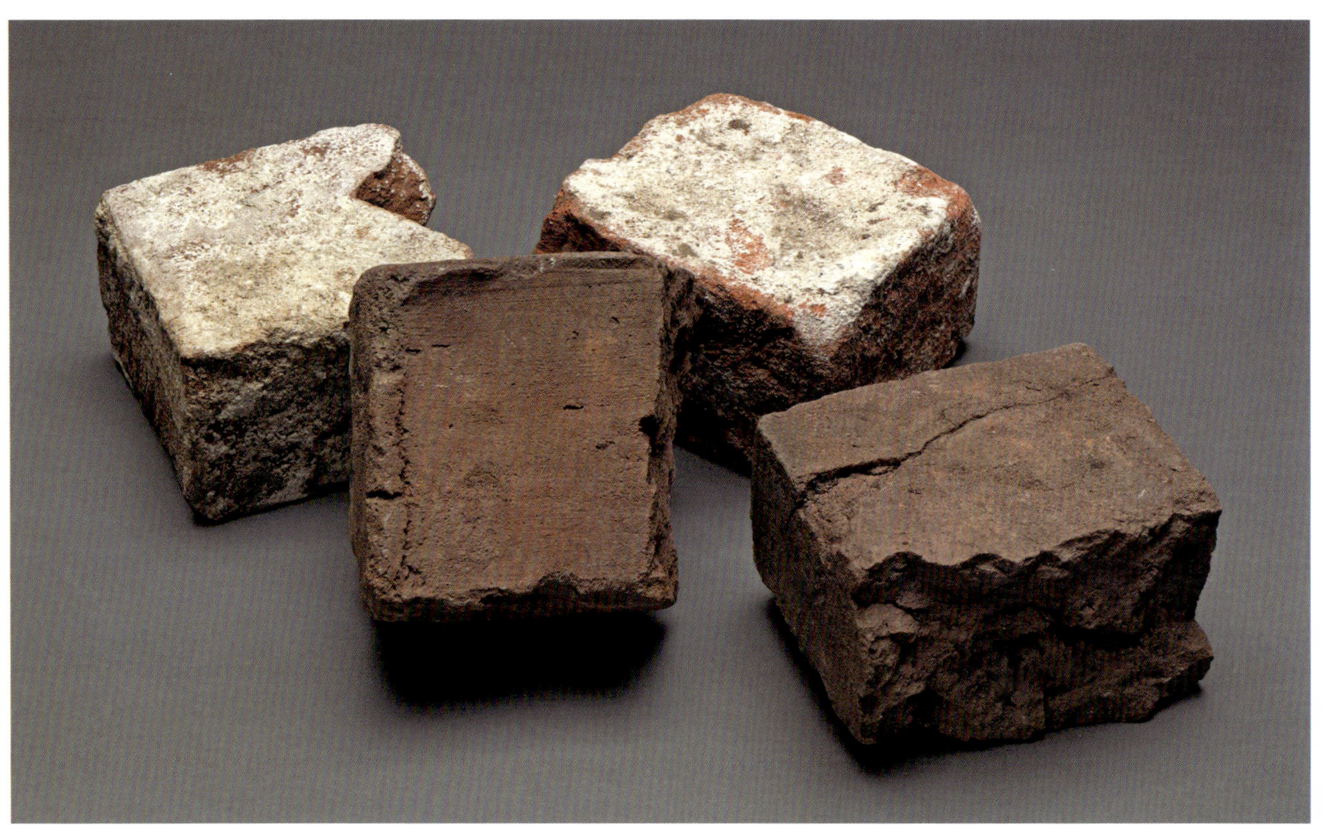

FIGURE 11
Unidentified craftspeople
Bricks, ca. 1753, Wilton Plantation, Henrico County, Virginia
Clay
Loan courtesy of private collection

Gazing at the facade of an eighteenth-century house, it is easy to overlook the immense labor and skill poured into making the foundational structure of the residence, the bricks. Often relegated as meaningless labor, the superiority of the skill set necessary to manufacture these bricks ensured that these structures composed of those crafted bricks were durable. In many cases, the names and lives of those who created everyday objects such as bricks of the eighteenth and nineteenth centuries remain unknown. Great houses, such as Wilton, in present-day Richmond, Virginia, are often spoken of in relation to their owners. Although Wilton was originally built for a branch of the Randolphs, enslaved labor was used throughout the building process that created this Georgian mansion.

Some bricks for Wilton, made on-site through enslaved labor, still bear the fingerprints of those who created them. Their fingerprints represent the toil of a tedious process of continuous handling before the firing process, thus indelibly etching some of those fingerprints into bricks that speak to a common yet all too often forgotten necessity of Black skill. Many of those fingerprints are those of enslaved children, commonly used in brickyards for moving bricks from the molds to drying areas and for stacking. Bricks also had to be flipped periodically to ensure they were well dried throughout. Although the lives of these enslaved workers are not as thoroughly documented as the Randolphs of Wilton, they are equally intertwined with the house.

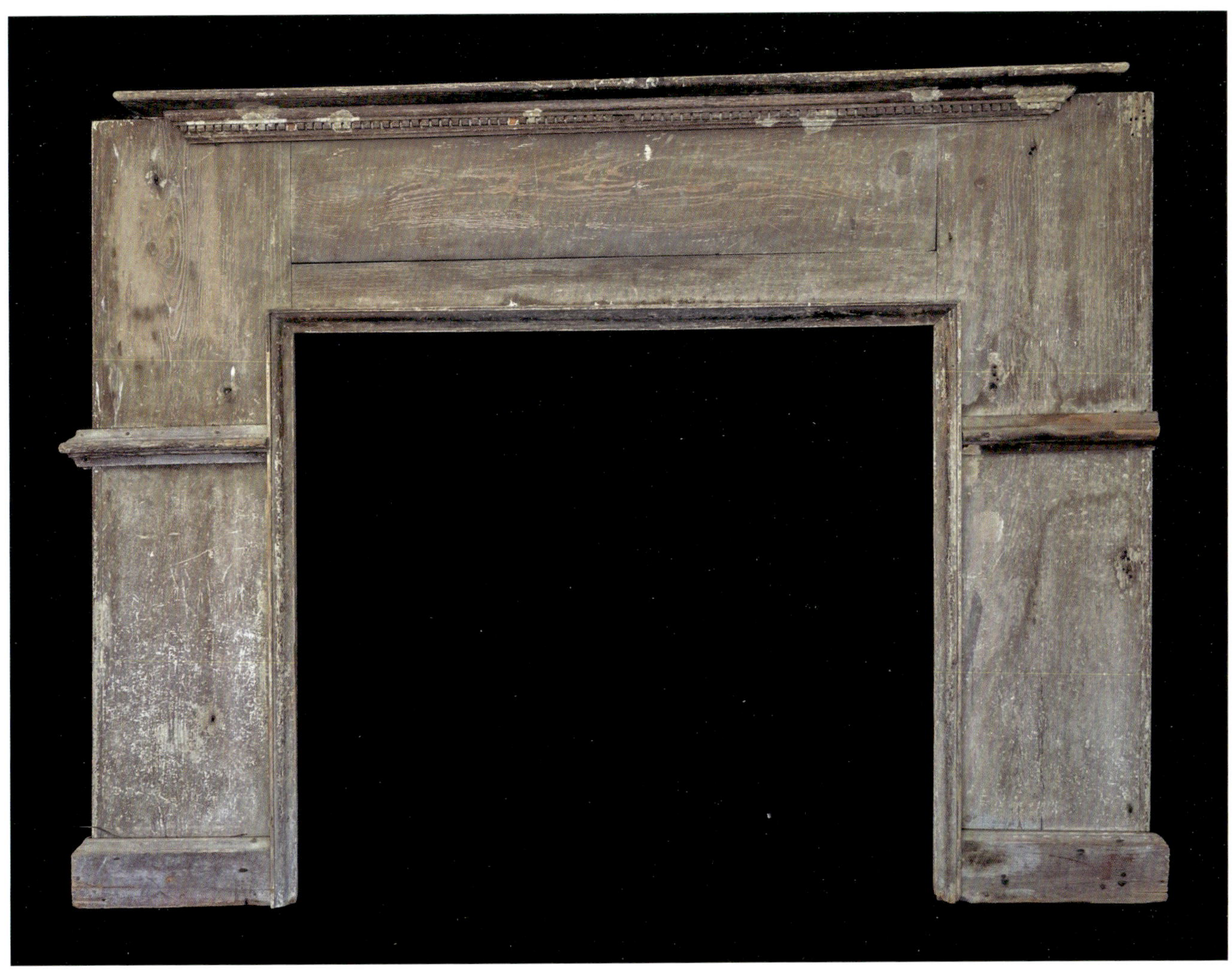

FIGURE 12
Unidentified craftsperson
Fireplace Mantel, ca. 1769, Richmond County, Virginia
Wood and paint
Loan courtesy of the Menokin Foundation,
Warsaw, Virginia, X-M1.2

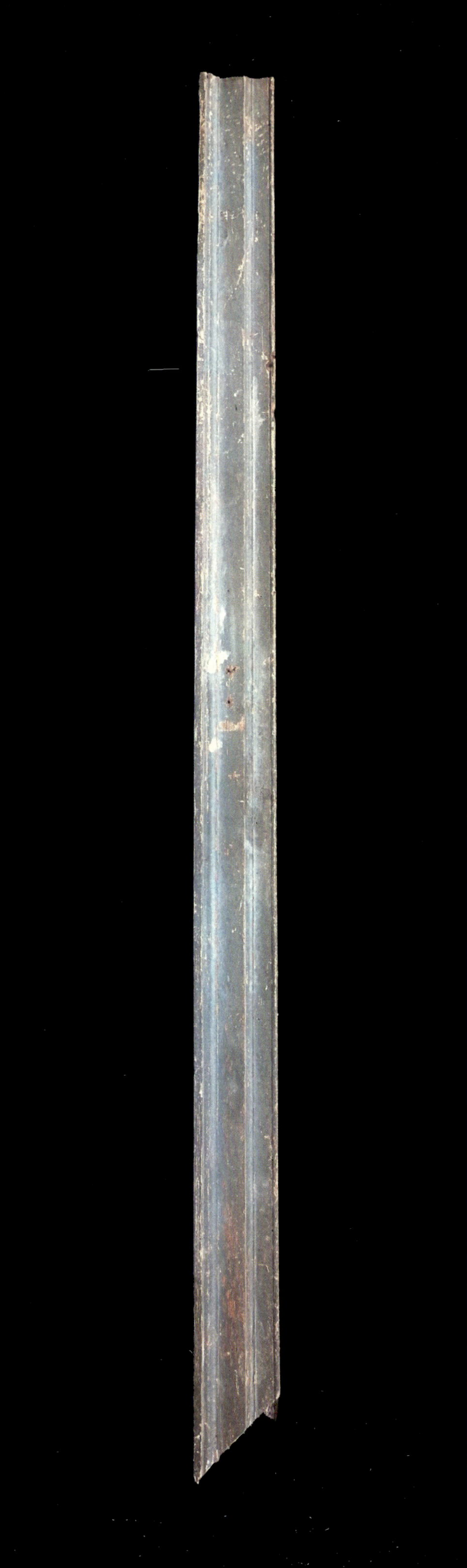

FIGURE 13
Unidentified craftsperson
Cornice Moulding, ca. 1769, Richmond County, Virginia
Wood and paint
Loan courtesy of the Menokin Foundation, Warsaw, Virginia, 103-S-DW-A

Figures 12–13. This mantel is from the National Historic Landmark Menokin Plantation, home of Declaration of Independence signer Francis Lightfoot Lee. Located in Richmond County, Virginia, Menokin was built of local materials such as sandstone. Approximately 80 percent of Menokin's original architectural matter has survived despite the house falling into disrepair. Unfortunately, the names of the architect and the free and enslaved craftspeople who erected the house have been lost to time. This mantel, made of yellow pine and tulip poplar, includes dentil molding and would have been one of five mantels in the house. Although Francis Lightfoot Lee signed his name to a declaration that proclaimed that "all men are created equal, that they are endowed by their Creator with certain unalienable Rights, that among these are Life, Liberty and the pursuit of Happiness," he held 200 enslaved people in bondage.

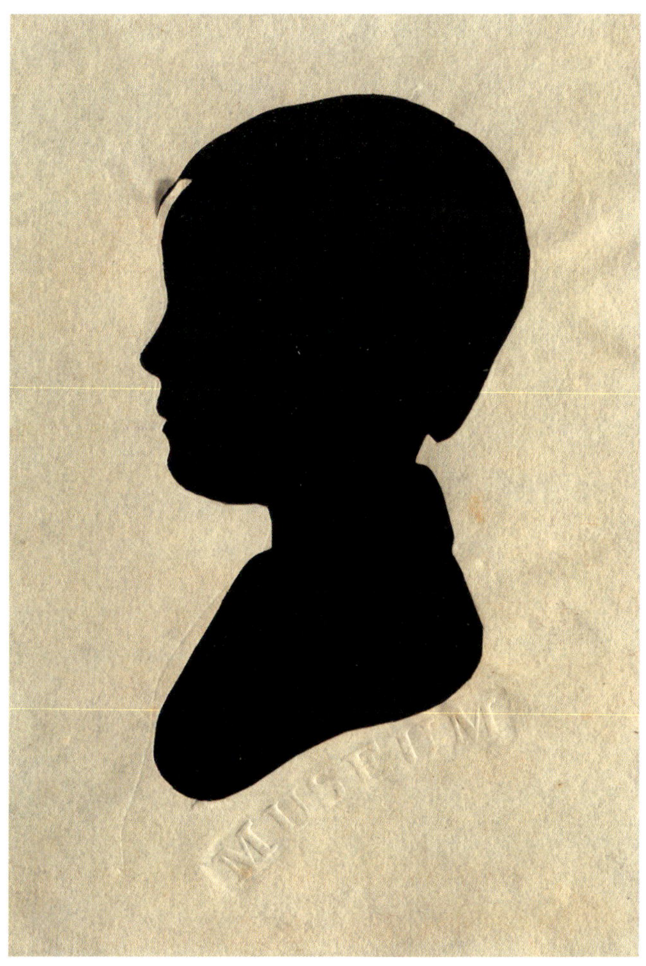

FIGURE 14
Moses Williams
Silhouette of a Boy, 1802–25, Philadelphia, Pennsylvania
Paper and silk
Loan courtesy of private collection

"The Physiognotrace is still in demand. . . . The perfection of Moses's cutting supports its reputation of correct likeness."
—CHARLES WILLSON PEALE, 1807

Moses Williams, enslaved by famous portrait artist Charles Willson Peale, learned and perfected the skill of creating silhouettes using a physiognotrace, a device for tracing profiles in miniature, while working at Peale's museum. The delicate work of creating a silhouette required Williams to cut a silhouette from its center and overlay the outline above black cardstock. The majority of Williams's customers were white museum patrons, and the operation of the physiognotrace required Williams to stand closely to seated patrons and guide the device carefully to their face.

"I have just spoken to a Gentleman who says he was at your Room in Norfolk which was so crouded [sic] *that he could not get his profiles," Peale wrote to his son Raphaelle. "Moses has made him a good one, being from Carolina he did not at first relish having it done by a Molatta* [sic], *however I convinced him that Moses could do it much better than I could."*
—CHARLES WILLSON PEALE TO RAPHAELLE PEALE, 1803

In 1803, Peale advertised in the *Philadelphia Aurora* newspaper that Williams could cut a profile in less than a minute. It is estimated that he crafted more than 8,000 silhouettes per year. Each silhouette sold for six to eight cents. Following his emancipation by Peale in 1803, Williams continued working at the museum and soon earned enough money to buy his family a two-story brick house in Philadelphia's Lower Delaware Ward neighborhood. Williams was listed in Philadelphia city directories as a profile cutter until 1833.

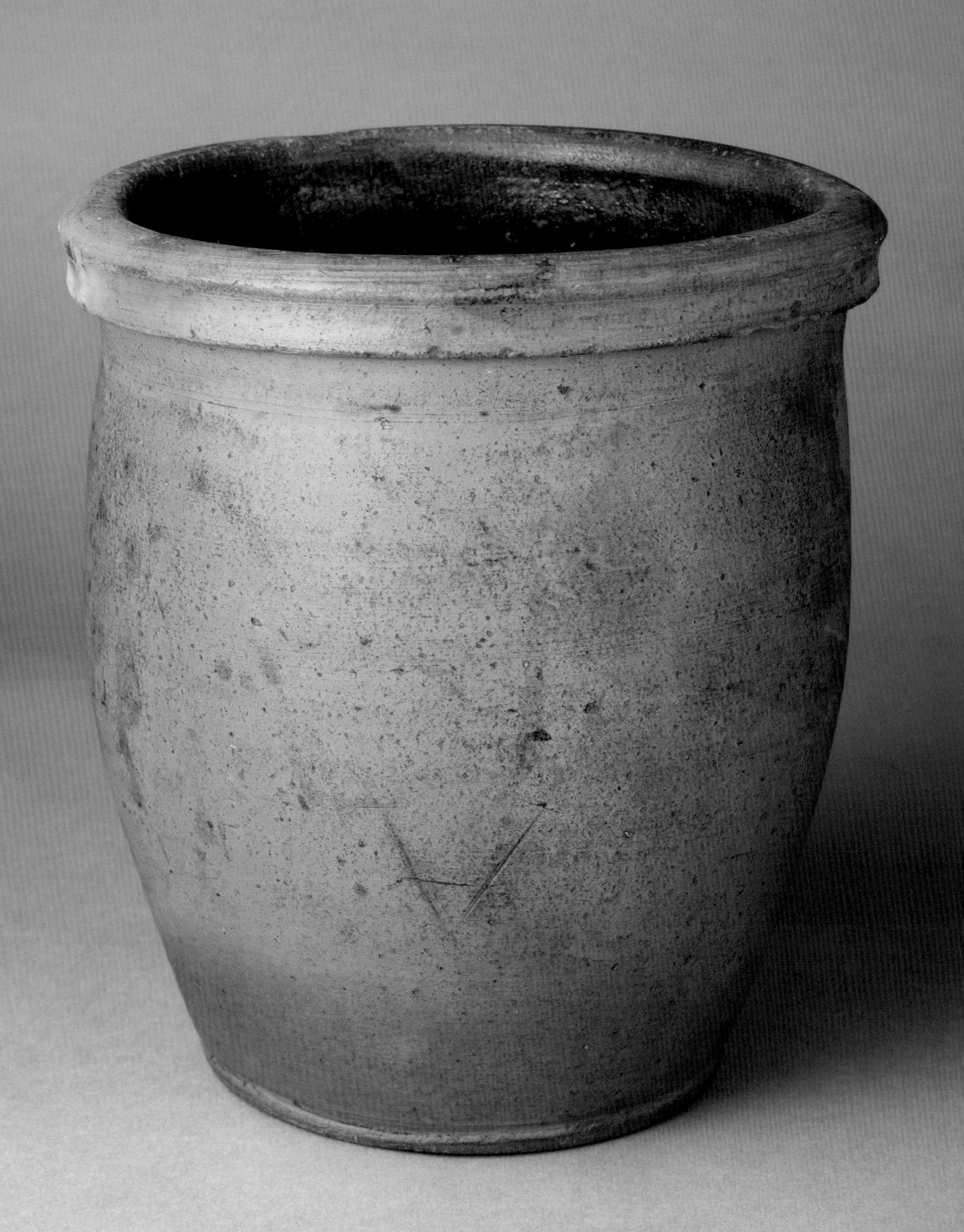

FIGURE 15
Abraham Spencer
Crock, 1860–73, Strasburg, Virginia
Earthenware with manganese-glazed interior
Loan courtesy of the Museum of the Shenandoah Valley, Winchester, Virginia, 2018.1.1

Born free in 1806, Abraham Spencer likely apprenticed as a child with potter George Bodel in New Market, Virginia. Spencer's father, Jesse, was emancipated in 1803, thus securing freedom for his future family. Jesse's emancipation came shortly before the passage of Virginia's Removal Law in 1806, requiring that individuals emancipated after May 1, 1806, leave the state or face reenslavement. The abundance of potters in New Market was fortuitous during Spencer's early years and undeniably aided in his taking up of the trade. On September 8, 1829, Spencer registered himself in Shenandoah County as a "free negro," asserting his status and securing his future.

Spencer's crocks are identified by the inverted "A" used to mark his work. During his lifetime, he produced numerous ceramic vessels in the Shenandoah Valley, working with white potters such as Solomon Bell. Bell family tradition proclaims that Spencer marked his wares with the letter "A" in order to receive appropriate compensation for his work. Spencer last appears in the 1870 United States Census living with his wife in Opequan, Frederick County, Virginia, and he died in 1873. The idea of prosperity was attainable for free people of color who possessed the ability to create and market their work.

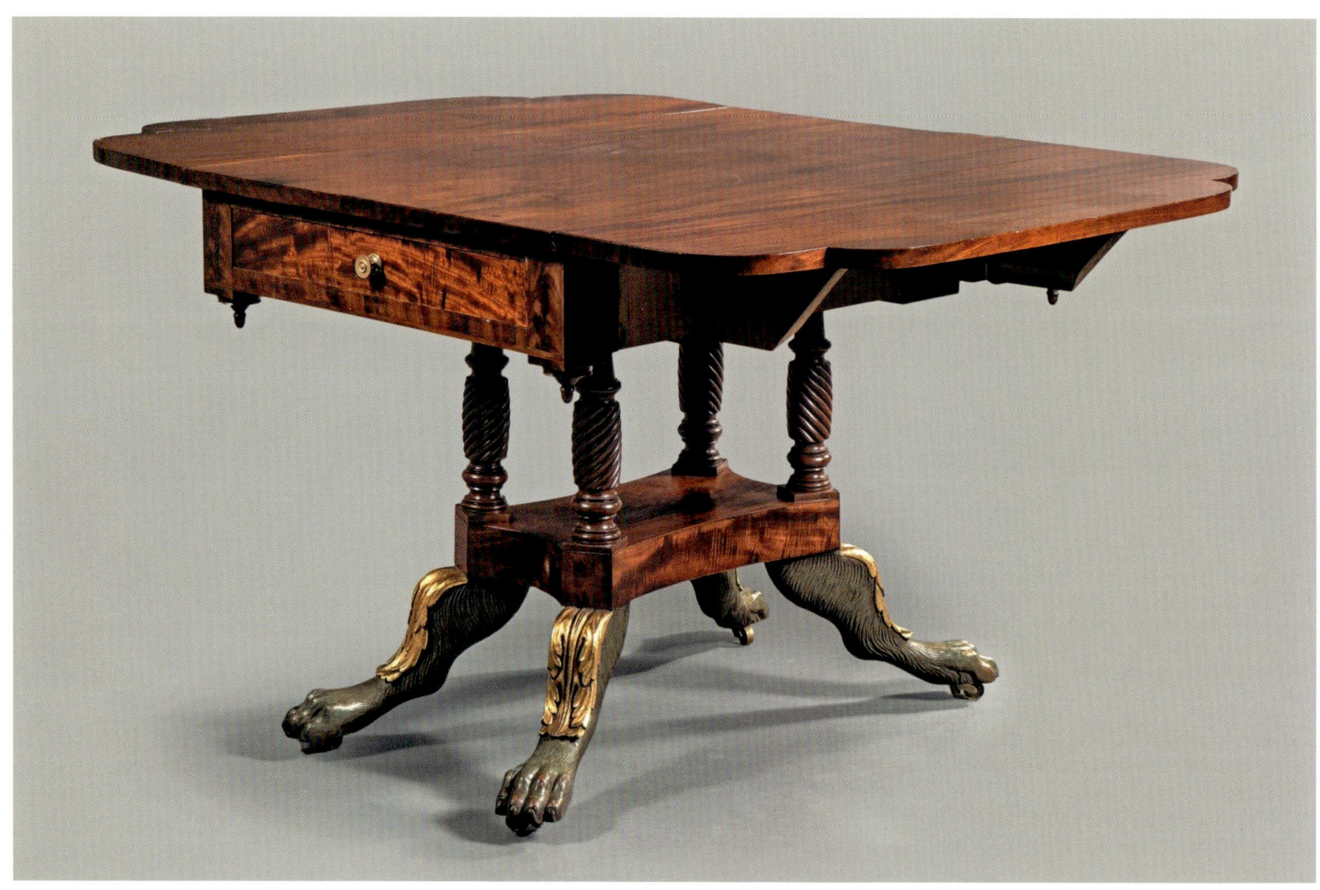

FIGURE 16
Shop of James Woodward
Breakfast Table, 1819, Norfolk, Virginia
Mahogany, poplar, white pine, sycamore, paint, and gilt
Loan courtesy of the Museum of Early Southern Decorative Arts (MESDA), Winston-Salem, North Carolina, 3813

For enslaved craftspeople apprenticed in a trade there was no expectation of securing freedom, but it was possible. Such was the case for James, an enslaved cabinetmaker who learned the skill of carving in the shop of Norfolk cabinetmaker James Woodward. Securing his freedom through working in Woodward's shop for one year, James was required "to work as a Journeyman Cabinetmaker . . . until the full value . . . shall be repaid."

This breakfast table, made in Woodward's shop in 1819, could have been one of the pieces James took part in making during his repayment period. Composed primarily of mahogany, the table features feet finished with green paint and gold leafage. These expensive elements not only added to the value of the table but served as a status symbol for the owner. Humberston Skipwith of Mecklenburg County, Virginia, purchased this "large [Pillar] & Claw Breakfast Table," for forty-five dollars on July 17, 1819. During his apprenticeship, James learned how to create each element in a piece of furniture and bring them together. He used his skill as a gateway to freedom, securing his independence after a year of work for his enslaver. After manumitting himself in 1819, James undertook his own commissions.

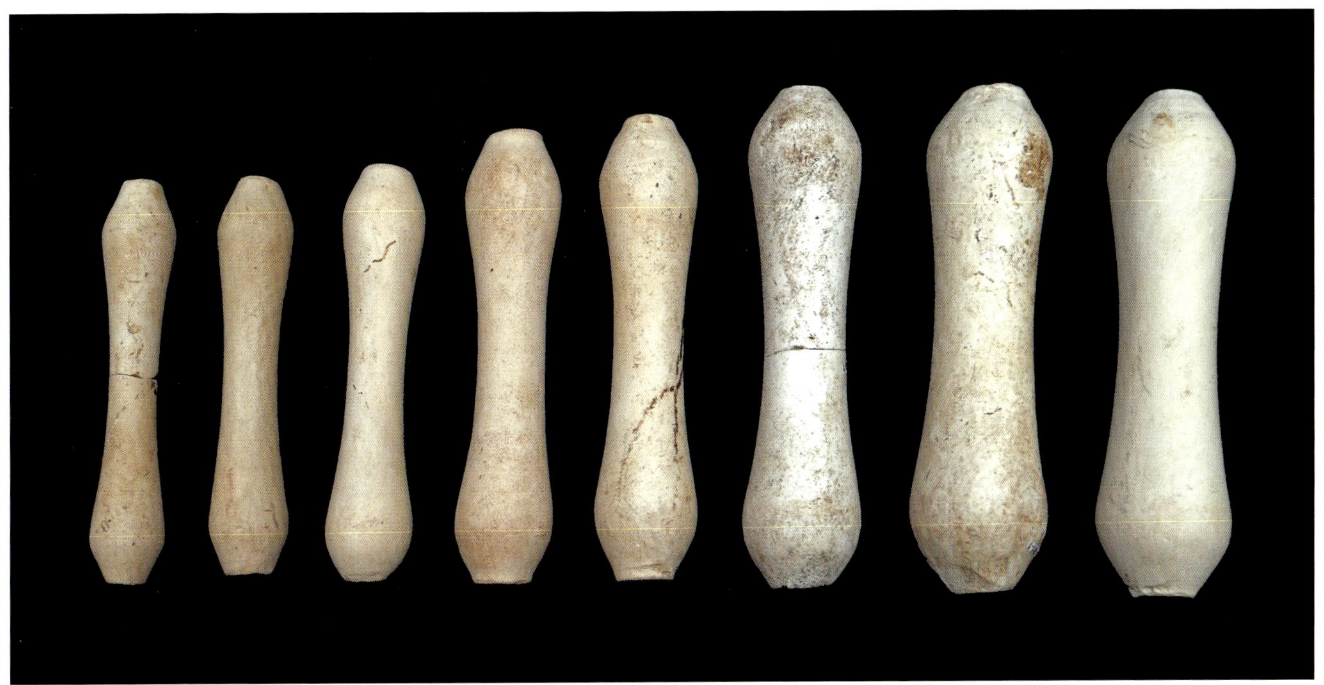

FIGURE 17
Unidentified craftspeople
Wig Curlers, 1738–72, Stafford County, Virginia
Clay
Loan courtesy of the George Washington Foundation, Fredericksburg, Virginia, FF-12-00423-11, FF-12-00181-1, FF-18-00333-1, FF-12-00449-1, FF-06-00001-1, FF-18-00170-1, FF-20-00067-1 mended with FF-06-00013-1, FF-18-00067-2 mended with FF-14-00228-8

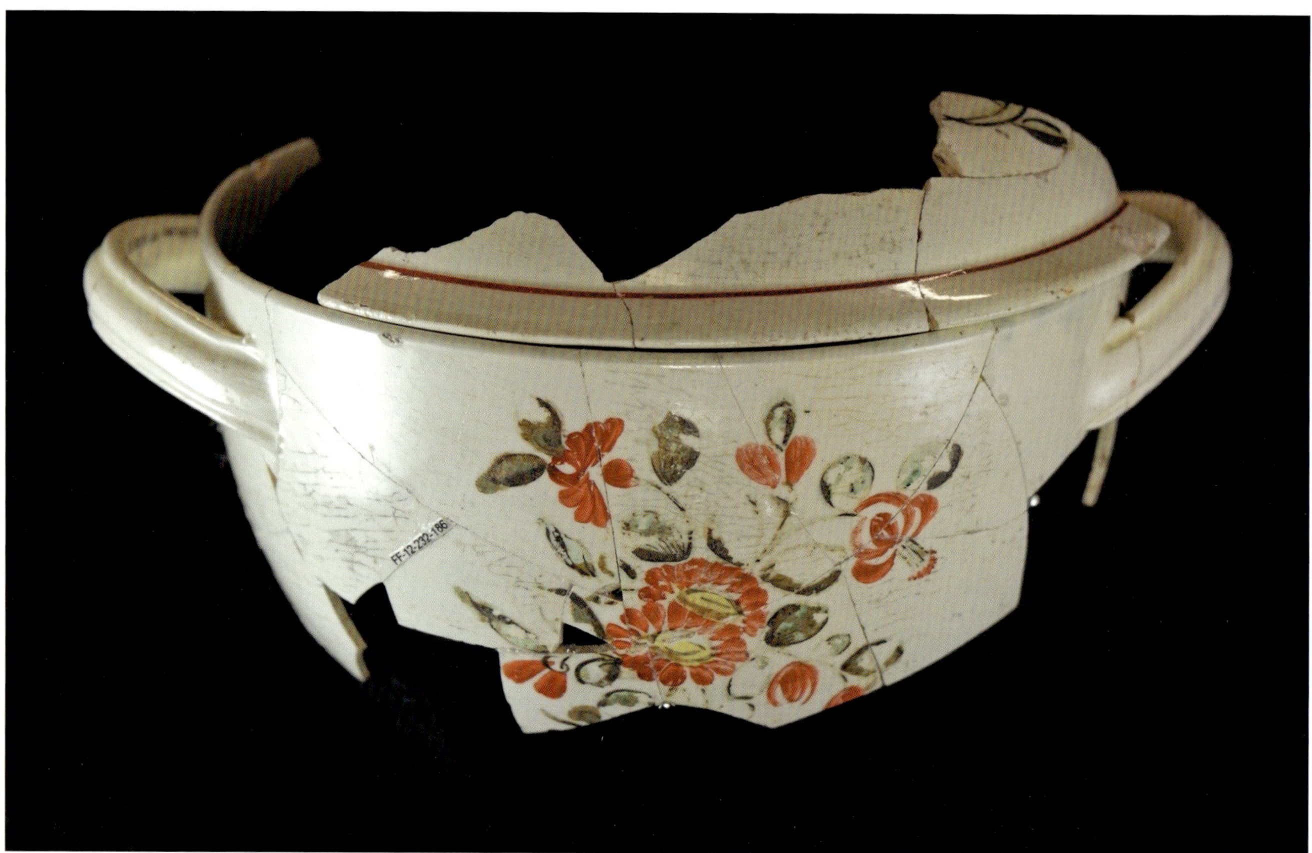

FIGURE 18
Unidentified craftsperson
Bowl, eighteenth century, China
Chinese soft paste porcelain
Loan courtesy of the George Washington Foundation, Fredericksburg, Virginia, 472

Figures 17–18. Affluency in the eighteenth century often surrounded appearance and dress. This included various wigs that, once styled, needed to be maintained. Enslaved hair workers performed the labor-intensive tasks required to clean and dress the wigs. This necessary maintenance brought wealthy members of society to visit Mary Washington's Ferry Farm, George Washington's childhood home.

The Washingtons operated a ferry across the Rappahannock River, bringing the enslaved community at Ferry Farm a steady stream of wealthy passengers to offer wig-dressing services; no known wigmakers resided across the river in Fredericksburg at this time.

Desperate to keep up appearances, Mary Washington often had enslaved craftspeople at Ferry Farm mend broken ceramics using their knowledge of glue-making recipes over an open fire. For the enslaved community, the art of mending ceramics required a scientific knowledge of the materials. Archaeological evidence has uncovered numerous valuable ceramics mended with glue made on-site.

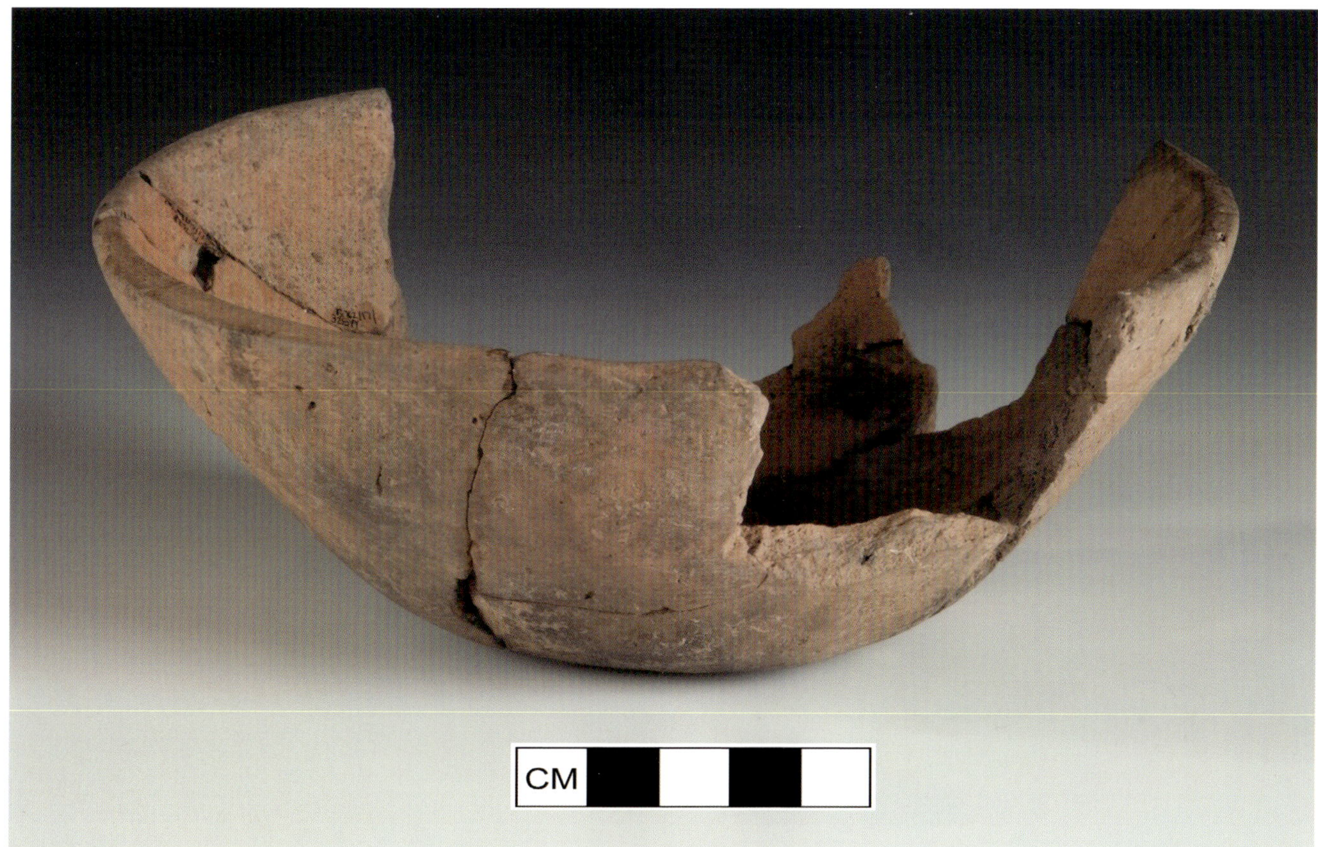

FIGURE 19
Unidentified craftsperson
Colonoware Bowl, eighteenth century,
Mount Vernon, Fairfax County, Virginia
Course earthenware
Loan courtesy of the Mount Vernon
Ladies' Association, 1694691

Many traditions of producing craft predate the Black presence in America. Archaeologists and historians have connected colonoware to West African pottery traditions that predate the 1700s. A low-fired, unglazed, coarse earthenware commonly found in Virginia, South Carolina, Georgia, and the Caribbean, colonoware vessels included bowls, jugs, plates, and pots. This colonoware bowl was found during an excavation of the South Grove section of Mount Vernon Plantation, often referred to as the "Houses for Families." Maintaining its shape with an intact base, body, and rim, this bowl depicts through its survival the legacies of craft tradition in foodways.

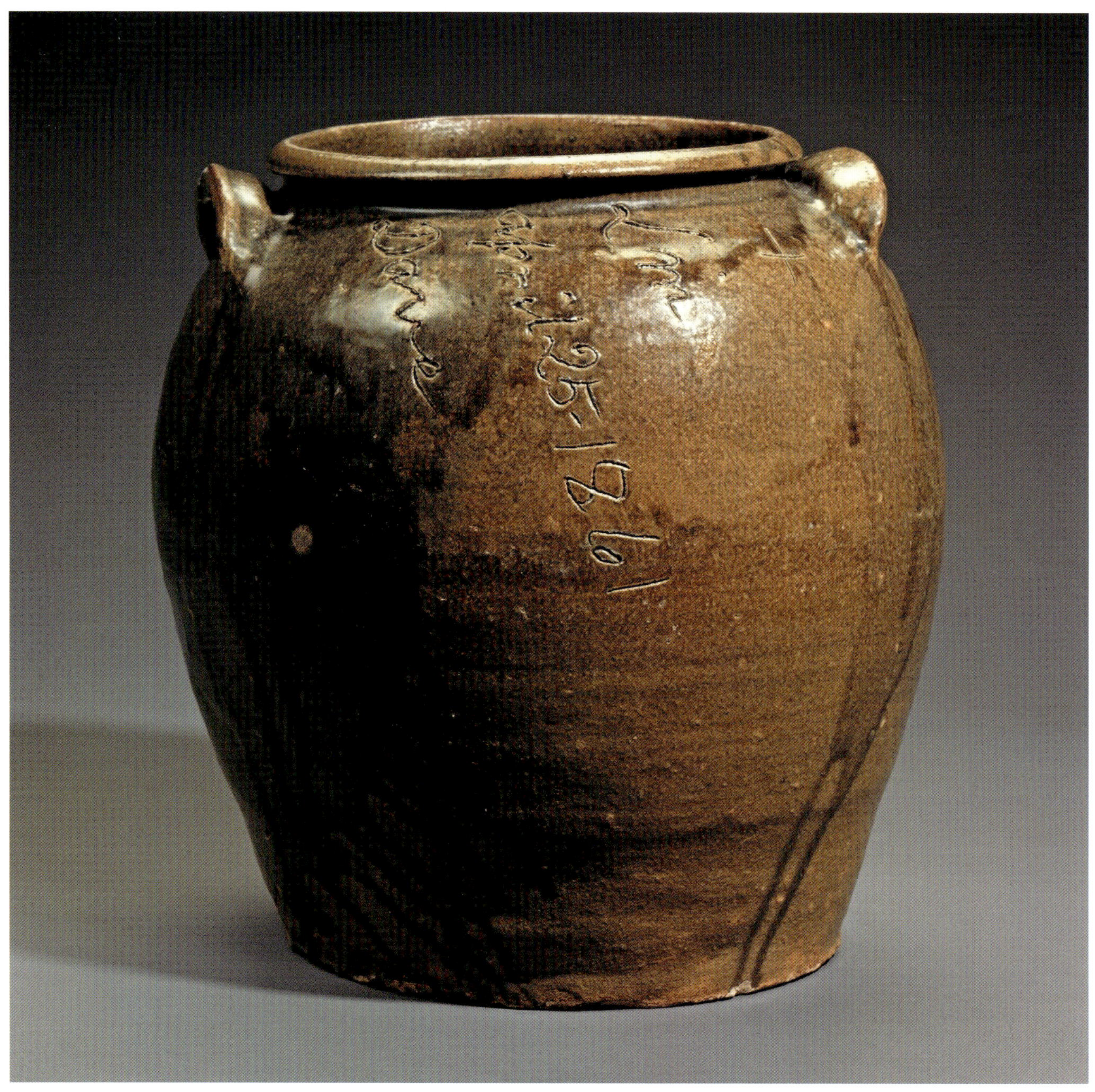

FIGURE 20
David Drake
Jar, April 25, 1861, Edgefield District, South Carolina
Alkaline-glazed earthenware
DAR Museum Collection, Friends of the Museum Purchase, 2007.24

Known for his elegant prose inscribed onto the exterior of his thrown pots, the ceramic creations of David Drake are perhaps the most celebrated Black decorative art form. Amid the turmoil and strife of his enslavement in South Carolina, David Drake's incorporation of poetry coupled with ornate, masterfully thrown pots signifies the presence of thought and intentional artistry in craft. This alkaline-glazed earthenware storage jar was made at the Lewis Miles Stoneware Factory at Stoney Bluff Plantation on Big Horse Creek in the Edgefield District of South Carolina by the hands of one of America's most celebrated potters, David Drake. This jar is olive-green and mottled brown in color with two deep-arched lug handles and a semi-rounded rim with varying levels of concentration of glaze application that create a variation in the color and gloss throughout the surface.

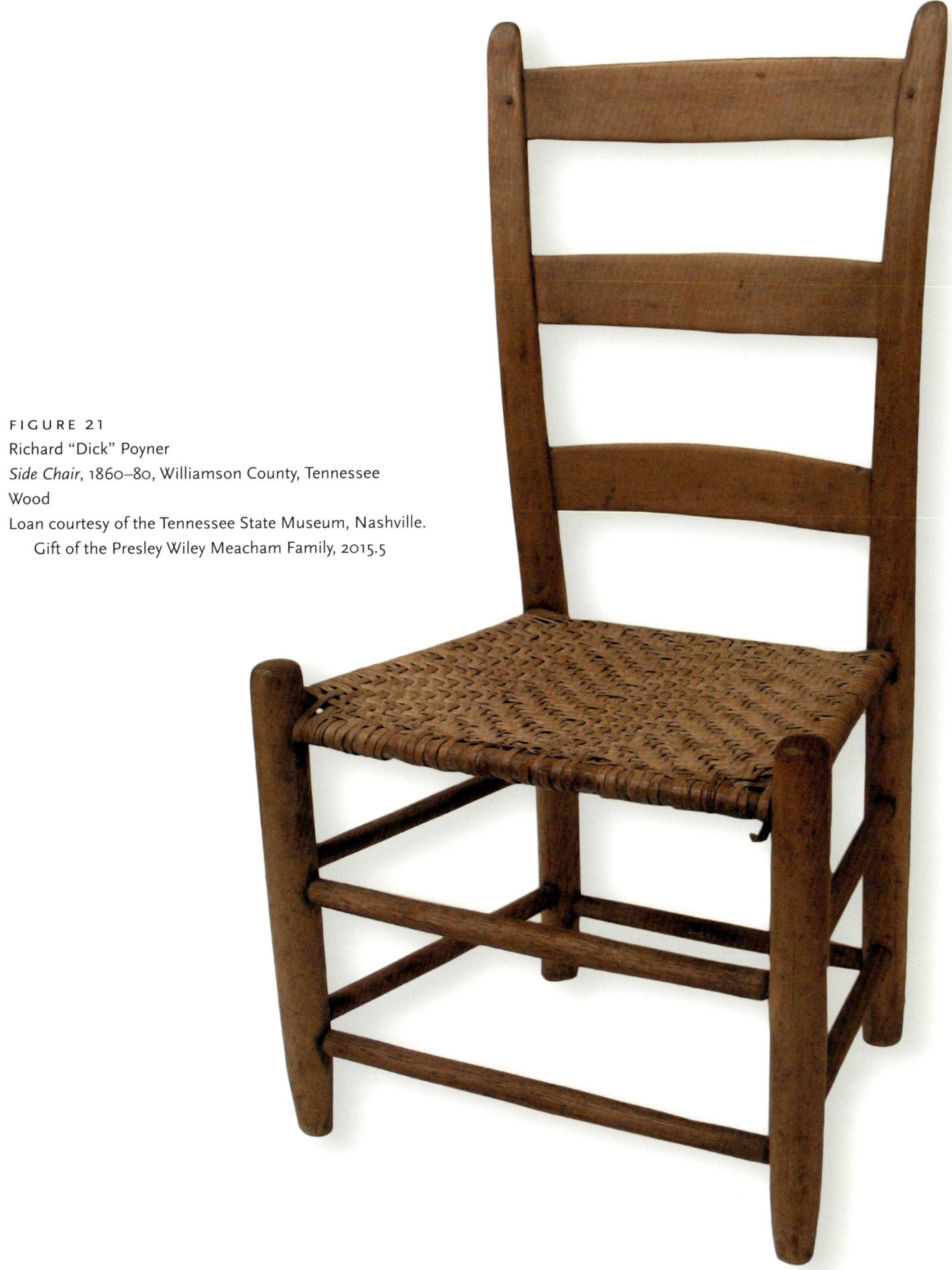

FIGURE 21
Richard "Dick" Poyner
Side Chair, 1860–80, Williamson County, Tennessee
Wood
Loan courtesy of the Tennessee State Museum, Nashville. Gift of the Presley Wiley Meacham Family, 2015.5

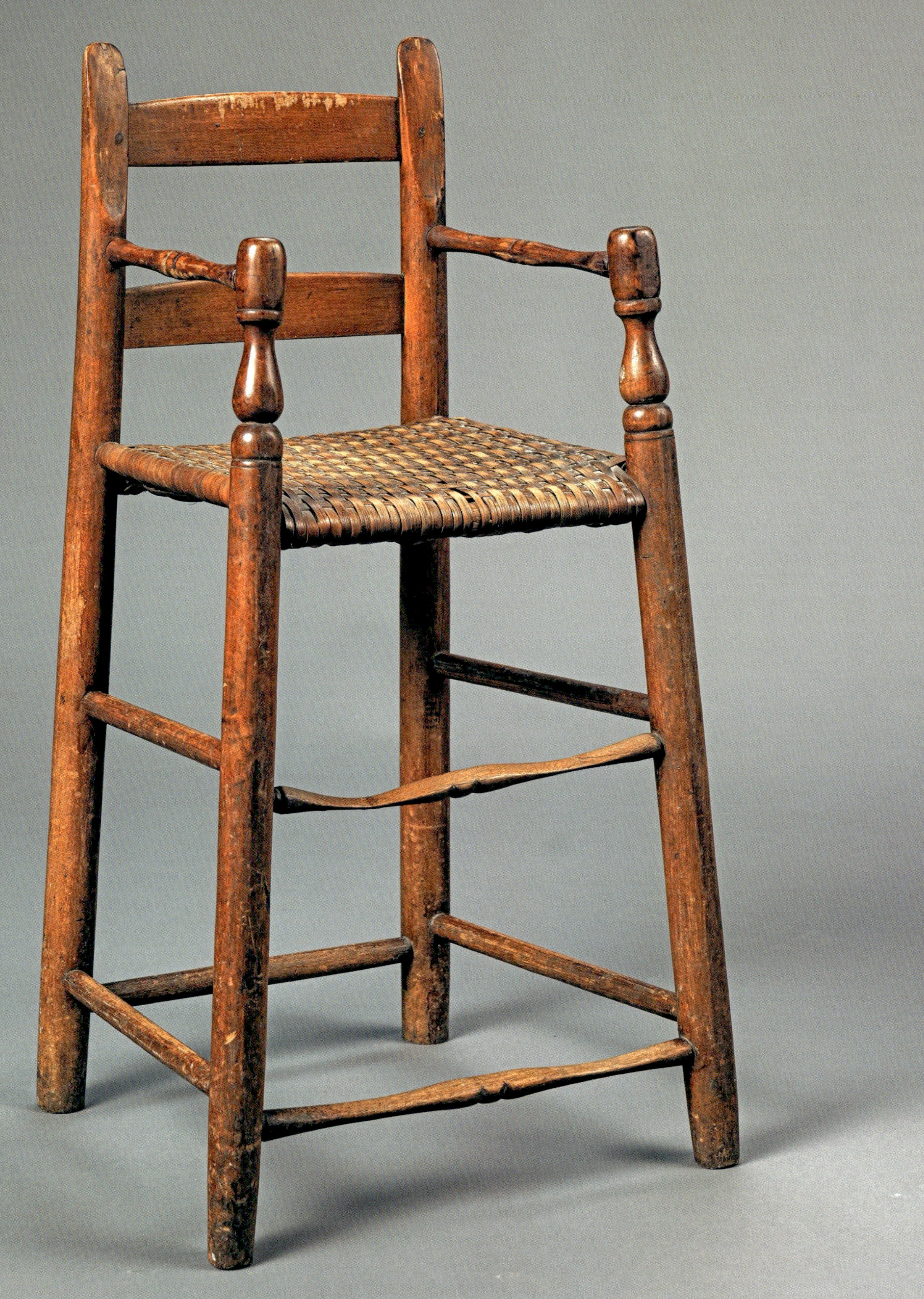

FIGURE 22
Richard "Dick" Poyner
Chair, late nineteenth century,
Williamson County, Tennessee
Wood
Loan courtesy of Battle of Franklin Trust. Gift of the
Family of Alma Parry Reilly West, BOFT 2014.3.1

Figures 21–22. In the November 16, 1849, edition of the *Western Weekly Review* newspaper, Richard "Dick" Poyner declared that he was "now on my own book." Poyner's declaration came shortly after his emancipation. He soon established a chair workshop complete with a horse-powered lathe used to create the posts and rungs of the chairs. Poyner used green woodworking methods to build sturdy chairs, eliminating the need for nails or glue. He made a variety of chairs, including rocking chairs, armchairs, children's highchairs, and sitting chairs. Poyner's chairs are distinctive because of their design, including mule-eared or curved back posts secured by wooden pegs. He used sugar maple and hickory woods to form the chairs and white oak splits to form the seats. Poyner taught the trade to his son James and established a family business, thus advancing the family's economic status in the years before the Civil War. Poyner died in 1882 at the age of eighty-one.

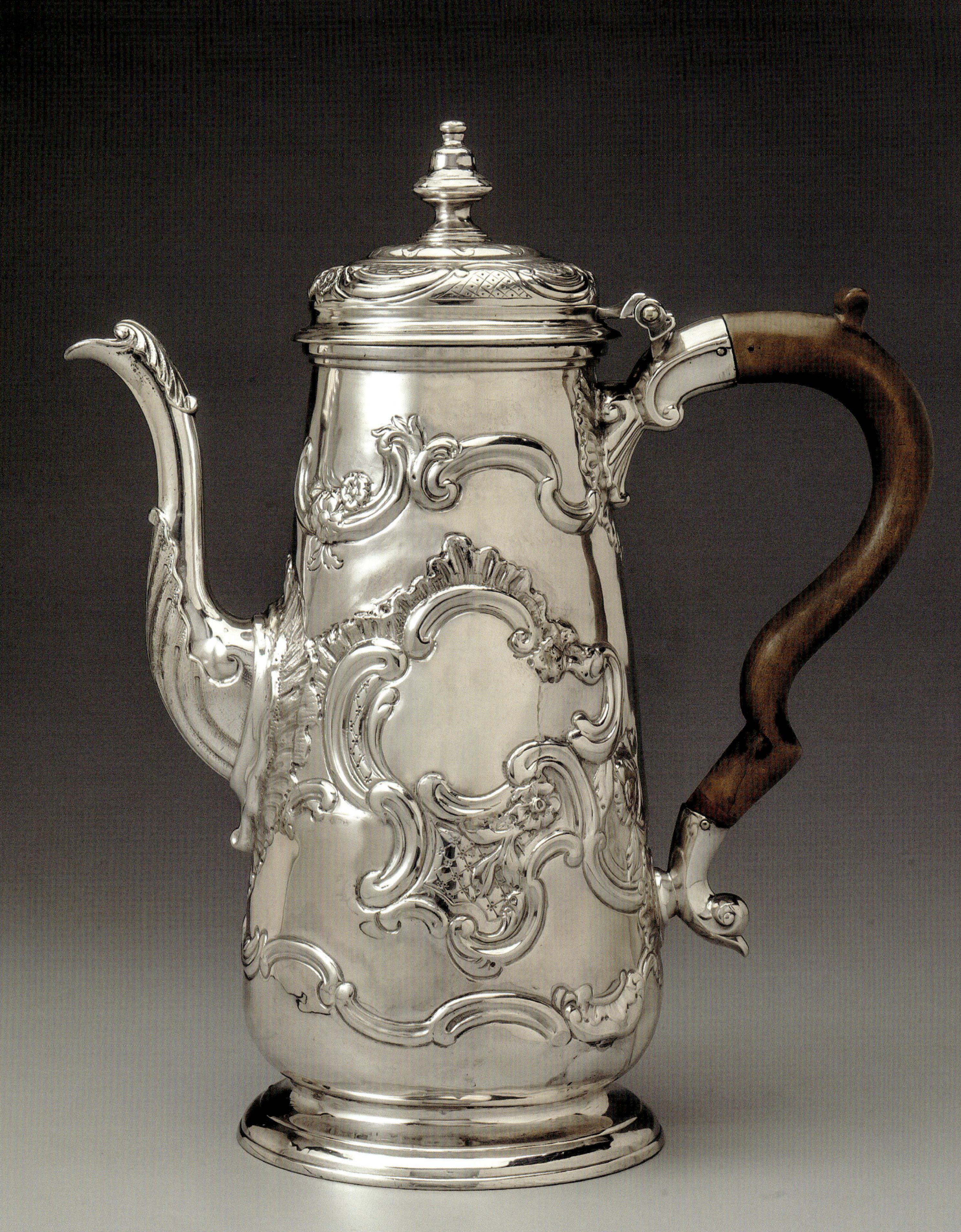

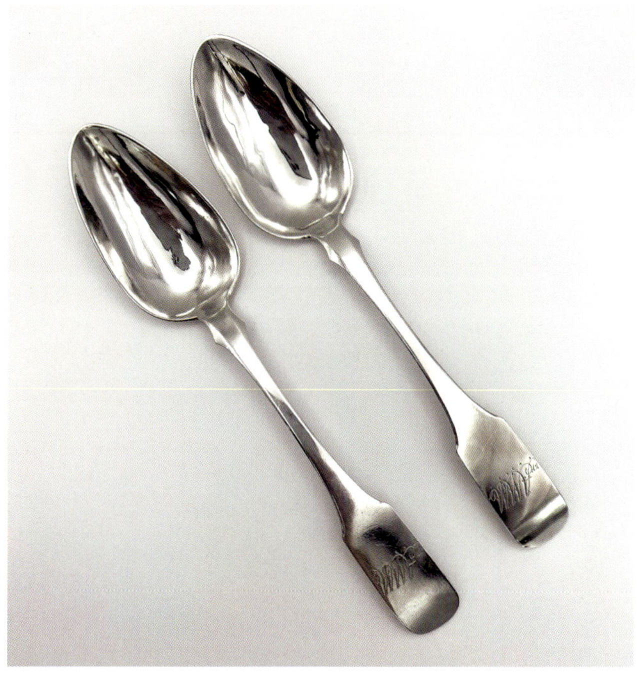

FIGURE 24
Peter Bentzon
Tablespoons, 1806–48, Philadelphia, Pennsylvania, or Saint Croix, Virgin Islands
Silver
DAR Museum Collection, Friends of the Museum Purchase, 2024.25.1-2

(*opposite*) FIGURE 23
Shop of Alexander Petrie
Coffeepot, 1742–68, Charleston, South Carolina
Silver with wooden handle
Loan courtesy of the Museum of Early Southern Decorative Arts (MESDA), Winston-Salem, North Carolina, 3996

Little is known of the enslaved craftsman Abraham's life outside of his forced labor in Alexander Petrie's silver shop in Charleston, South Carolina. Petrie was an established silversmith and ran a successful business selling Charleston-made silver items, jewelry, and imported English plate while also offering clock and watch repair services. It is likely that Petrie taught Abraham the silversmith trade and that Abraham participated in various shop activities, including creating Charleston-made silver. It is unclear when Petrie purchased Abraham, but Abraham's labor ensured the success of Petrie's shop. One of the only mentions of Abraham in the documentary record is an account of his purchase by Jonathan Sarrazin at Petrie's estate sale in 1768. Abraham commanded a price of £810, a testament to his skill. Listed on the same page as Abraham in Petrie's estate inventory was "1 New Chased Coffee pott," weighing 32½ ounces. In this instance, it is possible that the creator was also listed for sale alongside his creation.

Abraham represents the many Black craftspeople who labored in workshops and whose larger life stories remain unknown. Despite a lack of archival records documenting Abraham's life, his training in the trade prepared him to create delicate and refined work in silver that not only fulfilled a purpose but entertained the eye.

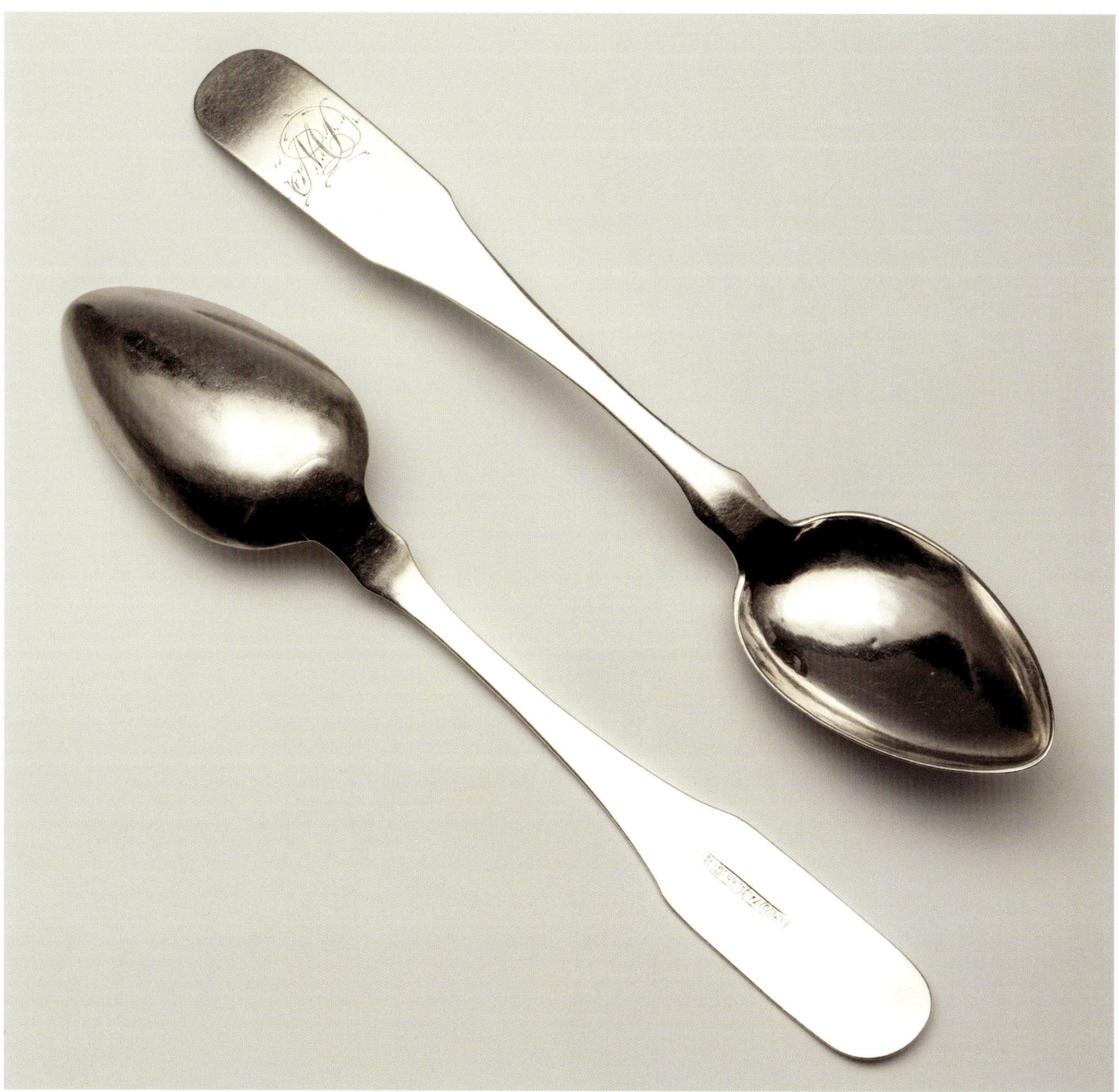

FIGURE 25
Peter Bentzon
Teaspoons, 1815–30, Philadelphia, Pennsylvania, or Saint Croix, Virgin Islands
Silver
Loan courtesy of The Colonial Williamsburg Foundation, Museum Purchase, Hugh Trumbull Adams Fund, 2017-2,1

Figures 25–26. Born in the Virgin Islands, Peter Bentzon learned the silversmith's trade in Philadelphia between 1799 and 1806. He worked in both Saint Croix and Philadelphia. His business was established in Saint Croix in 1807, but Bentzon frequently traveled back to Philadelphia. Philadelphia records indicate that Bentzon was "white." However, in Saint Croix, he is listed as "mustice," meaning that one of his parents was of African descent. Given this complex understanding of identity, Bentzon traveled back and forth between the two cities in search of regular business. Identifying as white at times allowed Bentzon to take advantage of the different markets and clientele.

His work, sophisticated and detailed, was sought-after by wealthy members of society for use at their tables. Bentzon's work differs from the majority of Black craftspeople in that he was creating pieces, not based on the orders of a shop master, but for the clients who sought out his work. His care and attention to etching decorations onto each piece separates his work from the monotonous and repetitive labor done by the majority of Black craftspeople.

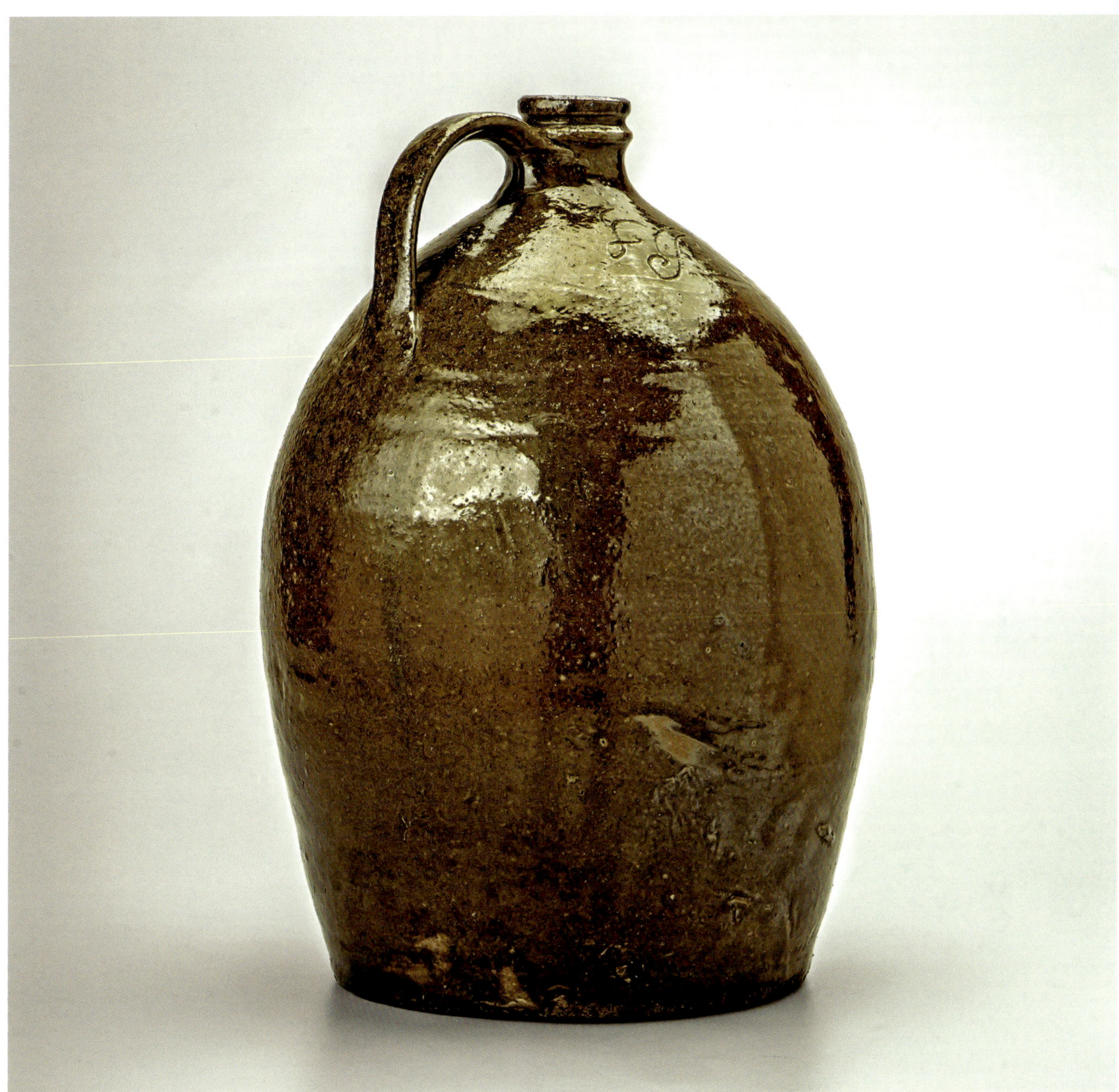

FIGURE 26
Lucius Jordan
Jug, 1850–60, Washington County, Georgia
Alkaline-glazed stoneware
Loan courtesy of the Museum of Early Southern Decorative Arts (MESDA), Winston-Salem, North Carolina, 5763

The Washington County, Georgia, tax records for 1836 open a window into the life of free potter Lucius Jordan. Listed first as a "free person of Cullor," Jordan later identified as "White" in the Washington County documents from the 1860s and 1870s. Jordan's ability to identify as Black and white could have helped him move more easily through Georgia society. Only 100 miles away from his home were the pottery factories of the Edgefield District, made successful by the enslavement of hundreds of Black potters. Based on Jordan's extant pottery, he most likely learned the trade in Edgefield or from other Edgefield-trained potters, such as the white potter Cyrus Cogburn. Unlike the many enslaved potters of the Edgefield District, Jordan had the freedom to throw jugs for his own clients and not a free factory owner. In addition, Jordan's jugs bear his maker's mark. Inscriptions by Black potters were quite rare and allowed their work to be identified. These marks also document how the migration of knowledge and ceramic traditions moved west from Edgefield throughout the nineteenth century.

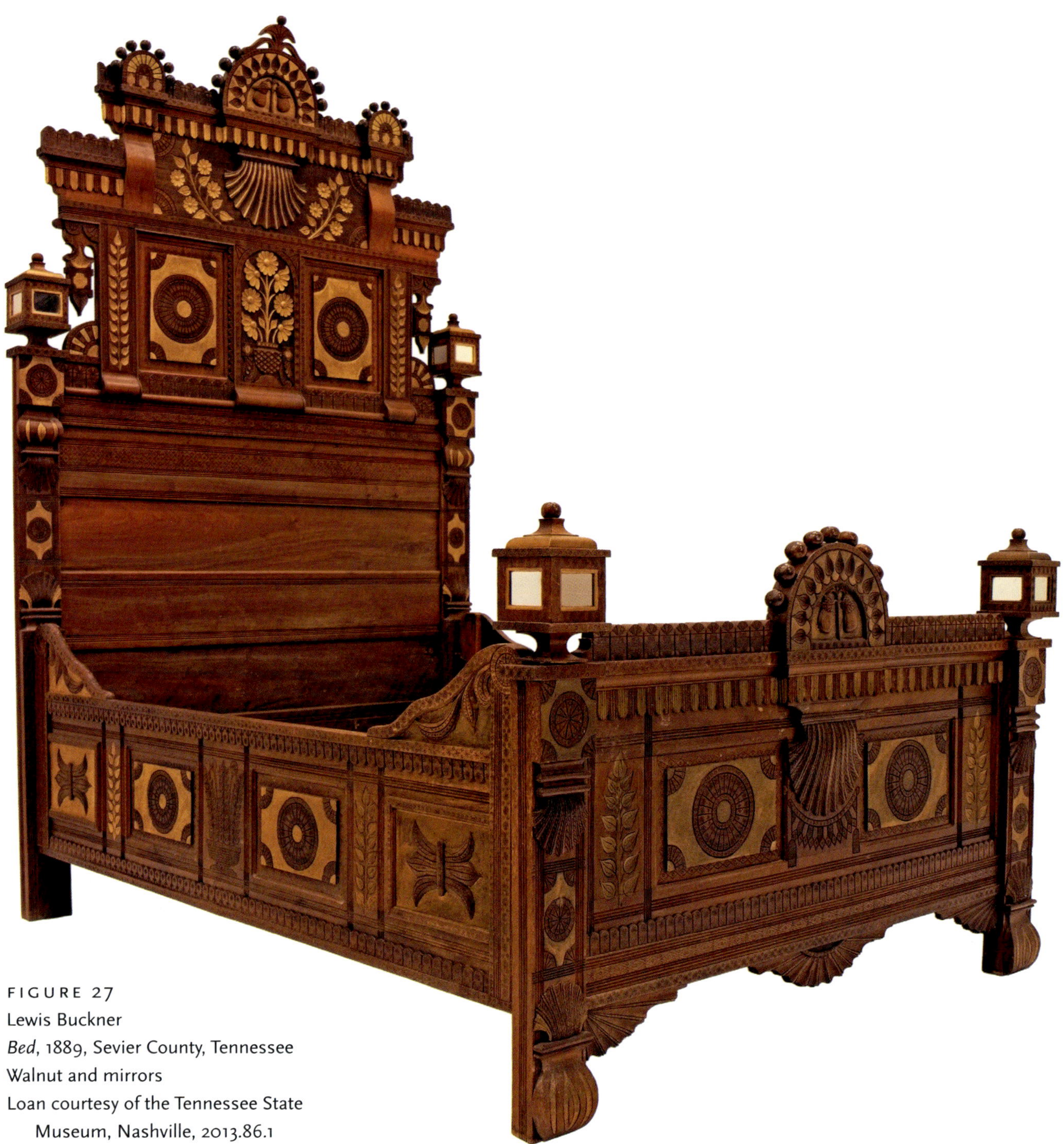

FIGURE 27
Lewis Buckner
Bed, 1889, Sevier County, Tennessee
Walnut and mirrors
Loan courtesy of the Tennessee State Museum, Nashville, 2013.86.1

Lewis Buckner is among the most distinguished Black cabinetmakers from Tennessee. Born enslaved in Jefferson County, Tennessee, in 1856, Buckner moved to Sevier County at the end of the Civil War, where he apprenticed with white craftsperson Christian Stump and trained as a cabinetmaker. By 1880, Buckner was working as a cabinetmaker on his own accord, joining a cadre of Black artisans in Sevier County. Buckner used his superior carving skills to create architectural features including mantels and trim work that adorned the homes of East Tennessee.

Among Buckner's best-known works is a bed and dresser created for William and Rebecca Henderson in 1889. According to family recollections, Henderson hired Buckner to make an entire furniture suite to furnish his home. Henderson's furniture featured Buckner's intricate carvings, which were largely inspired by Charles Eastlake and the aesthetic movement. Incorporating his creativity into his designs, Buckner added unique carvings and symbols that became a hallmark of his work. Lewis Buckner died on May 16, 1924, having left his mark on the decorative arts of Tennessee.

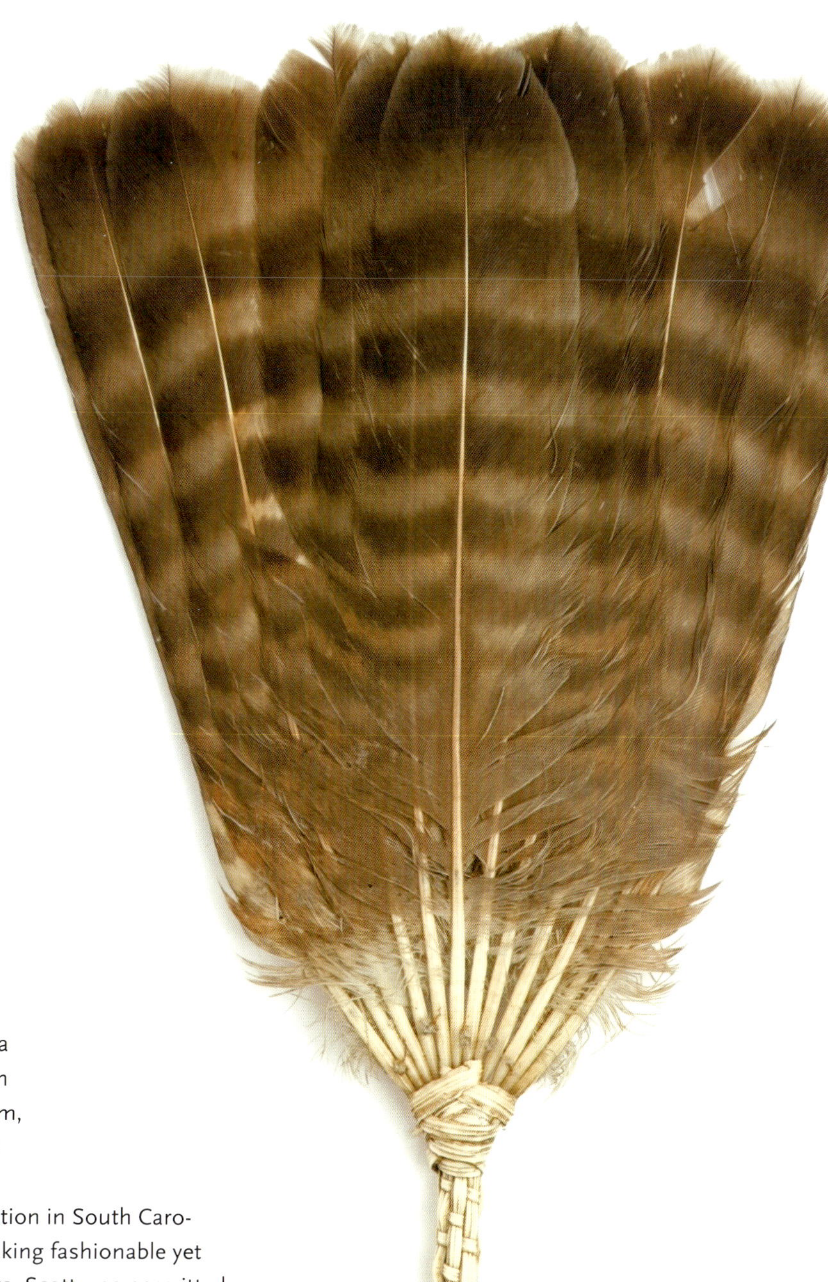

FIGURE 28
Tobias Scott
Fan, ca. 1880, Charleston, South Carolina
Hawk tail feathers, quill, wire, and ribbon
Loan courtesy of The Charleston Museum, Charleston, South Carolina, HT 4270

While enslaved on a James Island plantation in South Carolina, Tobias Scott mastered the art of making fashionable yet masterfully ornate fans from bird feathers. Scott was permitted to make and sell these fans in his spare time by his enslaver. Scott understood the value of his craft, eventually purchasing his freedom. After marrying, Scott continued producing fans as a freeman on James Island until the end of the Civil War. Scott, his wife, and their five children moved to Charleston after the war, where he opened a shop on Water Street. Local newspapers often captured both the sale and advertisement of Scott's fans and his civic engagement.

This fan, dated ca. 1880, captures the subtle yet vibrant character of his creations. The open fan, composed of hawk feathers with matching horizontal stripes and a hand-crafted handle made of woven quills, has a wire running through the handle, securing the feathers in place. A solid black, delicate grosgrain ribbon is tied to the handle.

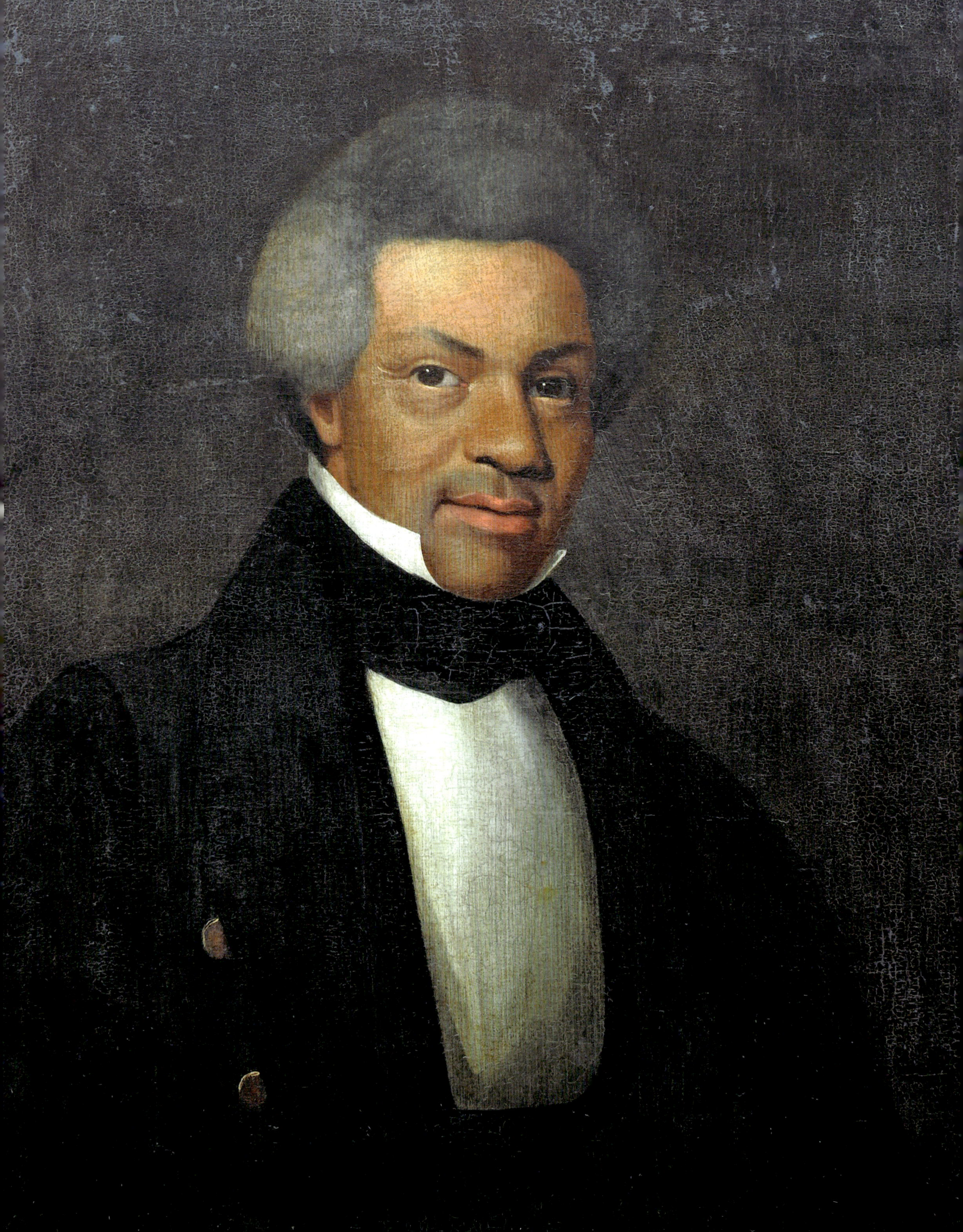

FIGURE 29
Patrick Henry Davenport
Dennis Doram, Jr., 1839, Kentucky
Oil on canvas
Loan courtesy of the Kentucky Historical Society, Frankfort, 2000.29.1

The freedom to own a business in nineteenth-century Kentucky gave Dennis and Diademia Doram the opportunity to elevate their status in society. Their portraits illustrate their unique social position compared to the many enslaved individuals of Kentucky. Painted by white artist Patrick Henry Davenport, Dennis's likeness is conveyed in the same manner as Davenport's white sitters, placing him on a plane equal to the artist's other paying customers. Dennis was born enslaved but was freed in 1797 along with his mother and later received an education. The success of the Dorams' rope factory, hemp business, and Caldwell School for Women opened opportunities for the couple. The freedoms Dennis and Diademia Doram enjoyed were defended during the Civil War; their son, Joshua, served as a Union soldier in Company F, 114th United States Colored Troops. Another son was a buffalo soldier in the Indian Wars.

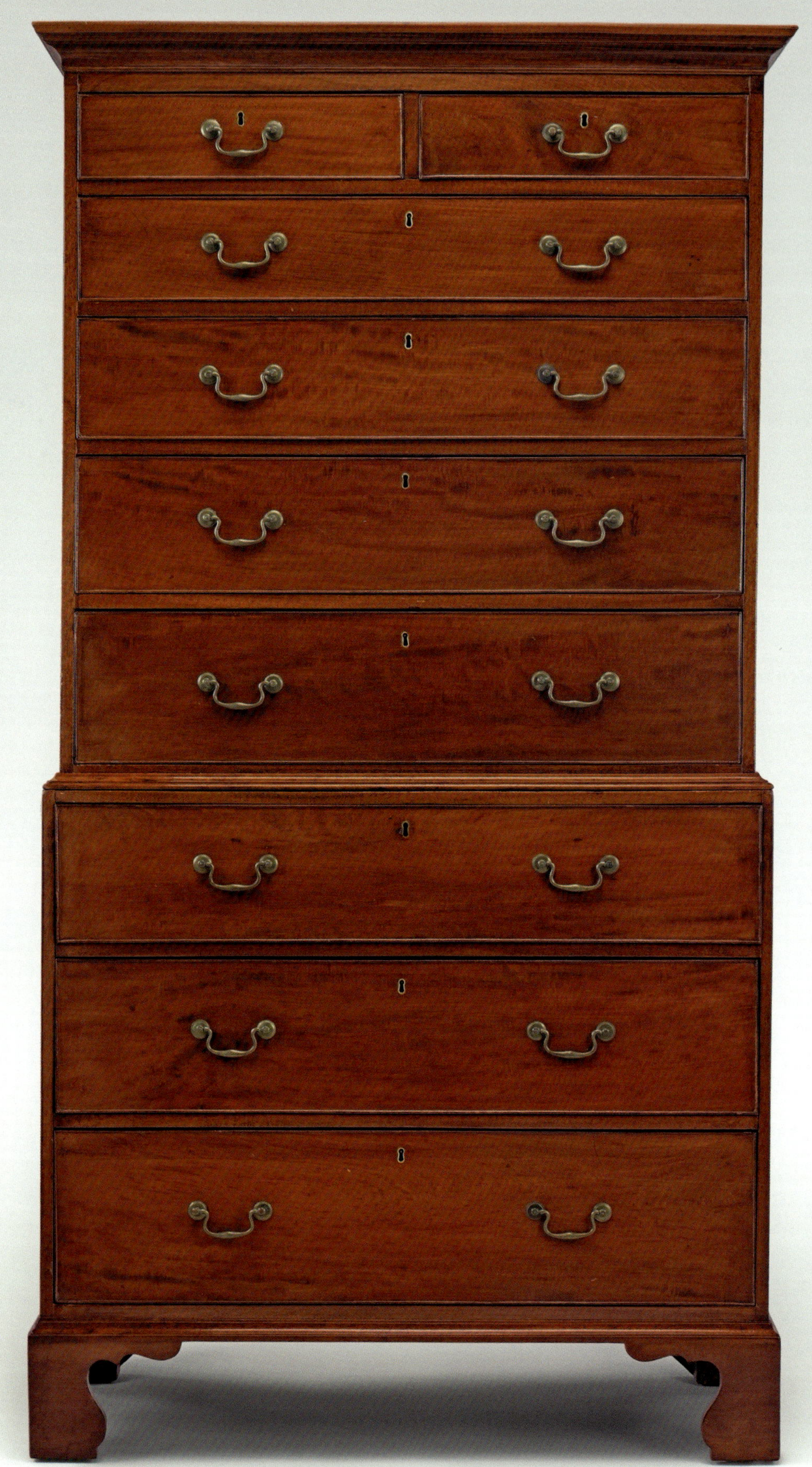

FIGURE 30
Thomas Gross
Double Chest, 1805–10, Philadelphia, Pennsylvania
Mahogany, tulip poplar, yellow pine, and brass
Loan courtesy of the Philadelphia Museum of Art. Gift of Mrs. Leslie Legum, 1983-167.a,b

Discovered after his inscription, "Thomas Gross / Maker," was found on the drawer bottom of a double chest, Thomas Gross rose to notoriety among furniture scholars. Subsequent research revealed that in the early 1800s, Gross operated a cabinetmaking shop in Philadelphia's Cedar Ward neighborhood, joining the many established cabinetmakers who gave Philadelphia its reputation as one of the furniture-making centers of the country. Born the free son of a Black carpenter, Gross likely learned his cabinetmaking and carpentry skills from his father. By all accounts, Gross was a successful cabinetmaker, creating fashionable furniture from imported mahogany. Like most cabinetmakers, Gross also worked as an undertaker and built coffins.

Gross's double chest is representative of the few Black artisans who boldly inscribed their works with their names. By placing the inscription in a location where it was never to be seen, Gross covertly claimed ownership and recognition of his work in a time when the works of many Black artisans went unrecognized and unrecorded.

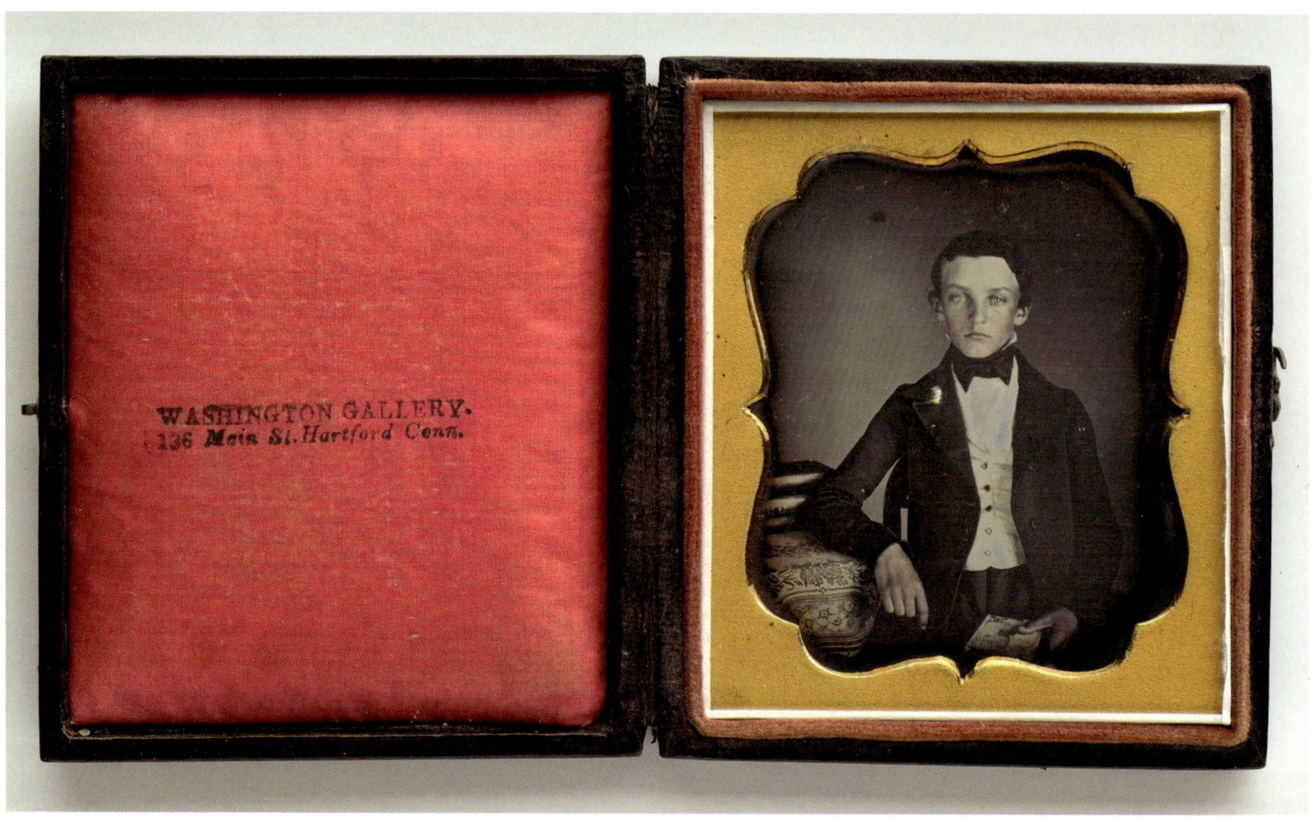

FIGURE 31
Augustus Washington
Boy with Books, 1847–53, Hartford, Connecticut
Sixth-plate daguerreotype in leather case
DAR Museum Collection, Friends of the Museum Purchase, 2019.7

The well-dressed, unidentified young male sitter in this daguerreotype made between 1847 and 1853 showcases the talent of an artist who not only framed identity but spotlighted their own skill and business prowess within the small case frame stamped onto a red silk pillow. The inscription, which reads, "Washington Gallery, 136 Main St., Hartford, Conn.," refers to the studio of Black photographer Augustus Washington. Born about 1820, in Trenton, New Jersey, Washington is believed to have been the product of an interracial family, with his mother being of South Asian descent and his father a former enslaved man from Virginia.

From the outset, Washington's upbringing and educational path set him apart from many Black children. His parents paid for his early education in New Jersey until an all too common backlash arose against the cause of abolition and the education of Black youth. This merely stifled Washington's schooling; it did not extinguish his ability to find education. In 1843, Washington entered Dartmouth College in New Hampshire. Washington was the only Black person to do so that year. Unsurprisingly, money was scarce, so Washington took to the new trade of making daguerreotype photographs. As Washington's skill set grew, he earned enough money to purchase a camera as well as lessons to refine his new craft. He did not, however, earn enough money to pay for his tuition and ultimately left Dartmouth College. Washington moved to Hartford, Connecticut, and there took charge of an African American school.

Washington thoroughly supported the abolition of slavery and was wary of the colonization movement, often a harbor for racists wishing to rid the United States of African Americans. However, convinced that Liberia might be the "last refuge of the oppressed colored man," Washington and his family sailed in 1853 to Liberia. Capturing the evolution of the young nation through his camera, those surviving photographs of prominent citizens and politicians are a rare lasting glimpse of Washington's skill. In Liberia, Washington eventually owned several businesses, including a newspaper and a 1,000-acre sugar plantation. He served in both the Liberian House of Representatives and Senate and was considered one of the best employers in the country. Washington died in Monrovia, Liberia, on June 7, 1875.

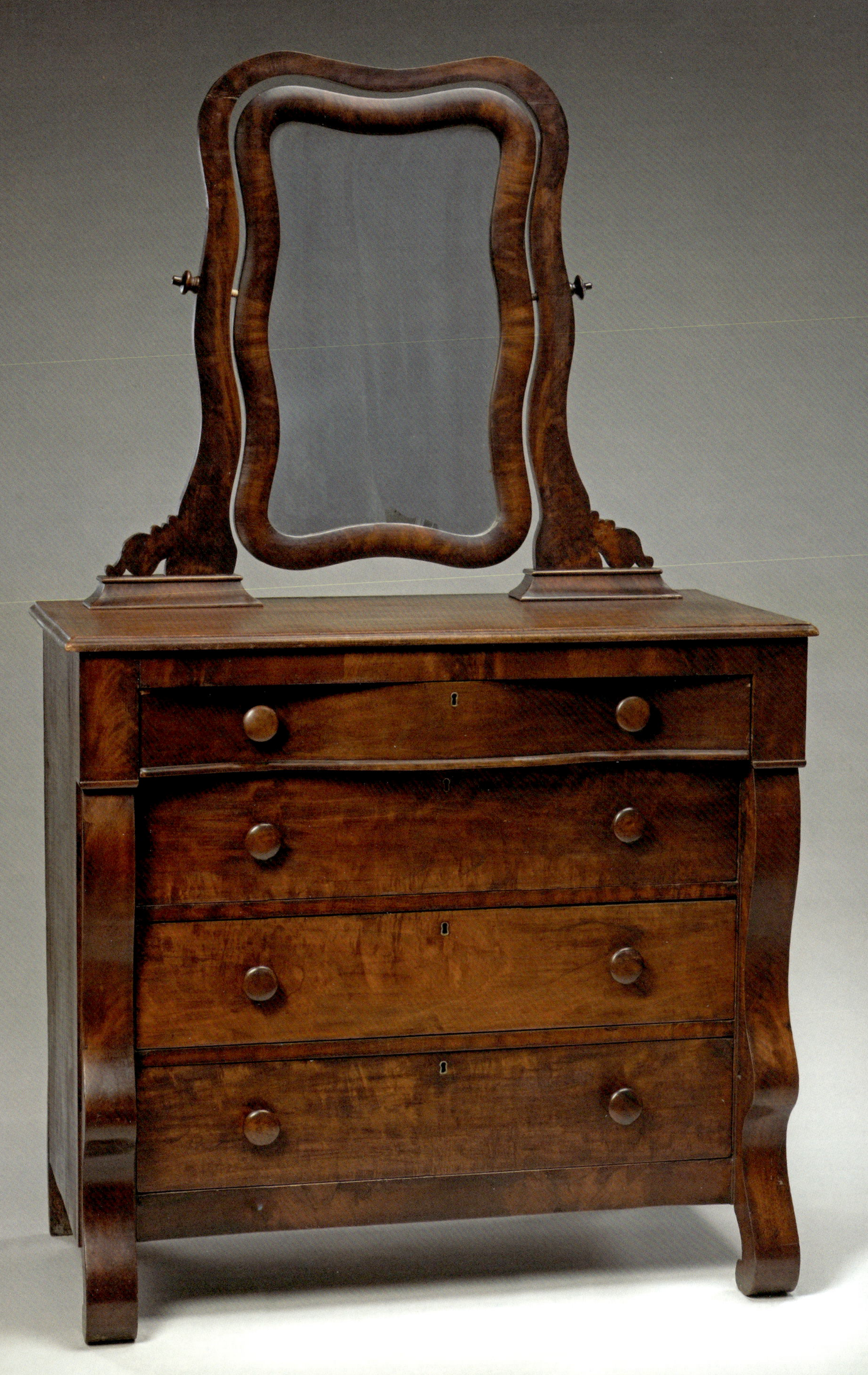

(*overleaf*) FIGURE 32
Thomas Day
Chest of Drawers, 1845–50, Milton, North Carolina
Mahogany, poplar, and yellow pine
DAR Museum Collection, Friends of the Museum Purchase, 2021.13

This popular chest incorporating four graduating drawers is the work of one of the most celebrated Black master craftspeople of the nineteenth century, Thomas Day. Day's masterful artistry is seen through this chest with a front featuring serpentine drawers and scrolled pilasters supported by incurved volute feet. From Milton, North Carolina, Day opened his shop there in 1827 and operated it until his death in 1861. The inscription on the back is not confirmed as Day's hand and in fact is more likely by an unidentified shop hand.

In the early 1850s, Day sought to increase his clientele. He began using auctions in Raleigh, North Carolina. His work garnered much praise in local Raleigh newspapers, with such pronouncements as "We notice for sale a lot of superior furniture, embracing bureaus, wardrobes, superfine bedsteads, chairs, &c. . . . made by Thomas Day so well known as a fine artisan in his profession." What is of utmost importance today is Day's ingenuity in design, incorporation of new industrial techniques, and desire to uplift his social status.

Day's shop was thoroughly modern. By 1855, he owned a steam engine, used to operate various belt-powered woodworking machines including a Daniels plane, circular saw, lathe, and jigsaw. Markings of each of these can be observed on this chest of drawers. Mechanization allowed Day to speed up production and thus profit. This also allowed Day to keep some fully finished furniture in stock for ready purchase. Day could fulfill ambitious orders such as the one for David Settle of Rockingham County, North Carolina, who ordered forty-seven items in 1855. Mechanized production meant that he could deliver this large order in only two months.

FIGURE 33
Dutreuil Barjon
Armoire, 1835–45, New Orleans, Louisiana
Mahogany, cherry, and cedar
Loan courtesy of The Historic New Orleans Collection. Gift of Mr. and Mrs. Robert J. Patrick, 2008.0088

Haitian-born Dutreuil Barjon relocated with his mother to New Orleans, Louisiana, in 1813, joining a large community of recently immigrated Haitians following the Haitian Revolution. Shortly after his arrival, he apprenticed with free person of color cabinetmaker Jean Rousseau for three years, where he learned the cabinetmaker's trade and business. In Rousseau's shop, Barjon possibly learned how to create furniture that appealed to the elite of New Orleans, including large, oversized furniture designed to fill plantation homes. In 1821, Barjon established his own cabinetmaking shop at 245 Royal Street, known as Furniture Row, where he produced fine furniture and imported furniture from Europe. In 1834, Barjon advertised that he had articles of furniture for sale that were "made in this city." Barjon's business prospered, and in later years he retired to Paris, leaving his shop under the leadership of his son, Dutreuil Barjon Jr.

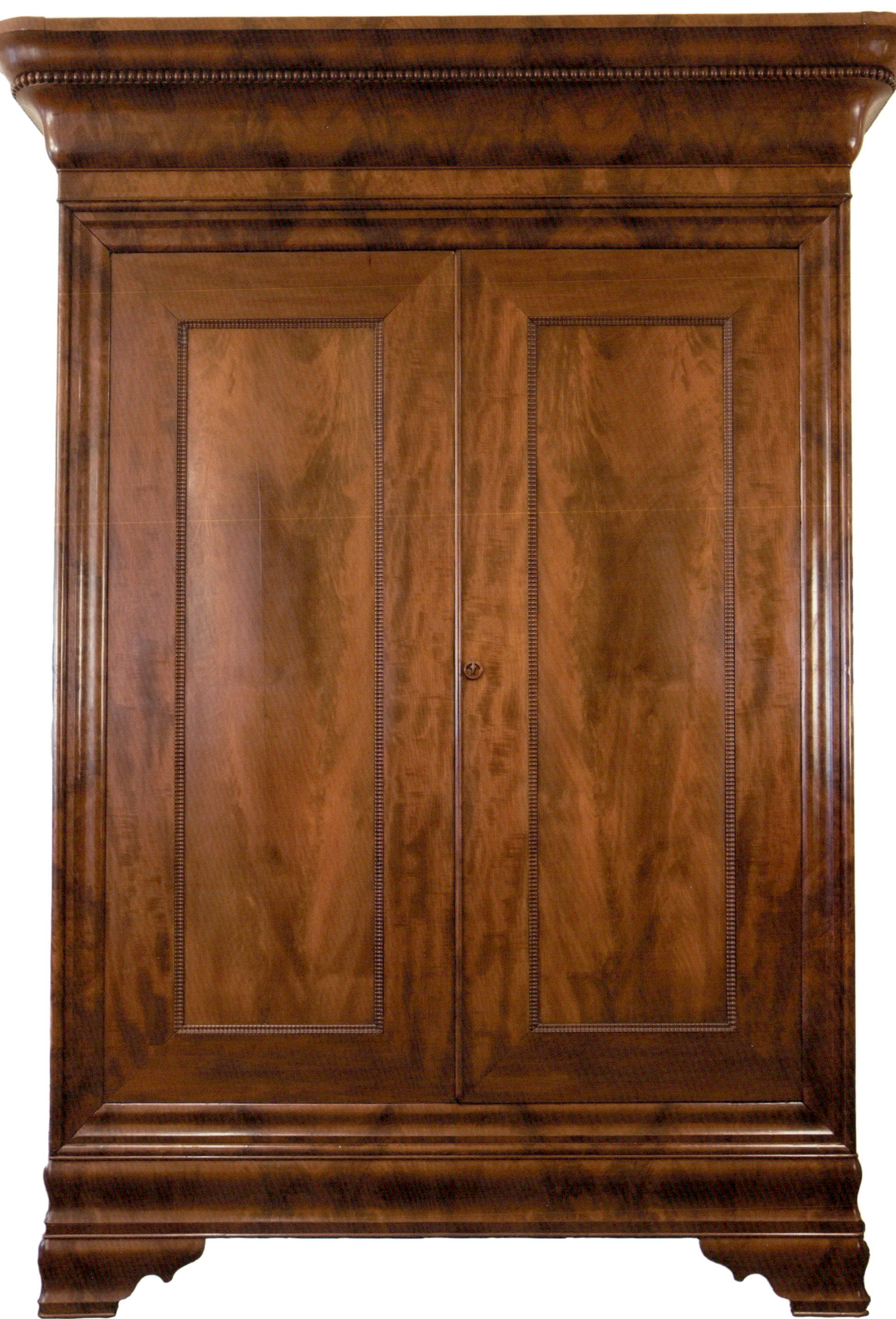

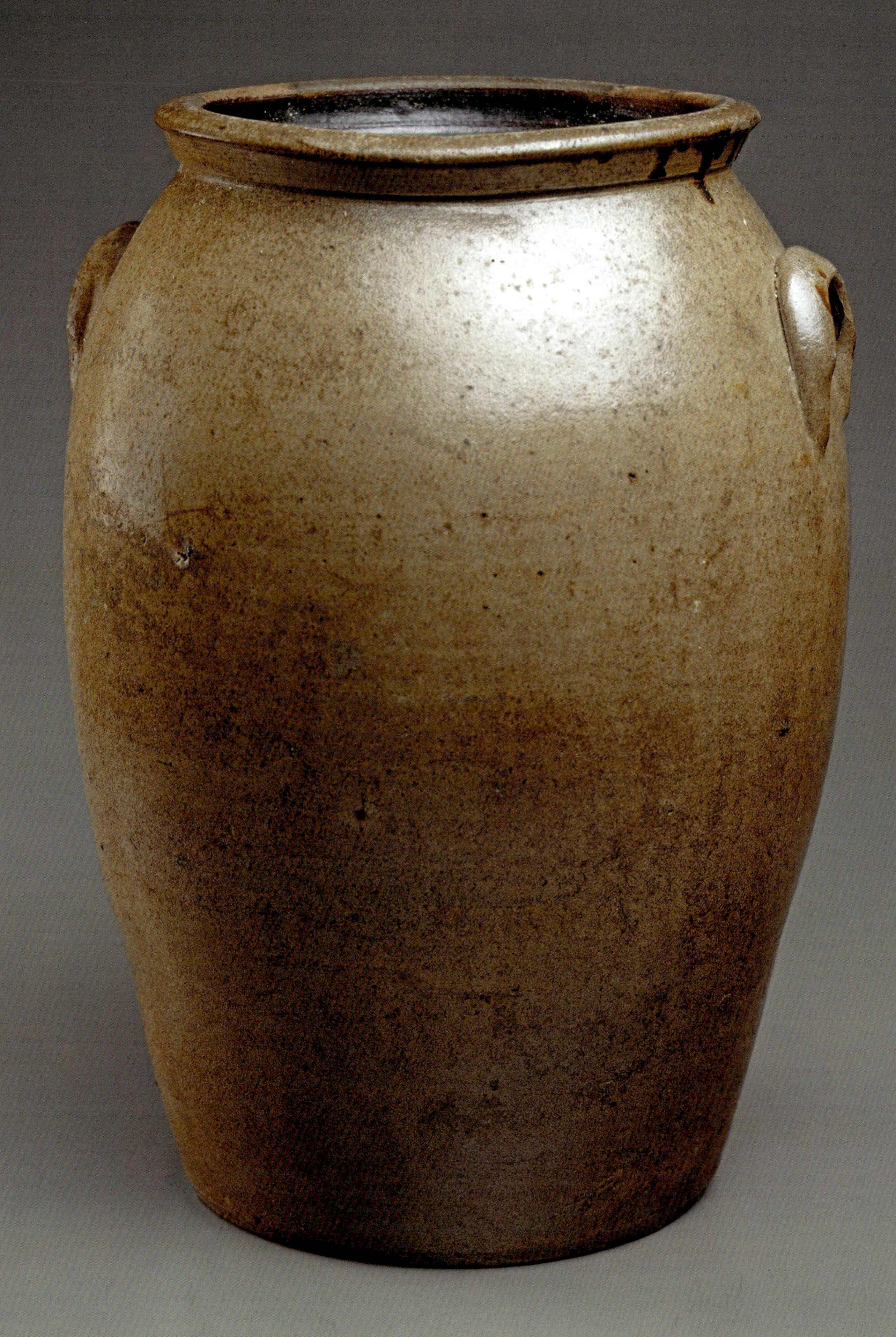

FIGURE 34
H. Wilson & Co.
Five-Gallon Jar, ca. 1869–84, Guadalupe, Texas
Salt-glazed stoneware
Loan courtesy of The Museum of Fine Arts, Houston, The Bayou Bend Collection, museum purchase funded by The Brown Foundation, Inc., B.93.1

Parallel with the power to create is the power of ownership. A testament to that power is found in this jar attributed to "H. Wilson & Co." Hiram Wilson (also seen as Hyrum), James Wilson, and Wallace Wilson opened a pottery in rural Guadalupe County, Texas, in March 1872. The Reverend John M. Wilson brought these three enslaved men to Texas in the 1830s. Although not related, all three took Wilson's last name.

The Wilson men mastered their craft from the nearby pottery established by their enslaver around 1857. It is believed that the J. M. Wilson firm incorporated techniques of manipulating alkaline glaze learned from potters in South Carolina. This glazing tradition migrated west into the Gulf South before reaching the east coast of Texas. From 1872 until the company's dissolution in 1884, H. Wilson & Company pottery flourished, employing a primarily salt-glaze technique in the production of ceramics. This five-gallon jar, impressed twice on the shoulder with the mark "H. WILSON & CO.," is a representation of the striking pottery created by H. Wilson & Company and a testament to what is widely believed to be the first Black-owned business in Texas.

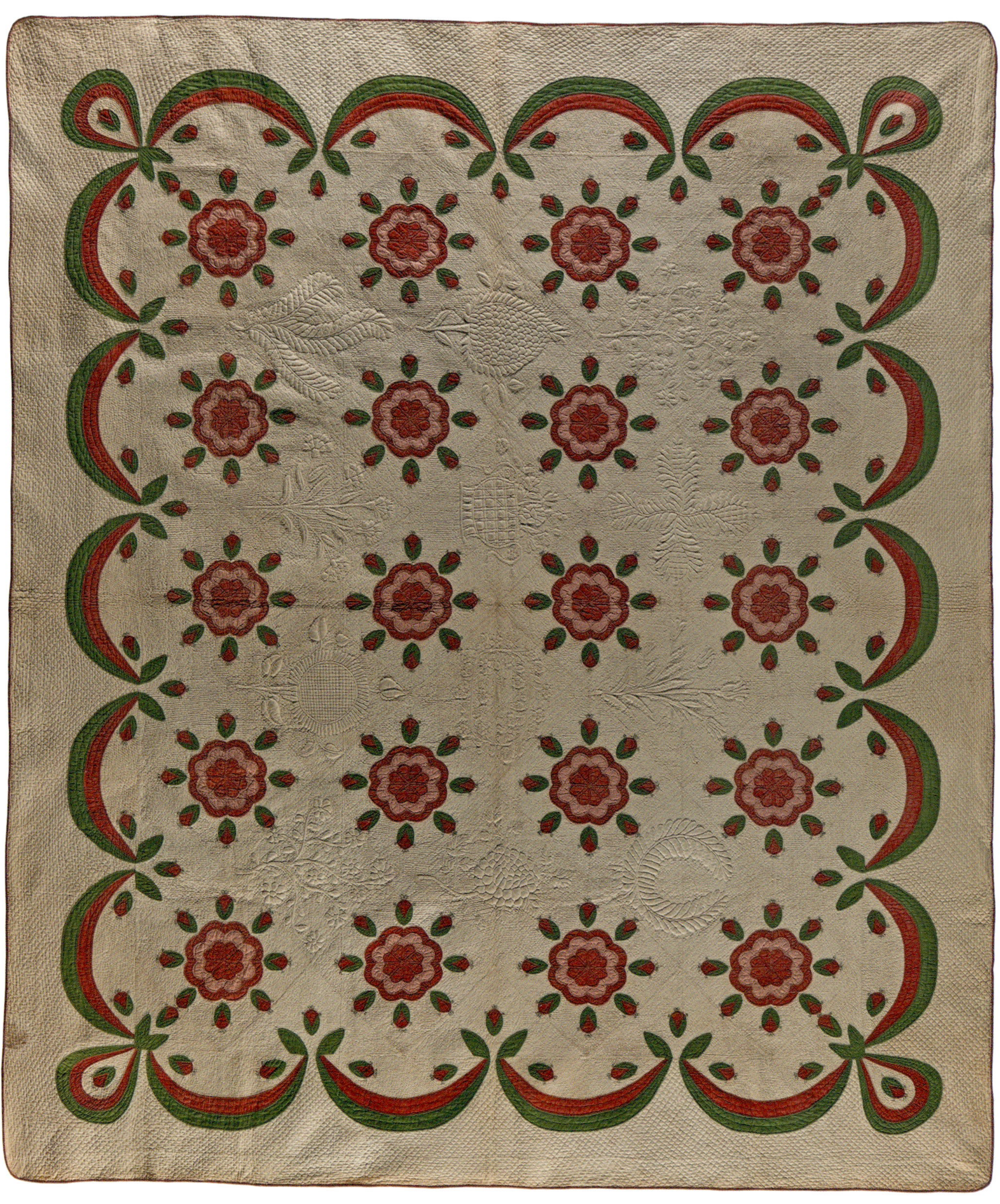

FIGURE 35
Ellen and Margaret Morton
Quilt, ca. 1850, The Knob Plantation, Russellville, Kentucky
Cotton
Loan courtesy of the American Folk Art Museum, New York City. Gift of Marijane Edwards Camp, 2012.8.1

Seldom are the names of the enslaved women who created quilts documented or recorded with their work. Such pieces are often attributed to the mistress of the plantation from which the covering descended. The descendants of Mr. and Mrs. Marmaduke Beckwith Morton, owners of The Knob, in Russellville, Kentucky, attached a note to this quilt, recording that it comes with a history of being made by two enslaved women on the plantation. Because of similarities in two other quilts from the same plantation, Ellen Morton and younger sister Margaret Morton are the names of the two makers associated with this quilt. Although Margaret was known largely for her cooking, Ellen was remembered for her sewing. When this quilt was being sewn around 1850, there were sixteen enslaved people living and working on the plantation. Ellen and Margaret likely worked this quilt while also performing other duties for the Morton family. Ellen remained on the plantation following emancipation and cared for Marmaduke Morton until he died in 1887.

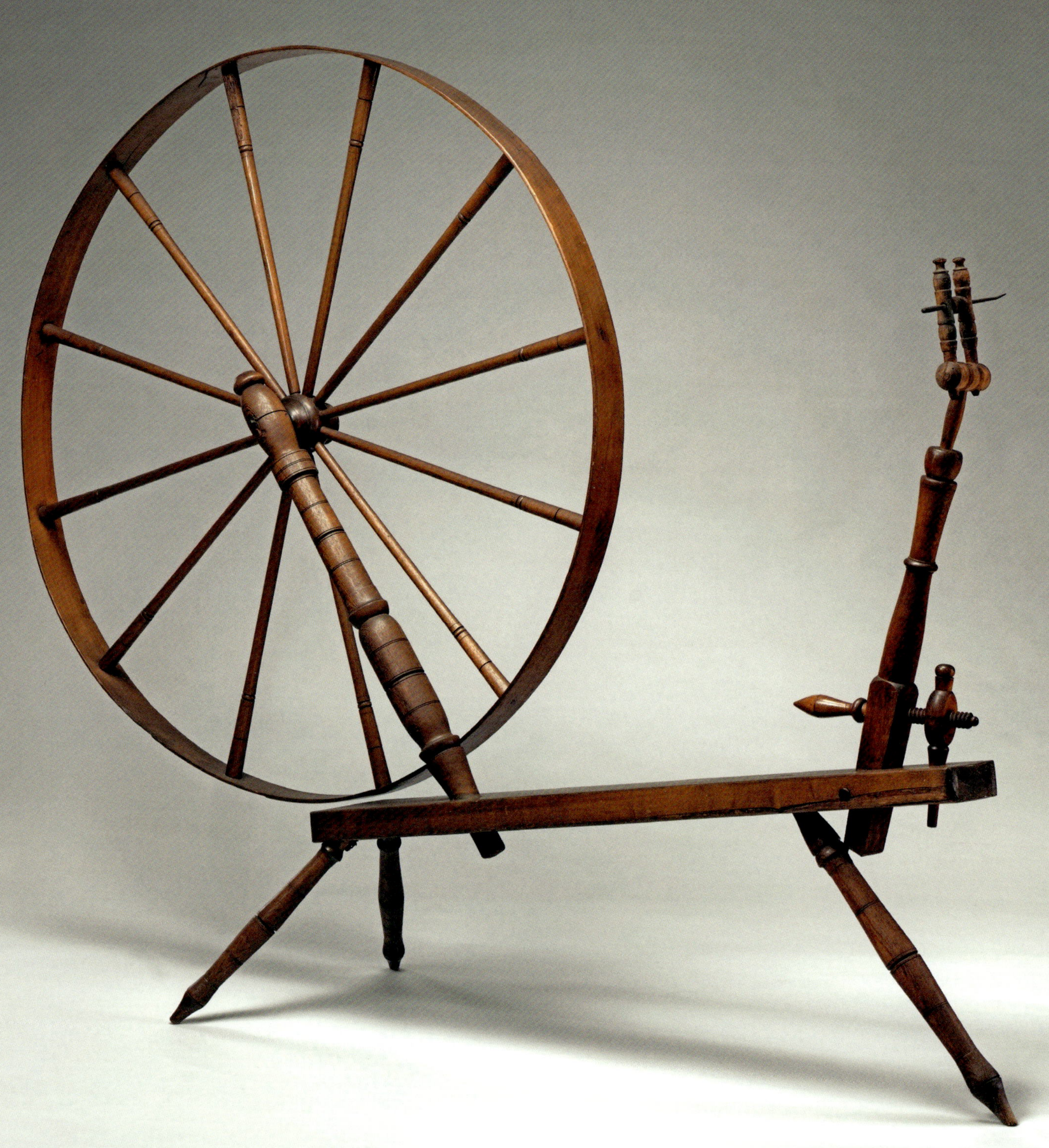

FIGURE 36
Unidentified maker
Spinning Wheel, 1816–25, Carthage, New York
Wood
DAR Museum Collection, 3139.1

Spinning wheels evoke images of white women in early America crafting yarn for their families. Over time, the spinning wheel has become a symbol of patriotic sentiment in colonial America. However, the truth is that many enslaved women also identified as spinners, laboring to produce yarn and thread to meet the needs of their enslavers and fellow enslaved individuals. Enslaved spinners were trained to spin flax, cotton, and wool, and their thread could be used in the home or sold for profit.

In the late 1930s, Lucindy Lawrence Jurdon sat for an interview with the Federal Writers' Project: Slave Narratives Project. The interviewer asked Ms. Jurdon about her life, and she recalled that her mother, Patsy, had been a fine weaver. Jurdon proudly posed for a photograph with Patsy's spinning wheel (see figure 0.1).

"Dis is her spinning wheel, an' it can still be used. I use it sometimes now. Us made our own cloth an' our stockings too."

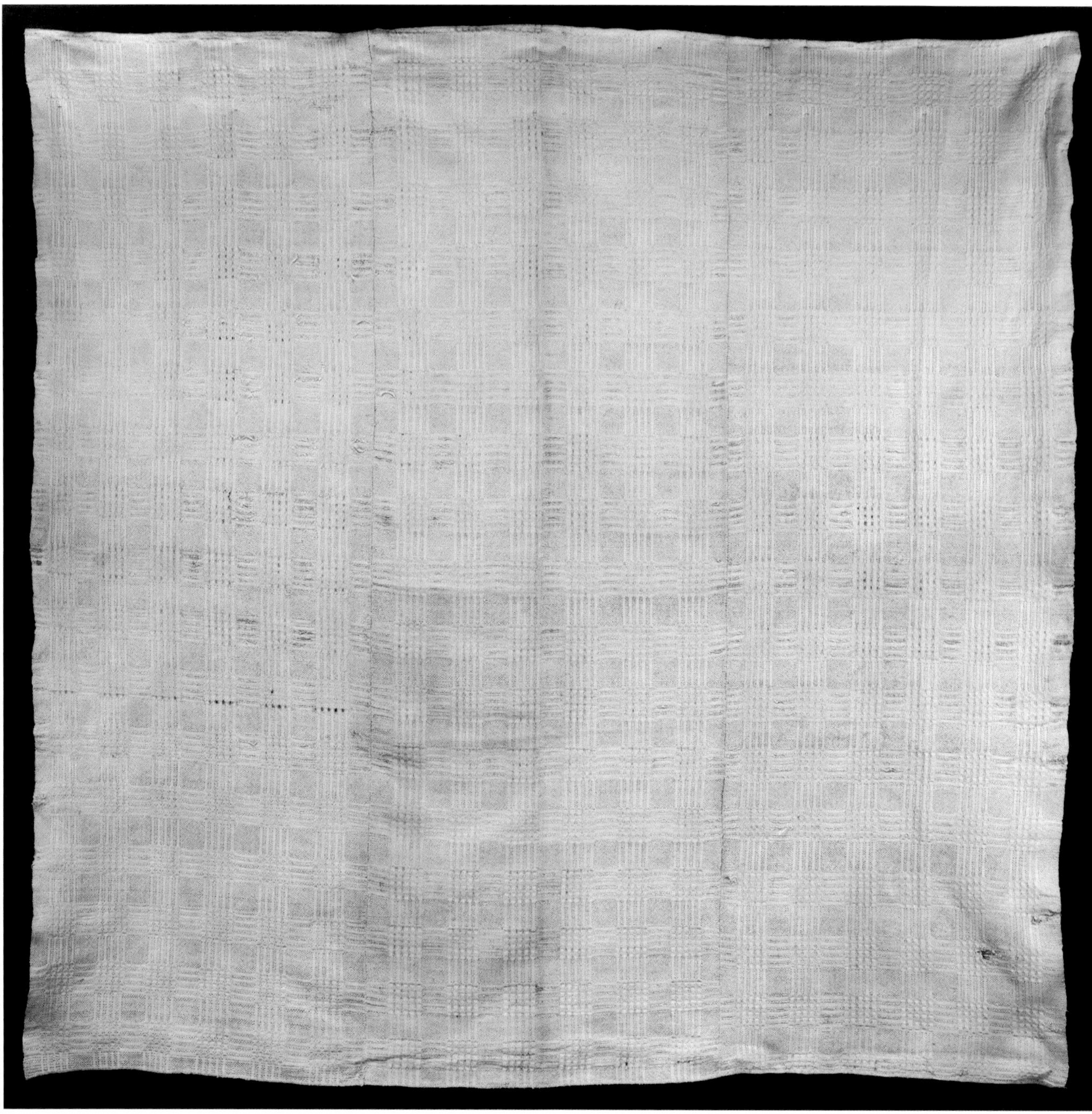

FIGURES 37A–B
Unidentified craftspeople
Coverlet, 1810–50, Rockbridge County, Virginia
Cotton
DAR Museum Collection. Gift of
Mrs. Morton E. Thomas, 6946

The 1820 US Census for Rockbridge County, Virginia, offers immense insight into the lives of those who resided in the Shenandoah Valley in the early nineteenth century. The entry for the estate of John Buchanan shows seven people living on the property when the census was taken. Only two of these individuals were Black, both females. The youngest person was listed as under fourteen years of age and the oldest, over forty-five years. According to the family, both of these unnamed women served multiple roles within the house, primarily caring for the two children and textile production. Their role as textile producers is further supported by the 1820 census, which lists two individuals as "Engaged in Manufacturing."

A fundamental part of an eighteenth- or nineteenth-century southern plantation could include textile production tools, such as a loom or spinning wheel. The family history goes on to state that there was a "loom house" on the property where this and another coverlet that had been passed down in the family were produced.

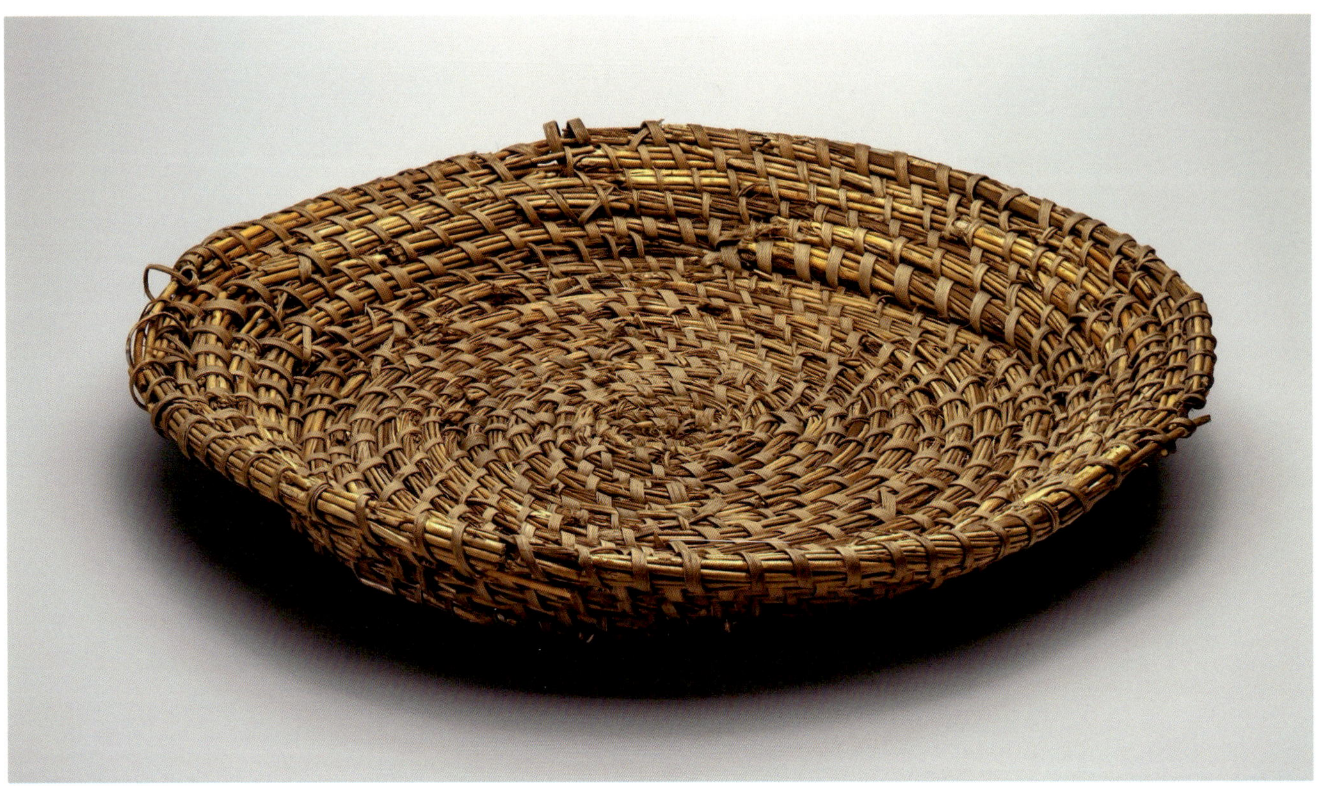

FIGURE 38
Unidentified craftsperson
Fanning Basket, 1850–60, Cat Island Plantation, Georgetown County, South Carolina
Sweetgrass
Loan courtesy of the Museum of Early Southern Decorative Arts (MESDA), Winston-Salem, North Carolina, 5764.1

A staple on Lowcountry rice plantations, sweetgrass fanner baskets aided in rice harvesting. Enslaved women crafted sweetgrass baskets by coiling and weaving materials such as sweetgrass, marsh grass, palmetto leaves, and split white oak. Because fanner baskets were used for winnowing rice after it had been hulled, they were wide with a shallow edge and often created with stronger materials such as split white oak to bind the coils. Their durability ensured that the baskets could be used season after season.

Historically, fanner baskets draw their form from rice harvesting in West Africa. When enslaved Africans arrived in the Americas, they brought their knowledge of rice growing and the essential tools to make the practice successful. Although beautiful, fanner baskets were a tool that not only winnowed rice and made rice production easier but also aided in the spread of rice as a cash crop in the Lowcountry.

(*opposite*) FIGURE 39
Unidentified craftsperson
Coverlet, ca. 1800, Washington (present-day Marion) County, Kentucky
Wool and cotton
DAR Museum Collection. Gift of Mrs. G. B. Puller, 3560

The Revolutionary War often evokes conversation of liberty, freedom, and separation from tyranny. Records often yield a murky reality as many colonists, although fighting for independence from the British, were eager to participate in the oppression of enslaved Africans and African Americans. William Crowdus is one such example. Crowdus received a pension and acreage of land in present-day Marion County, Kentucky, for three years of service during the Revolutionary War. Crowdus used his pension to secure a farm on which were enslaved twenty-eight people. At least one of these individuals, the "Head weaving woman," is responsible for creating this coverlet. According to census records, eleven women were working in close proximity to the family. It is likely that one or more of these women were involved in textile production on the farm.